ETHICS

Other works of Dietrich Bonhoeffer
published by SCM Press

LIFE TOGETHER
LETTERS AND PAPERS FROM PRISON
THE COST OF DISCIPLESHIP

Dietrich Bonhoeffer

ETHICS

Edited by
EBERHARD BETHGE

SCM PRESS LTD

Translated by Neville Horton Smith
from the German *Ethik*,
published by Chr. Kaiser Verlag, Munich 1949

The order followed in this edition is based on
the sixth German edition, 1963

334 00405 5

First published 1955
by SCM Press Ltd
56 Bloomsbury Street London
Second impression 1971

Printed in Great Britain by
Fletcher & Son Ltd, Norwich

CONTENTS

CONTENTS

CONTENTS

PART TWO

CONTENTS

PREFACE TO THE FIRST–FIFTH
GERMAN EDITIONS

THIS book is not the *Ethics* which Dietrich Bonhoeffer
intended to have published. It is a compilation of the
sections which have been preserved, some of them complete
and others not, some already partly rewritten and some
which had been committed to writing only as preliminary
studies for the work which was planned. These are the parts
of the work which it was possible to conceal in a place of
safety before they could be seized by the police. They have
been retrieved from their garden hiding-places in the same
disorder in which they were put there. And then there are
other parts which were already in the hands of the Gestapo
before 5th April 1943, the day of Dietrich Bonhoeffer's arrest.

Already at the time of completing his *Nachfolge*[1] Bonhoeffer
was planning a new approach to the problems of Christian
ethics. He thought of this as the beginning of his actual life-
work. In June 1939 he was invited by Professor John Baillie,
on behalf of the Croall Lectureship Trust, to lecture at
Edinburgh, and he hoped to make his lectures the basis for
his book. The war put an end to his preparations, and he
did not take up this work again until 1940, when he was
compelled to give up his clergy training duties and forbidden
to speak in public anywhere in the Reich. He was also
forbidden by the Reich Chamber of Literature to publish
any kind of written work, because, it was said, he had neither
'signed on' nor asked for exemption from 'signing on' as a
Nazi propagandist. The manuscripts which are now before
us were written between 1940 and 1943 in Berlin, at the
monastery of Ettal and at Kieckow. The work was inter-.

---

[1] Published 1937. Published in English as *The Cost of Discipleship*, S.C.M.
Press 1948.

rupted by various tasks undertaken on behalf of the Brotherhood Council of the Confessing Church, by various journeys
in connexion with political activities, and finally by Bonhoeffer's arrest.

Bonhoeffer's books did not progress chapter by chapter in
accordance with a fixed and unalterable plan. Each one
grew gradually by the coalescence of numerous separate
studies of the subject until it formed a whole. The titles and
the arrangement of the books were subject to constant
change in the course of this process. We possess a sketch for
the arrangement of the *Ethics*, dating from the autumn of
1940. It runs as follows:

I. THE FOUNDATIONS

Ethics as Formation
Inheritance and Decay
Guilt and Justification
The Church and the World, Christ and the Command-
  ments
The Things before the Last, and the Last Things
The New Man

II. THE STRUCTURE

Structure of Personal Life
Structure of Classes and Offices
Structure of Communities
Structure of the Church
Structure of Christian Life in the World.

As possible titles Bonhoeffer jotted down the following
characteristic phrases: 'The foundations and structure of a
world which is reconciled with God'; 'The foundations and
structure of a future world'; and 'The foundations and
structure of a united west'. His sub-title was: 'A tentative
Christian ethic'. A little later he wrote in a letter: 'Today I
have thought of a possible title for my book: "The preparing
of the way and the entry into possession". This would
correspond with the division of the book into the things
before the last and the last things.'

The material has come to us in such a form that there has been no possibility of working out a clear arrangement of the extant chapters in accordance with the subjects they treat. The first sections have been arranged according to the outline to which we have already referred. The remaining sections in many cases approach from a new angle some topic which had already been treated before; these have been placed in the order in which they appear to have been written. Roman figures indicate the sections which are clearly intended to form coherent units and in which there is a clear line of advance within the particular range of problems with which they deal. A few sub-headings have been added by the Editor, according to the demands of the material.

Of the essays contained in Part Two, numbers I and III were written as reports for the Reich Brotherhood Council and numbers IV and V were sketched out in the prison at Tegel. It is to be hoped that the theological parts of Bonhoeffer's letters from prison will later be published: they will show how he continued to concern himself with these matters until the very end.[1]

Special thanks are due to Frau Anni Lindner for her part in the laborious task of deciphering the manuscripts and arranging the innumerable small slips of paper in order.

On 18th November 1943 Dietrich Bonhoeffer wrote from Tegel: 'I for my part have been reproaching myself for not having finished the *Ethics*. No doubt part of it has been confiscated. It has been some comfort to me to know that I had already told you the gist of it. Even if you no longer have it in mind it will still somehow crop up again indirectly. And in any case my ideas were not yet altogether in shape.' And on 15th December 1943 he wrote: 'Sometimes I think I really have my life more or less behind me now and that all that would remain for me to do would be to finish my *Ethics* . . .'

9th April 1948   EBERHARD BETHGE

PREFACE TO THE REARRANGED SIXTH
GERMAN EDITION

DISCUSSIONS about the development in Bonhoeffer's thought
leading up to *Letters and Papers from Prison* made it seem
desirable to re-examine the chronology of the composition of
Ethics. The inclusion of this new edition in a uniform edition
of Bonhoeffer's works has been the occasion for a version of
Ethics which sets out to show Bonhoeffer's four fresh starts on
the book in chronological sequence. Some passages can be
dated accurately; others, however, can only be fixed with
some degree of probability.

A. Bonhoeffer's *first start* on *Ethics* was with two chapters,
'The Love of God and the Decay of the World' and 'The
Church and the World', which originally formed chapters IV
and V of the book. The thought and language of these chapters is very close to *The Cost of Discipleship*. Of course, there is
no absolutely certain proof that the work on ethics began
with these chapters. Among the notes for 'The Love of God
and the Decay of the World' are types of paper which
Bonhoeffer used for letters in spring and summer 1940.
Notes and key-words for 'The Church and the World' are
written on calendar pages marked May 1939, e.g. the two
fundamental scriptural passages, Mark 9.40 and Matt. 12.30.
The first pages of 'The Church and the World' are of the
same kind of paper as that used for the last pages of 'The
Love of God and the Decay of the World'. So these chapters
should be put about 1939/1940. They were probably interrupted before August 1940.

B. *The second attempt* can be dated more accurately. 'Ethics
as Formation', previously chapter I, was clearly begun in
September 1940 and the first pages were written on the
estate at Klein-Krössin (Kieckow). That means that its

themes took shape immediately after Bonhoeffer had had his
first successful meetings with Colonel Oster of the *Abwehr*.
During this period – up to October 1940 – he also wrote the
sketches mentioned in the preface to the first edition of
Ethics (see also *Gesammelte Schriften* II, p. 376). The confession of the guilt of the Church was thus written when
Hitler had achieved his most surprising victory.

C. 'The Last Things and the Things Before the Last', which
used to form chapter III, is the *third fresh start*. It was com-
posed at Ettal between the end of November 1940 and the
middle of February 1941, was interrupted by the first journey
to Switzerland and not taken up again. It is, however, the
most compact part of the *Ethics*. The key-phrase 'The Last
Things and the Things Before the Last' is to be found earlier
on notes from Klein-Krössin. Bonhoeffer never managed
such a long period of work again.

It is difficult to date 'Christ, Reality and Good', which
used to be chapter II. It appeared at that point because in
some ways it seemed to match the sketches from Klein-
Krössin of 1940. The paper used is that which Frau von
Kleist in Klein-Krössin used to collect and prepare for
Bonhoeffer (rough paper was very difficult to get hold of at
that time). So the chapter could have been written either in
summer 1940 or during a new stay in Pomerania in summer
1941. I am inclined to think that 1941 is the right date. The
manuscript pages end with page 14 in Bonhoeffer's writing,
and 'History and Good' begins on page 15, but on quite a
different kind of paper. The latter chapter was begun during
the course of 1941.

D. If this arrangement is correct, then the first theological
starting-point would be *The Cost of Discipleship*, the second
'identification' and the third justification. These are now
followed by the fourth starting-point, which is the incarnation. 'History and Good', which used to be chapter VI, will
have been begun in summer 1941, as is indicated by the
paper from Klein-Krössin used in August 1941. Then followed the second journey to Switzerland in September and
pneumonia in November. Work then continued, with inter-

ruptions, until a long and intensive period of travelling which began in April 1942. Bonhoeffer worked on this most political chapter at the height of his involvement with the conspiracy. He rejected a first, quite extensive outline (now to be found in *Gesammelte Schriften* III, pp. 455 ff.), and began again in much more detail. As far as the general problem indicated is concerned, however, the first shorter effort went much further than its successor. The second version quotes Bultmann's *Commentary on John*, which appeared in 1941.

Chapter VII, 'The "Ethical" and the "Christian" as a Theme', will then have been written during the winter of 1942/43. At the time of Bonhoeffer's arrest, his desk was overflowing with notes on this theme. They also contained the phrase 'being there for the world'.

This arrangement of the *Ethics* makes rather more visible Bonhoeffer's inward development from *The Cost of Discipleship* to the threshold of *Letters and Papers from Prison*; for this reason, the re-ordering may seem justifiable.

Part Two is so to speak an appendix. 'The Doctrine of the Primus Usus Legis' was written as a study document for a synodal commission preparing a declaration on the fifth commandment. This commission sat under the presidency of G. Harder, in Magdeburg, on 10 August 1942 and 15 March 1943. Bonhoeffer probably presented his work at the second session, i.e. shortly before his arrest. At the conclusion it contains a clear repudiation of excessively apocalyptic proclamation and strikes a note of true worldliness over against a perversion of worldly ordinances by Christianity or the Church (see p. 000); it goes so far as to demand collaboration between Christians and non-Christians on certain material questions and concrete tasks. ' "Personal" and "Real" Ethos' was written as a critique of Dilschneider's *Ethics*, shortly after they appeared in 1940. So far there has unfortunately been no indication of the occasion for and circumstances of the composition of 'State and Church'; two notes only are written on the kind of paper used at Klein-Krössin. 'On the Possibility of the Word of the Church to the World' is written on very bad paper, of a kind only used at a late stage, on which only pencil writing was possible; I therefore guess that it was written in Tegel, but that is not certain. 'What is meant by "Telling the Truth"?' does, however, clearly belong to the Tegel period.

Among Bonhoeffer's ethical work in those years can also be included 'Thoughts on William Paton's *The Church and the New Order*' of September 1941 (see *Gesammelte Schriften* I, pp. 356–371) and the two literary fragments from *Tegel* (see *Gesammelte Schriften* III, pp. 478 ff.).

With the manuscripts are also more than a hundred notes of various kinds, some with only phrases, others with sentences and outlines.

July 1962   EBERHARD BETHGE

STATIONS ON THE WAY TO FREEDOM

SELF-DISCIPLINE

If you set out to seek freedom, you must learn before all things
Mastery over sense and soul, lest your wayward desirings,
Lest your undisciplined members lead you now this way, now that way.
Chaste be your mind and your body, and subject to you and obedient,
Serving solely to seek their appointed goal and objective.
None learns the secret of freedom save only by way of control.

ACTION

Do and dare what is right, not swayed by the whim of the moment.
Bravely take hold of the real, not dallying now with what might be.
Not in the flight of ideas but only in action is freedom.
Make up your mind and come out into the tempest of living.
God's command is enough and your faith in Him to sustain you.
Then at last freedom will welcome your spirit amid great rejoicing.

SUFFERING

See what a transformation! These hands so active and powerful
Now are tied, and alone and fainting, you see where your work ends.
Yet you are confident still, and gladly commit what is rightful
Into a stronger hand, and say that you are contented.
You were free for a moment of bliss, then you yielded your freedom
Into the hand of God, that He might perfect it in glory.

DEATH

Come now, highest of feasts on the way to freedom eternal,
Death, strike off the fetters, break down the walls that oppress us,
Our bedazzled soul and our ephemeral body,
That we may see at last the sight which here was not vouchsafed us.
Freedom, we sought you long in discipline, action, suffering.
Now as we die we see you and know you at last, face to face.

PART ONE

I

THE LOVE OF GOD AND THE
DECAY OF THE WORLD

The World of Conflicts

THE knowledge of good and evil seems to be the aim of all ethical reflection.[1] The first task of Christian ethics is to invalidate this knowledge. In launching this attack on the underlying assumptions of all other ethics, Christian ethics stands so completely alone that it becomes questionable whether there is any purpose in speaking of Christian ethics at all. But if one does so notwithstanding, that can only mean that Christian ethics claims to discuss the origin of the whole problem of ethics, and thus professes to be a critique of all ethics simply as ethics.

Already in the possibility of the knowledge of good and evil Christian ethics discerns a falling away from the origin. Man at his origin knows only one thing: God. It is only in the unity of his knowledge of God that he knows of other men, of things, and of himself. He knows all things only in God, and God in all things. The knowledge of good and evil shows that he is no longer at one with this origin.

In the knowledge of good and evil man does not understand himself in the reality of the destiny appointed in his origin, but rather in his own possibilities, his possibility of being good or evil. He knows himself now as something apart from God, outside God, and this means that he now knows only himself and no longer knows God at all; for he can

[1] For the purposes of our present discussion it makes no difference if modern ethics replaces the concepts of good and evil by those of moral and immoral, valuable and valueless or (in the case of existential philosophy) of actual or proper being and not actual or proper being.

3

know God only if he knows only God. The knowledge of good and evil is therefore separation from God. Only against God can man know good and evil.

But man cannot be rid of his origin. Instead of knowing himself in the origin of God, he must now know himself as an origin. He interprets himself according to his possibilities, his possibilities of being good or evil, and he therefore conceives himself to be the origin of good and evil. *Eritis sicut deus.* 'The man is become as one of us, to know good and evil', says God (Gen. 3.22).

Originally man was made in the image of God, but now his likeness to God is a stolen one. As the image of God man draws his life entirely from his origin in God, but the man who has become like God has forgotten how he was at his origin and has made himself his own creator and judge. What God had given man to be, man now desired to be through himself. But God's gift is essentially *God's* gift. It is the origin that constitutes this gift. If the origin changes, the gift changes. Indeed the gift consists solely in its origin. Man as the image of God draws his life from the origin of God, but the man who has become like God draws his life from his own origin. In appropriating the origin to himself man took to himself a secret of God which proved his undoing. The Bible describes this event with the eating of the forbidden fruit. Man now knows good and evil. This does not mean that he has acquired new knowledge in addition to what he knew before, but the knowledge of good and evil signifies the complete reversal of man's knowledge, which hitherto had been solely knowledge of God as his origin. In knowing good and evil he knows what only the origin, God Himself, can know and ought to know. It is only with extreme reserve that even the Bible indicates to us that God is the One who knows of good and evil. It is the first indication of the mystery of predestination, the mystery of an eternal dichotomy which has its origin in the eternally One, the mystery of an eternal choice and election by Him in whom there is no darkness but only light. To know good and evil is to know oneself as the origin of good and evil, as the origin of an eternal choice and

4

election. How this is possible remains the secret of Him in whom there is no disunion because He is Himself the one and eternal origin and the overcoming of all disunion. This secret has been stolen from God by man in his desire to be an origin on his own account. Instead of knowing only the God who is good to him and instead of knowing all things in Him, he now knows himself as the origin of good and evil. Instead of accepting the choice and election of God, man himself desires to choose, to be the origin of the election. And so, in a certain sense, he bears within himself the secret of predestination. Instead of knowing himself solely in the reality of being chosen and loved by God, he must now know himself in the possibility of choosing and of being the origin of good and evil. He has become like God, but against God. Herein lies the serpent's deceit. Man knows good and evil, but because he is not the origin, because he acquires this knowledge only at the price of estrangement from the origin, the good and evil that he knows are not the good and evil of God but good and evil against God. They are good and evil of man's own choosing, in opposition to the eternal election of God. In becoming like God man has become a god against God.

This finds its expression in the fact that man, knowing of good and evil, has finally torn himself loose from life, that is to say from the eternal life which proceeds from the choice of God. 'And now, lest he put forth his hand, and take also of the tree of life, and eat, and live for ever . . . he drove out the man; and he placed at the east of the garden of Eden Cherubims, and a flaming sword which turned every way, to keep the way of the tree of life' (Gen. 3.22 and 24). Man knows good and evil, against God, against his origin, godlessly and of his own choice, understanding himself according to his own contrary possibilities; and he is cut off from the unifying, reconciling life in God, and is delivered over to death. The secret which man has stolen from God is bringing about man's downfall.

Man's life is now disunion with God, with men, with things, and with himself.

5

Shame

Instead of seeing God man sees himself. 'Their eyes were opened' (Gen. 3.7). Man perceives himself in his disunion with God and with men. He perceives that he is naked. Lacking the protection, the covering, which God and his fellow-man afforded him, he finds himself laid bare. Hence there arises shame. Shame is man's ineffaceable recollection of his estrangement from the origin; it is grief for this estrangement, and the powerless longing to return to unity with the origin. Man is ashamed because he has lost something which is essential to his original character, to himself as a whole; he is ashamed of his nakedness. Just as in the fairy-story the tree is ashamed of its lack of adornment, so, too, man is ashamed of the loss of his unity with God and with other men. Shame and remorse are generally mistaken for one another. Man feels remorse when he has been at fault; and he feels shame because he lacks something. Shame is more original than remorse. The peculiar fact that we lower our eyes when a stranger's eye meets our gaze is not a sign of remorse for a fault, but a sign of that shame which, when it knows that it is seen, is reminded of something that it lacks, namely, the lost wholeness of life, its own nakedness. To meet a stranger's gaze directly, as is required, for example, in making a declaration of personal loyalty, is a kind of act of violence, and in love, when the gaze of the other is sought, it is a kind of yearning. In both cases it is the painful endeavour to recover the lost unity by either a conscious and resolute or else a passionate and devoted inward overcoming of shame as the sign of disunion.[1]

1 Shame isn't spontaneous . . . it's artificial, it's acquired. You can make people ashamed of anything. Agonizingly ashamed of wearing brown boots with a black coat, or speaking with the wrong sort of accent. . . . The Christians invented it, just as the tailors in Savile Row invented the shame of wearing brown boots with a black coat' (Aldous Huxley, *Point Counter Point*, Chapter X). To this it must be replied that first, embarrassment and diffidence are not to be confused with shame, and, secondly, shame may also find expression in quite external matters in a way which will depend on the character of the individual. The point is that shame may arise wherever there is experience of man's disunion—so why not also in connexion with dress?

'They made themselves aprons.' Shame seeks a covering as a means of overcoming the disunion. But the covering implies the confirmation of the disunion that has occurred, and it cannot therefore make good the damage. Man covers himself, conceals himself from men and from God. Covering is necessary because it keeps awake shame, and with it the memory of the disunion with the origin, and also because man, disunited as he is, must now withdraw himself and must live in concealment. Otherwise he would betray himself. 'Every profound mind requires a mask', said Nietzsche. Yet this mask is not a disguise; it is not intended to deceive the other man, but it is a necessary sign of the actual situation of disunion. For that reason it is to be respected. Beneath the mask there is the longing for the restoration of the lost unity. Whenever this longing forces its way towards fulfilment, in the partnership of sex when two human beings become one flesh (Gen. 2.24), and in religion, when a human being seeks for his union with God, whenever, that is to say, the covering is broken through, then, more than ever, shame creates for itself the very deepest secrecy. The fact that he was ashamed when he was discovered praying was for Kant an argument against prayer. He failed to see that prayer by its very nature is a matter for the strictest privacy, and he failed to perceive the fundamental significance of shame for human existence.

Shame implies both a positive and a negative attitude to man's disunion, and that is why man lives between covering and discovering, between self-concealment and self-revelation, between solitude and fellowship. This means that in his positive attitude to his disunion, that is to say in solitude, he may have a more intense experience of fellowship than in fellowship itself, though certainly only of a disunited fellowship. But both must always be present. And not even the closest fellowship must be allowed to destroy the secret of the disunited man. It may, therefore, be felt to be a repudiation of shame if one's relation to another is expressed in a free exchange of words, for one thereby reveals oneself and lays oneself bare before oneself. Nor will the most profound and intimate joy or grief allow itself to be disclosed in words. In the same way shame preserves a man against making any kind of display of his relation to God. Finally, man protects himself against any ultimate disclosure, he keeps his own secret even from himself when, for example, he refuses to become conscious of himself in everything that arises within him.

The covering of shame conceals everything nascent that proceeds from man's yearning for the reattainment of the unity which he has lost.[1] The secrecy of shame remains outspread over the creative power of man which comes to him in the self-sought union of the disunited. It is the memory of the disunion from the Creator, and of the robbery from the Creator, which is here disclosed. This is true of the coming into being of human life, just as it is true of the coming into being of a work of art, of a scientific discovery, and indeed of any creative work which arises from the union of man with the world of things. Only when life is born, when the work is perfected, is the secret broken through by jubilant open joy. But the secret of its coming into being it bears within itself for ever.

The dialectic of concealment and exposure is only a sign of shame. Yet shame is not overcome by it; it is rather confirmed by it. Shame can be overcome only when the original unity is restored, when man is once again clothed by God in the other man, in the 'house which is from heaven', the Temple of God (II Cor. 5.2ff.). Shame is overcome only in the enduring of an act of final shaming, namely the becoming

1 *Editor's note.* In a letter from prison, dated 26th November 1943, Bonhoeffer asks the following question after an air raid: 'The people here are talking quite openly about how frightened they have been. I don't quite know what to make of it, for after all fear is properly something of which a man is ashamed. I have the feeling that properly one ought to be able to speak of it only when one makes one's confession. Otherwise there can so very easily be something shameless about it. That does not mean at all that one need pretend to be a hero. And, on the other hand, a naive frankness can be somehow quite disarming; but the point is that there is also a cynical, godless kind of frankness which can just as well express itself in an orgy of drinking and whoring and which gives one an impression of utter chaos. Isn't fear perhaps one of the *pudenda*, something which ought to be kept hidden?'

manifest of knowledge before God. 'That thou mayest remember, and be confounded, and never open thy mouth any more because of thy shame, when I am pacified toward thee for all that thou hast done, saith the Lord God' (Ezek. 16.63). 'I will do this . . . You will have to be ashamed and to blush for shame at your behaviour' (Ezek. 36.32).[1] Shame is overcome only in the shaming through the forgiveness of of sin, that is to say, through the restoration of fellowship with God and men. This is accomplished in confession before God and before other men. Man's being clothed with the forgiveness of God, with the 'new man' that he puts on, with the Church of God, with the 'house which is from heaven', all this is comprised in the lines of the Leipzig hymn of 1638: 'Christ's blood and righteousness, that is my adornment and my fine raiment.'

Shame and Conscience

In shame man is reminded of his disunion with God and with other men; conscience is the sign of man's disunion with himself. Conscience is farther from the origin than shame, it presupposes disunion with God and with man and marks only the disunion with himself of the man who is already disunited from the origin. It is the voice of apostate life which desires at least to remain one with itself. It is the call to the unity of man with himself. This is evident already from the fact that the call of conscience is always a prohibition. 'Thou shalt not.' 'You ought not to have.' Conscience is satisfied when the prohibition is not disobeyed. Whatever is not forbidden is permitted. For conscience life falls into two parts: what is permitted and what is forbidden. There is no positive commandment. For conscience permitted is identical with good, and conscience does not register the fact, that even in this, man is in a state of disunion with his origin. It follows from this also that conscience does not, like shame, embrace the whole of life; it reacts only to certain definite actions. In one sense it is inexorable; in forbidden actions it sees a peril

---

1 *Translator's note.* Luther's version.

to life as a whole, that is to say, disunion with oneself; it recalls what is long past and represents this disunion as something which is already accomplished and irreparable, but the final criterion remains precisely that unity with oneself which is imperilled only in the particular instances in which the prohibition is disobeyed. The range of experience of conscience does not extend to the fact that this unity itself presupposes disunion with God and with men and that consequently, beyond the disobedience to the prohibition, the prohibition itself, as the call of conscience, arises from disunion with the origin. This means that conscience is concerned not with man's relation to God and to other men but with man's relation to himself. But a relation of man to himself, in detachment from his relation to God and to other men, can arise only through man's becoming like God in the disunion.

Conscience itself reverses this relation. It derives the relation to God and to men from the relation of man to himself. Conscience pretends to be the voice of God and the standard for the relation to other men. It is therefore from his right relation to himself that man is to recover the right relation to God and to other men. This reversal is the claim of the man who has become like God in his knowledge of good and evil. Man has become the origin of good and evil. He does not deny his evil; but in conscience man summons himself, who has become evil, back to his proper, better self, to good. This good, which consists in the unity of man with himself, is now to be the origin of all good. It is the good of God, and it is the good for one's neighbour. Bearing within himself the knowledge of good and evil, man has become judge over God and men, just as he is judge over himself.

Knowing of good and evil in disunion with the origin, man begins to reflect upon himself. His life is now his understanding of himself, whereas at the origin it was his knowledge of God. Self-knowledge is now the measure and the goal of life. This holds true even when man presses out beyond the bounds of his own self. Self-knowledge is man's interminable striving to overcome his disunion with himself by thought;

by unceasingly distinguishing himself from himself he endeavours to achieve unity with himself.

All knowledge is now based upon self-knowledge. Instead of the original comprehension of God and of men and of things there is now a taking in vain of God and of men and of things. Everything now is drawn in into the process of disunion. Knowledge now means the establishment of the relationship to oneself; it means the recognition in all things of oneself and of oneself in all things. And thus, for man who is in disunion with God, all things are in disunion, what is and what should be, life and law, knowledge and action, idea and reality, reason and instinct, duty and inclination, conviction and advantage, necessity and freedom, exertion and genius, universal and concrete, individual and collective; even truth, justice, beauty and love come into opposition with one another, just as do pleasure and displeasure, happiness and sorrow. One could prolong the list still further and the course of human history adds to it constantly. All these disunions are varieties of the disunion in the knowledge of good and evil. 'The point of decision of the specifically ethical experience is always conflict.'[1] But in conflict the judge is invoked; and the judge is the knowledge of good and evil; he is man.

The World of Recovered Unity

Now anyone who reads the New Testament even superficially cannot but notice the complete absence of this world of disunion, conflict and ethical problems. Not man's falling apart from God, from men, from things and from himself, but rather the rediscovered unity, reconciliation, is now the basis of the discussion and the 'point of decision of the specifically ethical experience'. The life and activity of men is not at all problematic or tormented or dark: it is self-evident, joyful, sure and clear.

1 Spranger, *Lebensformen*, 7th edition, p. 283. Spranger, of course, takes the concept of conflict in a narrower sense than we do.

The Pharisee

It is in Jesus's meeting with the Pharisee that the old and the new are most clearly contrasted. The correct understanding of this meeting is of the greatest significance for the understanding of the gospel as a whole. The Pharisee is not an adventitious historical phenomenon of a particular time. He is the man to whom only the knowledge of good and evil has come to be of importance in his entire life; in other words, he is simply the man of disunion. Any distorted picture of the Pharisees robs Jesus's argument with them of its gravity and its importance. The Pharisee is that extremely admirable man who subordinates his entire life to his knowledge of good and evil and is as severe a judge of himself as of his neighbour to the honour of God, whom he humbly thanks for this knowledge. For the Pharisee every moment of life becomes a situation of conflict in which he has to choose between good and evil. For the sake of avoiding any lapse his entire thought is strenuously devoted night and day to the anticipation of the whole immense range of possible conflicts, to the reaching of a decision in these conflicts, and to the determination of his own choice. There are innumerable factors to be observed, guarded against and distinguished. The finer the distinctions the surer will be the correct decision. This observation extends to the whole of life in all its manifold aspects. The Pharisee is not opinionated; special situations and emergencies receive special consideration; forbearance and generosity are not excluded by the gravity of the knowledge of good and evil; they are rather an expression of this gravity. And there is no rash presumption here, or arrogance or unverified self-esteem. The Pharisee is fully conscious of his own faults and of his duty of humility and thankfulness towards God. But, of course, there are differences, which for God's sake must not be disregarded, between the sinner and the man who strives towards good, between the man who becomes a breaker of the law out of a situation of wickedness and the man who does so out of necessity. If anyone disregards these differences, if he fails to take every factor into account in each of the innumerable cases of conflict, he sins against the knowledge of good and evil.

These men with the incorruptibly impartial and distrustful vision cannot confront any man in any other way than by examining him with regard to his decisions in the conflicts of life. And so, even when they come face to face with Jesus, they cannot do otherwise than attempt to force Him, too, into conflicts and into decisions in order to see how He will conduct Himself in them. It is this that constitutes their temptation of Jesus. One need only read the twenty-second chapter of St Matthew, with the questions about the tribute money, the resurrection of the dead and the first and great commandment, and then the story of the good Samaritan (Luke 10.25) and the discussions about the keeping of the Sabbath (Matt. 12.11), and one will be most intensely impressed by this fact. The crucial point about all these arguments is that Jesus does not allow Himself to be drawn in into a single one of these conflicts and decisions. With each of His answers He simply leaves the case of conflict beneath Him. When it is a matter of conscious malice on the part of the Pharisees Jesus's answer is the still cleverer avoidance of a cleverly laid trap, and as such it may well have caused the Pharisees to smile. But that is not essential. Just as the Pharisees cannot do otherwise than confront Jesus with situations of conflict, so, too, Jesus cannot do otherwise than refuse to accept these situations. Just as the Pharisees' question and temptation arises from the disunion of the knowledge of good and evil, so, too, Jesus's answer arises from unity with God, with the origin, and from the overcoming of the disunion of man with God. The Pharisees and Jesus are speaking on totally different levels. That is why their words so strikingly fail to make contact, and that is why Jesus's answers do not appear to be answers at all, but rather attacks of His own against the Pharisees, which is what they, in fact, are.

What takes place between Jesus and the Pharisees is only a repetition of that first temptation of Jesus (Matt. 4.1–11), in which the devil tries to lure Him into a disunion in the word of God, and which Jesus overcomes by virtue of His essential unity with the word of God. And this temptation of Jesus in its turn has its prelude in the question with which the serpent in Paradise ensnares Adam and Eve and brings about their downfall: 'Yea, hath God said?' It is the question which implies all the disunion against which man is powerless, because it constitutes his essential character; it is the question which can be overcome (but not answered) only from beyond this disunion. And, finally, all these temptations are repeated in the questions which we, too, always put to Jesus when we appeal to Him for a decision in cases of conflict, in other words when we draw Him in into our problems, conflicts and disunions, and demand that He shall provide the solution to them. Already in the New Testament there is no single question put by men to Jesus which Jesus answers with an acceptance of the human either-or that every such question implies. Every one of Jesus's answers, to the questions of His enemies and of His friends alike, leaves this either-or behind it in a way which shames the questioner. Jesus does not allow Himself to be invoked as an arbiter in vital questions; He refuses to be held by human alternatives. 'Man, who made me a judge or a divider over you?' (Luke 12.14).

Jesus often seems not to understand at all what men are asking Him. He seems to be answering quite a different question from that which has been put to Him. He seems to be missing the point of the question, not answering the question but addressing Himself directly to the questioner. He speaks with a complete freedom which is not bound by the law of logical alternatives. In this freedom Jesus leaves all laws beneath Him; and to the Pharisees this freedom necessarily appears as the negation of all order, all piety and all belief. Jesus casts aside all the distinctions which the Pharisee so laboriously maintains; Jesus bids His disciples eat of the ears of the field on the Sabbath, although they would certainly not have starved without them; He heals a sick woman on the Sabbath, although she has been ill for eighteen years already and could certainly have waited a day longer (the Pharisee, too, has left room in his system for the genuine case of

emergency); Jesus replies evasively to all the clear questions
which are intended to determine His position once and for
all. All this means that, for the Pharisee, He is a nihilist, a
man who knows and respects only his own law, an egotist and
a blasphemer of God. On the other hand, no one can discern
in Jesus the uncertainty and the timidity of one who acts
arbitrarily, but His freedom gives to Him and to His followers
in all their actions a peculiar quality of sureness, unquestion-
ableness and radiance, the quality of what is overcome and of
what overcomes. The freedom of Jesus is not the arbitrary
choice of one amongst innumerable possibilities; it consists
on the contrary precisely in the complete simplicity of His
action, which is never confronted by a plurality of possibilities,
conflicts or alternatives, but always only by one thing. This
one thing Jesus calls the will of God. He says that to do this
will is His meat. This will of God is His life. He lives and
acts not by the knowledge of good and evil but by the will of
God. There is only one will of God. In it the origin is
recovered; in it there is established the freedom and the
simplicity of all action.

In interpreting some of Jesus's sayings we will try to show
what is new in that which He has brought with Him.

'Judge not, that ye be not judged' (Matt. 7.1). This is not
an exhortation to prudence and forbearance in passing
judgement on one's fellow-men, such as was also recognized
by the Pharisees. It is a blow struck at the heart of the man
who knows good and evil. It is the word of Him who speaks
by virtue of his unity with God, who came not to condemn
but to save (John 3.17). For man in the state of disunion
good consists in passing judgement, and the ultimate criterion
is man himself. Knowing good and evil, man is essentially a
judge. As a judge he is like God, except that every judgement
he delivers falls back upon himself. In attacking man as a
judge Jesus is demanding the conversion of his entire being,
and He shows that precisely in the extreme realization of his
good he is ungodly and a sinner. Jesus demands that the
knowledge of good and evil shall be overcome; He demands
unity with God. Judgement passed on another man always

15

presupposes disunion with him; it is an obstacle to action. But the good of which Jesus speaks consists entirely in action and not in judgement. Judging the other man always means a break in one's own activity. The man who judges never acts himself; or, alternatively, whatever action of his own he may be able to show, and sometimes indeed there is plenty of it, is never more than judgement, condemnation, reproaches and accusations against other men. The Pharisee's action is clearly a judgement of the other man; it seeks for a public judgement, even though it be only in the public view of his own self; it desires to be seen, to be judged, and, if only in the sight of his own self, to be acknowledged as good. 'All their works they do for to be seen of men' (Matt. 23.5). The Pharisee's action is only a particular form of expression of his knowledge of good and evil, that is to say of his disunion with other men and with himself. It is consequently the gravest impediment to the achievement of that real action which arises from the rediscovered unity of man with other men and with himself. In this sense therefore, in the sense in which it arises from his disunited existence and not in the sense of conscious malevolence, the action of the Pharisee, that is to say, of the man who realizes his knowledge of good and evil to the very extreme, is false action or hypocrisy.

To this extent there is now indeed a profound contradiction between the speech and the action of the Pharisee. 'They say, and do not' (Matt. 23.3). It is not as though the Pharisees did nothing, or as though they were backward in the performance of good works. The opposite is the case. But their action is not genuine action; for indeed the action which is intended to overcome the disunion of man in good and evil does not achieve this aim but only aggravates the disunion still further. And in this way, for the Pharisee, the doing of the good which is intended to heal the inner disunion of man and his disunion with other men leads only to still greater disunion and to persistence in the defection from the origin. Finally, this same disunion of the man who sits in judgement over other men reveals itself in forms which can

16

be understood in terms of psychology. The serious man, for example, in this way abreacts his instincts of revenge against the frivolous man, whom he secretly envies; it is precisely when a man discerns his own foible in another man that he is impelled to condemn him with particular severity; in other words the spirit of judgement brings forth particularly poisonous fruit when it springs from the soil of inward mendacity, desperate indignation and resigned laxness with regard to a man's own weakness. All these facts must not, however, be allowed to distort the true picture; the passing of judgement does not spring from these vices of the human heart or from its wickednesses, be they never so rebellious; on the contrary, the passing of judgement is the origin of all these psychologically intelligible phenomena. It is not, as Nietzsche supposed, because it arises from these dark motives that judgement is wrongful; judgement is evil because it is itself apostasy, and that is also the reason why it brings forth evil fruit in the human heart. It cannot, of course, be denied that from the psychological point of view extremely noble motives may also be disclosed as determining the thought of the man who judges, but this fact can have no bearing on the character of judgement itself. 'Judging' is not a special vice or wickedness of the disunited man; it is his essence, manifesting itself in his speech, his action and his sentiment. It is true that the Pharisee is seen in this light only from the standpoint of unity already recovered, from the standpoint of Jesus. The Pharisee himself can know himself only in his virtues and vices, but not in his essence, in his apostasy from the origin. Only the overcoming of the knowledge of good and evil can bring about the conversion of the entire existence of the Pharisee; only Jesus can overthrow the authority of the Pharisee which is founded upon the knowledge of good and evil. In the mouth of Jesus 'judge not' is the summons addressed to disunited man by Him who is reconciliation; it is the call to reconciliation.

There is a spurious activity of man which is itself a judgement, and there is also, astonishingly enough, a judgement which is a true activity of man, that is to say, a 'judging' which springs from the achievement of union with the origin, with Jesus Christ. There is a 'knowing' which arises from the knowledge of Jesus Christ as the Reconciler. 'He that is spiritual judgeth all things, yet he himself is judged of no man' (I Cor. 2.15), and again, 'Ye have an unction from the Holy One, and ye know all things' (I John 2.20). This judgement and this knowledge spring from unity, not from disunion. They therefore create not further disunion, but reconciliation. Jesus Christ's judgement consisted precisely in His having come not to condemn but to save; 'And this is the judgement, that the light is come into the world' (John 3.19. *Cf.* verses 17 and 18), and likewise men who are reconciled with God and man in Christ will judge all things, as men who do not judge, and will know all things, as men who do not know good and evil. Their judgement will consist in brotherly help, in lifting up the falling and in showing the way to the straying, in exhortation and in consolation (Gal. 6; Matt. 18.15ff.), and also, if the need arises, in a temporary suspension of fellowship, but in such a manner that the spirit may be saved in the day of the Lord Jesus (I. Cor. 5.5). It will be a judgement of reconciliation and not of disunion, a judgement by not judging, a judgement which is the act of reconciling. No longer knowing good and evil, but knowing Christ as origin and as reconciliation, man will know all. For in knowing Christ man knows and acknowledges God's choice which has fallen upon this man himself; he no longer stands as the chooser between good and evil, that is to say, in disunion; he is the chosen one, who can no longer choose, but has already made his choice in his being chosen in the freedom and unity of the deed and will of God. He thus has a new knowledge, in which the knowledge of good and evil is overcome. He has the knowledge of God, yet no longer as the man who has become like God, but as the man who bears the image of God. All he knows now is 'Jesus Christ, and him crucified' (I Cor. 2.2), and in Him he knows all. As one who is without knowledge he has become the one who knows only God and all things in Him. Whoever knows God in His revelation in Jesus Christ, whoever knows the crucified and risen God, he knows all things that are in heaven, on earth and beneath the earth. He knows God as the ending of all disunion, all judgement and all condemnation, as the One who loves and as the One who lives. The knowledge of the Pharisees was dead and barren, but the knowledge of Jesus and of those who are allied with Him is alive and fruitful; the knowledge of the Pharisees is disruptive, but the new knowledge is redemptive and propitiatory; the knowledge of the Pharisees is the negation of all true action, but the knowledge of Jesus and of His own consists solely in action.

'But when thou doest alms, let not thy left hand know what thy right hand doeth: that thine alms may be in secret' (Matt. 6.3ff.). The Pharisee, too, knew that he was not to boast of his almsgiving, but that he owed thanks to God for all the good that he did. If Jesus had wanted to say no more than that, His saying would have been superfluous. But what Jesus wished to express was not this reasonable and pious thought, but something quite different and indeed exactly the opposite. The Pharisee who rendered thanks to God for his own good deed (Luke 18) was still the man who lived in the knowledge of good and evil, who passed judgement upon himself and then indeed thanked God that he was able to do so. The Pharisee knows the good that he has done. Jesus's saying is not directed against the boastfulness or the self-satisfaction of the man who has done good; but once again He is striking at the heart of the man who lives in disunion. He forbids the man who does good to know of this good. The new knowledge of the reconciliation which is accomplished in Jesus, the knowledge of the voiding of the disunion, itself entirely voids man's own knowledge of his own goodness. The knowledge of Jesus is entirely transformed into action, without any reflection upon a man's self. A man's own goodness is now concealed from him. It is not merely that he is no longer obliged to be the judge of his own goodness; he must no longer desire to know of it at all; or rather he is no longer permitted to know of it at all, and indeed he does no longer know of it. His deed has become entirely

unquestioning; he is entirely devoted to his deed and filled
with it; his deed is no longer one possibility among many,
but the one thing, the important thing, the will of God.
Knowledge can therefore no longer intervene and impede
him, and now quite literally no time can be lost in delaying
the deed, rendering it doubtful and judging it. The judgement remains hidden not only from other men, but even from
the forum of a man's own knowledge. The situation is quite
clear: knowing of Jesus a man can no longer know of his own
goodness, and knowing of his own goodness he can no longer
know of Jesus. Man cannot live simultaneously in reconciliation and in disunion, in freedom and under the law, in
simplicity and in discordancy. There are no transitions or
intermediate stages here; it is one thing or the other. But it is
impossible for a man by his own power to void and to overcome his knowledge of his own goodness, though he may
deceive himself and mistake the methodical repression of this
knowledge for the actual overcoming of it. That is why when
Jesus speaks of the right hand which must not know what the
left hand is doing, in other words of the concealment of a
man's own goodness, it is once again the summons to forsake
disunion, apostasy and the knowledge of good and evil, and
to return to unity and to the origin, to the new life which is in
Jesus alone. It is the call of liberation, the call to simplicity and
to conversion; it is the call which nullifies the old knowledge
of the apostasy and which imparts the new knowledge of
Jesus, that knowledge which is entirely contained in the
doing of the will of God. The deep impression which this
saying of Jesus made upon His disciples is clearly shown by
the fact that wherever in the apostolic exhortation there is
reference to giving, we always find added the requirement
that it shall be done 'with simplicity' (Rom. 12.8; II Cor.
8.2, 9.11, 9.13, etc.). One cannot fail to see in this a remi-
niscence of the saying in the sermon on the mount. But
indeed even God Himself gives 'simply' (Jas. 1.5) to him who
asks Him 'without divided thoughts' ($\mu\eta\delta\grave{\epsilon}\nu$ $\delta\iota\alpha\kappa\rho\iota\nu\acute{o}\mu\epsilon\nu\sigma$).
Though indeed the 'double-minded man', the $\grave{a}\nu\acute{\eta}\rho$ $\delta\acute{\iota}\psi\nu\chi\sigma$,
the opposite of the simple man, cannot expect to receive

gifts from God (Jas. 1.7). And whoever receives simply will also give simply.

The parable of the last judgement (Matt. 25.31ff.) completes and concludes what has so far been said. When Jesus sits in judgement His own will not know that they have given Him food and drink and clothing and comfort. They will not know their own goodness; Jesus will disclose it to them. Then the time will have come for which there was no time here on earth, the time which will lay bare what is concealed so that it may then receive its public reward, the time of judgement. But even then all judging and all knowing will be on the part of God and of Jesus Christ, and we ourselves shall be filled with wonder at what we receive. The Pharisee, who thought that through impartial and earnest judgement of himself he could anticipate and prepare for the last judgement, cannot but regard as unintelligible and wrongful the message that he is to receive goodness solely from the knowledge, from the judgement and from the hand of Jesus.

The overcoming of the knowledge of good and evil, which is accomplished in Jesus, as well as everything which has been said here concerning freedom and simplicity, would, of course, be completely misunderstood if they were to be regarded as psychologically observable data, in other words if one were to begin again to reflect upon the presence of these things in oneself or in other men. From the psychological point of view it is, in fact, impossible for the left hand not to know what the right hand is doing and for simplicity always to do the one and only thing without knowing of any other possibilities. The reason for this is that the psychological view is itself always subject already to the law of disunion. Psychology, therefore, will never be able to discover the simplicity, the freedom and the deed of which Jesus speaks; behind the supposed simplicity, freedom and absence of reflexion it will always find a final reflexion, a final lack of freedom, a final disunion. And precisely this is to fail to grasp what Jesus means. From the psychological standpoint the man who has become simple and free in the discipleship of Jesus can still be a man of very complicated reflexion, just as,

conversely, there is a psychological simplicity which has
nothing whatever to do with the simplicity of the life which is
reconciled with God. Thus the Bible speaks of an entirely
proper and necessary questioning with regard to the will of
God and of an equally proper and necessary examination of
oneself, without thereby coming into contradiction with the
fact that those for whom the knowledge of good and evil is
nullified are no longer confronted with a choice between
many different possibilities, but always only with their own
election to the simple performance of the one single will of
God, and that for the disciples of Jesus there can no longer
be any knowledge of their own goodness.

Proving

'Be ye transformed by the renewing of your mind, that ye
may prove what is the will of God' (Rom. 12.2). 'I pray that
your love may abound yet more and more in knowledge and
in all discernment, that ye may prove the different situations
(*i.e.* what is in each case right)' (Phil. 1.9 and 10; *cf.* Rom.
2.18). 'Walk as children of light . . . proving what is acceptable unto the Lord' (Eph. 5.8ff.). These sayings show the
error of the view that the simple recognition of the will of
God must take the form of an intuition which excludes any
sort of reflexion and that it must be the naive grasping of the
first thought or feeling to force itself upon the mind, the
error, in other words, of that psychologizing misrepresentation of the new life which has begun in Jesus. It is not said at
all that the will of God forces its way into the human heart
without further ado, charged with the accent of uniqueness,
or that it is simply obvious, and identical with whatever
the heart may think. The will of God may lie very deeply
concealed beneath a great number of available possibilities.
The will of God is not a system of rules which is established
from the outset; it is something new and different in each
different situation in life, and for this reason a man must
ever anew examine what the will of God may be. The heart,
the understanding, observation and experience must all col-
laborate in this task. It is no longer a matter of a man's own

knowledge of good and evil, but solely of the living will of God; our knowledge of God's will is not something over which we ourselves dispose, but it depends solely upon the grace of God, and this grace is and requires to be new every morning. That is why this proving or examining of the will of God is so serious a matter. The voice of the heart is not to be confused with the will of God, nor is any kind of inspiration or any general principle, for the will of God discloses itself ever anew only to him who proves it ever anew.

Now how does a man set about this 'proving what is the will of God'? The crucial precondition for this is that this proving takes place solely on the basis of a 'metamorphosis', a complete inward transmutation of one's previous form, a 'renewing of the mind' (Rom. 12.2), a 'walking·as children of light' (Eph. 5.8). This metamorphosis of man can only be the overcoming of the form of the fallen man, Adam, and conformation with the form of the new man, Christ. This is shown quite clearly by the use which the Bible makes of these concepts on other occasions. The new form, by virtue of which alone the proving of the will of God is possible, has left behind and beneath it the man who in his defection from God won for himself the knowledge of good and evil. It is the form of the child of God who lives in unity with the will of the Father in the conformation of the one true Son of God. In the passage which we have quoted from Philippians St Paul describes exactly the same situation when he says that living and increasing in love is the precondition of proving, because to live and to increase in love is to live in reconciliation and unity with God and with men, it is to live the life of Jesus Christ. One cannot, therefore, prove what is the will of God simply from one's own resources, from one's own knowledge of good and evil; on the contrary, only that man can do this who has lost all knowledge of his own of good and evil and who therefore abandons any attempt to know the will of God by his own means, who lives already in the unity of the will of God because the will of God has already been accomplished in him. Proving what is God's will is possible only on the foundation of the knowledge of God's will

23

in Jesus Christ. Only upon the foundation of Jesus Christ, only within the space which is defined by Jesus Christ, only 'in' Jesus Christ can man prove what is the will of God.

What does this proving mean? Why is it needed? This question may appear to be logically necessary, yet it is in itself wrongly conceived. The knowledge of Jesus Christ, metamorphosis, renewal, love, or whatever other name we may give it, is something living, and not something which is given, fixed and possessed once and for all. For this reason there arises every day anew the question how here, today and in my present situation I am to remain and to be preserved in this new life with God, with Jesus Christ. And it is just this question which is involved in proving what is the will of God. Knowledge of Jesus Christ implies ignorance of a man's own good and evil; knowledge of Jesus Christ refers the man entirely to Jesus Christ; and from this it follows that there must every day arise a new authentic proving which will consist precisely in the exclusion of all other sources of the knowledge of the will of God. This proving springs from the knowledge that a man is preserved, sustained and guided by the will of God, the knowledge that he has already been endowed with the merciful union with the will of God; and it seeks to confirm this knowledge every day afresh in his actual concrete life. It is not, therefore, a defiant or desperate proving; it is a humble and a trustful proving, a proving in freedom for the ever new word of God, in the simplicity of the ever one word of God. It is a proving which no longer calls in question that unity with the origin which is regained in Jesus; it presupposes this unity, and yet it must always recover it anew.

But when all this has been said it is still necessary really to examine what is the will of God, what is rightful in a given situation, what course is truly pleasing to God; for, after all, there have to be concrete life and action. Intelligence, discernment, attentive observation of the given facts, all these now come into lively operation, all will be embraced and pervaded by prayer. Particular experiences will afford correction and warning. Direct inspirations must in no case be

24

heeded or expected, for this could all too easily lead to a man's abandoning himself to self-deception. In view of what is at stake there must be a lofty spirit of sober self-control. Possibilities and consequences must be carefully assessed. In other words, the whole apparatus of human powers must be set in motion when it is a matter of proving what is the will of God. But in all this there will be no room for the torment of being confronted with insoluble conflicts, or for the arrogant notion that one can master every conflict, or even for the enthusiastic expectation and assertion of direct inspiration. There will be the belief that if a man asks God humbly God will give him certain knowledge of His will; and then, after all this earnest proving, there will also be the freedom to make a real decision, and with it the confidence that it is not man but God Himself who, through this proving, gives effect to His will. Anxiety as to whether one has done the right thing will not now become a desperate clinging to one's own goodness or swing round into the assuredness of the knowledge of good and evil, but it will be dispelled in the knowledge of Jesus Christ who alone delivers the judgement of mercy; it will cause a man's own goodness to lie hidden until the proper time in the knowledge and the mercy of the Judge.

Union with the will of God does not exclude the proving of what is the will of God on each particular occasion, but rather demands it, and in the same way, side by side with Jesus's saying about not letting the left hand know what the right hand is doing, there is St Paul's admonition to prove oneself with regard to one's faith and works. 'Examine yourselves whether ye be in the faith; prove your own selves. Know ye not your own selves, how that Jesus Christ is in you?' (II Cor. 13.5; cf. Gal. 6.4). The simplicity of not knowing of one's own goodness, because one is entirely taken up with one's deed and looks only to Jesus Christ, does not mean frivolousness or heedlessness with regard to one's own self. There is a Christian as well as a pharisaical self-proving; that is to say, a self-proving which is not directed towards one's own knowledge of good and evil and towards its realization in practical life but which every day afresh renews the knowledge that 'Jesus Christ is in us'. The Christian cannot now indeed examine himself in any other way than on the basis of this possibility which is decisive for him, the possibility that Jesus Christ has entered into his life, nay more than that, that Jesus Christ lives for him and in him, and that Jesus Christ occupies within him exactly the space which was previously occupied by his own knowledge of good and evil. Christian self-proving is possible only on the basis of this foreknowledge that Jesus Christ is within us, and when this name is spoken in its entirety it is evident indeed that this is not some neutral concept but that it is the historical person Jesus. In this self-examination, therefore, the Christian's gaze is not directed away from Jesus Christ and towards his own self; it remains fixed entirely on Jesus Christ since Jesus Christ is already present and active within us; since He belongs to us, the question can and must certainly now arise, whether and how in our daily lives we belong to Him, believe in Him and obey Him. But the answer to this question cannot be given by us ourselves; in the nature of the case it can be given to us only by Jesus Christ Himself. No particular sign of our own steadfastness and loyalty can answer the question which we ask when we prove ourselves, for we no longer have at our disposal any criterion by which to judge ourselves, or rather our only criterion is the living Jesus Christ Himself. Consequently our self-examination will always consist precisely in our delivering ourselves up entirely to the judgement of Jesus Christ, not computing the reckoning ourselves but committing it to Him of whom we know and acknowledge that He is within ourselves. This process of self-proving is not superfluous, because indeed Jesus Christ really is and desires to be in us and because Jesus Christ's being in us is not simply a mechanical operation but is an event which occurs and is verified ever anew precisely in this self-proving. 'I judge not mine own self. For I know nothing by myself; yet am I not hereby justified: but he that judgeth me is the Lord' (I Cor. 4.3 and 4). The will of God requires to be proved ever anew just because it is the will of the living God; and it is in this proving that it takes effect. So, too, Jesus Christ is in us precisely by virtue of the fact that we ourselves prove ourselves ever anew in Him. Thus the Christian's proving of the will of God is to a certain extent part of the will of God, just as the Christian's self-proving is part of the will of Jesus Christ in us.

But this will in no case disrupt or even disturb the new unity with the will of God and the simplicity of doing. In order to understand this we must make clear to ourselves what is really meant by 'doing' in the sense of the gospel.

Doing

It is evident that the only appropriate conduct of men before God is the doing of His will. The sermon on the mount is there for the purpose of being done (Matt. 7.24ff.). Only in doing can there be submission to the will of God. In doing God's will man renounces every right and every justification of his own; he delivers himself humbly into the hands of the merciful Judge. If the Holy Scripture insists with such great urgency on doing, that is because it wishes to take away from man every possibility of self-justification before God on the basis of his own knowledge of good and evil. The Bible does not wish man's own deed to be set side by side with the deed of God, even as a thank-offering or sacrifice, but it sets man entirely within the action of God and subordinates human action to God's action. The error of the Pharisees, therefore, did not lie in their extremely strict insistence on the necessity for action, but rather in their failure to act. 'They say, and do not do it.'

When the Bible calls for action it does not refer a man to his own powers but to Jesus Christ Himself. 'Without me ye can do nothing' (John 15.5). This sentence is to be taken in its strictest sense. There is really no action without Jesus Christ. All the innumerable different activities which in general assume the appearance of action are, in the judgement of Jesus, as though nothing had been done. This saying of Jesus demonstrates more clearly than any other saying in the Bible that all action is entirely bound up with Jesus

Christ and no clearer distinction can be drawn than this between true action and all kinds of false action.

Our definitions are designed to ward off possible mis-understandings of the action of which the Bible speaks and to display the peculiar character of this action.

The irreconcilable opposite of action is judgement. 'He that speaketh evil of his brother, and judgeth his brother, speaketh evil of the law, and judgeth the law: but if thou judge the law, thou art not a doer of the law, but a judge' (Jas. 4.11). There are two possible attitudes to the law: judgement and action. The two are mutually exclusive. The man who judges envisages the law as a criterion which he applies to others, and he envisages himself as being respon-sible for the execution of the law. He forgets that there is only one lawgiver and judge 'who is able to save and to destroy' (Jas. 4.12). If a man employs his knowledge of the law in accusing or condemning his brother, then in truth he accuses and condemns the law itself, for he mistrusts it and doubts that it possesses the power of the living word of God to establish itself and to take effect by itself. In making himself the lawgiver and the judge he invalidates the law of God. Hence there arises the irreparable cleavage between knowledge and action. If by his knowledge of the law a man has become the judge of his brother and so eventually of the law itself, then he can no longer perform the law, however much else he may appear to perform. The 'doer of the law', unlike the judge, submits to the law; the law never becomes a criterion for him such as he might apply to his brother; the law never confronts him otherwise than in summoning him personally to action. Even when he has to deal with a brother who is at fault, the 'doer of the law' has only one possible means of giving effect to the law, and that is by performing it himself. It is precisely in this way that the law is held in honour and is rendered effective, and is acknowledged to be the living word of God which takes effect by its own power and which has need of no human assistance. This does not mean, then, that the doer of the law is content with his own doing and that with a sidelong glance he calls upon God to

28

be the judge of his sinful brother whom he himself is, unfortunately, not permitted to judge. There is really no such
sidelong glance here, but there is the only conduct which is
appropriate to the law of God, namely the doing of the law,
and it is only in this exclusive concentration upon one's own
doing of the law, without any other thought in mind, that
the law is given its due and is allowed to exercise its power
also upon one's brother. There does not therefore remain, in
addition to action or through action, some ultimate possibility of judgement; action is and must continue to be the
only possible attitude towards the law of God; any residue of
judgement would disrupt this action entirely and transmute
it into false action, into hypocrisy.

Doing the law, of course, presupposes hearing the law.
Yet even this formulation is questionable, because it might
be taken to imply a differentiation and separation of hearing
as the prerequisite and doing as the consequence. But if
hearing is made independent of doing and if it acquires a
right of its own, this means that the doing itself is once again
already disrupted. Certainly the doer of the law must also
be a hearer, but only in the sense that the hearer is always
at the same time the doer (Jas. 1.22). A hearing which does
not at the same instant become a doing becomes once again
that 'knowing' which gives rise to judgement and so leads to
the disruption of all action. If what is heard does not become
doing, but if it becomes this 'knowing', then, paradoxical as
this may sound, it is already 'forgotten' (Jas. 1.25). No matter
how long it may be stored up, reconsidered and elaborated
as knowledge, it is forgotten as that which it essentially is,
namely, as that which points solely and entirely towards
action. The hearer of the word who is not at the same time
the doer of the word thus inevitably falls victim to self-
deception (Jas. 1.22). Believing himself to know and to
possess the word of God, he has, in fact, already lost it again,
because he imagines that a man can possess the word of God
for a single instant otherwise than in doing it. St James's
polemic against the hearer of the word corresponds exactly
to Jesus's polemic against the Pharisees. It is not that the

29

zealous hearer of the word to whom St James refers does not engage in many kinds of action, just as the Pharisee indeed was certainly not backward in action, but this doing is secondary to the hearing; it is connected with it through the intermediacy of knowing; the hearing is in itself an independent entity and the doing is now added to it as another; it is therefore false doing, self-deception, or, as Jesus calls it, hypocrisy. It is self-deception because the man who performs this false action does, in fact, suppose himself to be the one who is acting genuinely and cannot but utterly reject the reproach of hypocrisy. One is making the mistake of psychologizing the antithesis between the hearer and the doer of the word if one represents it as an antithesis between thinking and willing or between theory and practice. The Pharisee, too, knew that the word of God demands not only the thought but also the will, not only the theory but also the practice, and accordingly he exercised his will no less than his understanding in obedience to the word. It was not the thought and the will that the Pharisee failed to unite, but precisely the hearing and the doing. For the hearer of the word who makes the hearing independent there is the saying that 'the doer shall be blessed in his doing' (Jas. 1.25). The doer is here the man who simply knows of no other possible attitude to the word of God when he has heard it than to do it; who therefore continues to concern himself strictly with the word itself and does not derive from it a knowledge for himself on the basis of which he might become the judge of his brother, of himself, and eventually also a judge of the word of God.

What is meant here becomes completely clear in that saying of Jesus to Mary and Martha which appears to assert exactly the opposite (Luke 10.38ff.). Mary sat at Jesus's feet and heard His word, but Martha 'was cumbered about much serving'. Martha asked Jesus to point out to her sister that doing goes together with hearing. 'Bid her therefore that she help me. And Jesus answered and said unto her, Martha, Martha, thou art careful and troubled about many things: but one thing is needful: and Mary hath chosen that

good part, which shall not be taken away from her.' Here
Jesus quite clearly says that the hearer is right, and not the
doer. 'Blessed is the doer in his deed,' says St James; 'Blessed
are they that hear God's word and keep it,' says Jesus, and
they both say the same thing. For just as hearing must not
be made independent of doing, so, too, doing must not make
itself independent of hearing. The beatification of the doer
includes his hearing, just as the beatification of the hearer
includes his doing. One thing is needful: not to hear or to do,
but to do both in one, in other words to be and to continue
in unity with Jesus Christ, to be directed towards Him, to
receive word and deed from Him, and not, on the basis
either of hearing or of doing, to become the accuser and
judge of one's brother or even, like Martha, to become the
accuser of Jesus Christ, but in hearing and in doing to
entrust everything to the decision of Jesus Christ and to live
through Him, by His grace and by His merciful judgement
which He will deliver in His own time. In the blessing of the
doer and in the blessing of the hearer alike that man is
blessed who is freed from the disunion of his own knowledge
of good and evil and who is in unity with Jesus Christ.
Jesus recognizes neither doing in itself, the busy activity of a
Martha, nor hearing in itself. There is a false doing and a
false hearing. We cannot ourselves examine whether our
hearing and our doing are true or false; indeed this will
depend precisely on whether or not we entrust this examination entirely to the knowledge and the judgement of Jesus.

Two further definitions will make the biblical conception
of doing still clearer. 'Not every one that saith unto me, Lord,
Lord, shall enter into the kingdom of heaven; but he that
doeth the will of my Father which is in heaven' (Matt. 7.21).
This means that there is a profession of allegiance to Christ
which He rejects, even at a time when such a profession is
not at all fashionable and may indeed quite possibly entail
suffering and persecution. Jesus rejects it because it conflicts
with the doing of the will of God. One need not jump to the
conclusion that this is a case of hypocrisy, of covering an evil
deed with pious words; on the contrary, this profession may

31

well spring from a personally upright heart, and with this brave profession there may well be associated an equally brave and devoted action. This profession and this action may arise from the determination of a steadfast character to give his support to that which he has recognized to be good. And yet Jesus will reject this profession and this action precisely because they arise from the man's own knowledge of good and evil; for indeed what takes place here, even though it may bear a striking outward resemblance to the will of God, is fundamentally the will of the man, who is in a state of disunion with God. God's will is not done; and so it is of no avail for the man to appeal to his action: 'Have we not in thy name done many wonderful works?' (Matt. 7.22); it is of no avail even if he thinks he has performed it in the name of Christ. And again it would be wrong to assume that there are all kinds of human wickedness attached to or contained in this action, and that it is on their account that the action is wrongful. On the contrary, precisely when the action arises from the purest motives, when the most pious and selfless deeds are performed, the danger is especially great that this is the ungodly antithesis to the will of God which resembles the will of God to the point of being entirely indistinguishable from it, but which springs from a man's own knowledge of good and evil, from his disunion with God. There can be an honest profession of faith in Christ and a discipleship of Christ with all its consequences, and these may be rejected by Christ Himself with the words: 'I never knew you: depart from me, ye that work iniquity' (Matt. 7.23). That this is possible is a dark enigma which has its basis in the stolen likeness of man to God, but it is, nevertheless, a fact which Jesus and St Paul took into account.

Love

'And though I have the gift of prophecy, and understand all mysteries, and all knowledge; and though I have all faith, so that I could remove mountains, and have not love, I am nothing. And though I bestow all my goods to feed the poor, and though I give my body to be burned, and have not love, it profiteth me nothing' (I Cor. 13.2 and 3). This is the decisive word which marks the distinction between man in disunion and man in the origin. The word is love. There is a recognition of Christ, a powerful faith in Christ, and indeed a conviction and a devotion of love even unto death—all without love. That is the point. Without this 'love' everything falls apart and everything is inacceptable, but in this love everything is united and everything is pleasing to God. What is this love?

Everything that we have so far seen to be true excludes all those definitions which endeavour to represent the essence of love as a human attitude, as conviction, devotion, sacrifice, the will to fellowship, feeling, brotherhood, service or action. All these, without exception, can, as we have just heard, arise without 'love'. Everything that we are accustomed to call love, that which lives in the depths of the soul and in the visible deed, and even the brotherly service of one's neighbour which proceeds from a pious heart, all this can be without 'love', not because there is always a 'residue' of selfishness in all human conduct, entirely overshadowing love, but because love as a whole is something entirely different from what the word designates here. Nor is love the direct relationship between persons, the acceptance of the personal and the individual in contrast to the law of the objective and impersonal institution. Quite apart from this thoroughly unbiblical and abstract wrenching apart of the 'personal' and the 'objective' or 'real', love here becomes an attitude of man, and only a partial one at that. 'Love' now becomes the superior ethos of the personal, which perfects and completes the inferior ethos of the purely real and institutional. It is, for example, in accordance with this view that one regards love and truth as mutually conflicting and gives priority to love as the personal principle over truth as the impersonal principle, thereby coming into direct contradiction with St Paul's saying that love 'rejoiceth in the truth' (I Cor. 13.6). For indeed love knows nothing of the very conflict in terms of which one seeks to define it. On the contrary, it is of the essence of love that it should lie beyond all disunion. A love which violates or even merely neutralizes truth is called by Luther, with his clear biblical vision, an 'accursed love', even though it may present itself in the most pious dress. A love which embraces only the sphere of personal human relations and which capitulates before the objective and real can never be the love of the New Testament.

If, then, there is no conceivable human attitude or conduct which, as such, can unequivocally be designated by the name of 'love', if love lies beyond all the disunion in which man lives, and if at the same time anything that men can understand and practise as love is conceivable only as human conduct within this actual disunion, then it is an enigma and an open question what else the Bible can mean by 'love'. The Bible does not fail to give us the answer. We know this answer well enough, but we continually misinterpret it. It is this: 'God is love' (I John 4.16). First of all, for the sake of clarity, this sentence is to be read with the emphasis on the word God, whereas we have fallen into the habit of emphasizing the word love. *God* is love; that is to say not a human attitude, a conviction or a deed, but God Himself is love. Only he who knows God knows what love is; it is not the other way round; it is not that we first of all by nature know what love is and therefore know also what God is. No one knows God unless God reveals Himself to him. And so no one knows what love is except in the self-revelation of God. Love, then, is the revelation of God. And the revelation of God is Jesus Christ. 'In this was manifested the love of God toward us, because that God sent his only begotten Son into the world, that we might live through him' (I John 4.9). God's revelation in Jesus Christ, God's revelation of His love, precedes all our love towards Him. Love has its origin not in us but in God. Love is not an attitude of men but an attitude of God. 'Herein is love, not that we loved God, but that he loved us, and sent his Son to be the propitiation for our sins' (I John 4.10). Only in Jesus Christ do we know what love is, namely, in His deed for us. 'Hereby perceive we the love of God, because he laid down his life for us' (I John

34

3.16). And even here there is given no general definition of love, in the sense, for example, of its being the laying down of one's life for the lives of others. What is here called love is not this general principle but the utterly unique event of the laying down of the life of Jesus Christ for us. Love is inseparably bound up with the name of Jesus Christ as the revelation of God. The New Testament answers the question 'What is love?' quite unambiguously by pointing solely and entirely to Jesus Christ. He is the only definition of love. But again it would be a complete misunderstanding if we were to derive a general definition of love from our view of Jesus Christ and of His deed and His suffering. Love is not what He *does* and what He *suffers,* but it is what *He* does and what *He* suffers. Love is always He Himself. Love is always God Himself. Love is always the revelation of God in Jesus Christ.

When all our ideas and principles relating to love are concentrated in the strictest possible manner upon the name of Jesus Christ this must, above all, not be allowed to reduce this name to a mere abstract concept. This name must always be understood in the full concrete significance of the historical reality of a living man. And so, without in any way contradicting what has been said so far, it is only the concrete action and suffering of this man Jesus Christ which will make it possible to understand what love is. The name of Jesus Christ, in which God reveals Himself, gives the explanation of itself in the life and the words of Jesus Christ. For, after all, the New Testament does not consist in an endless repetition of the name of Jesus Christ, but that which this name comprises is displayed in events, concepts and principles which are intelligible to us. And so, too, the choice of the concept of 'love', ἀγάπη, is not simply arbitrary; this concept acquires an entirely new connotation in the New Testament message, yet it is not entirely without connexion with what we understand by 'love' in our own language. Certainly it is not true to say that the biblical concept of love is a particular form of what we have already in general understood by this word. Precisely the opposite turns out to be the case, namely, that the biblical concept of love, and it alone, is the foundation, the truth and the reality of love, in the sense that any natural thought about love contains truth and reality only in so far as it participates in this its origin, that is to say, in the love which is God Himself in Jesus Christ.

We can now continue to follow the Bible in answering the question 'What is love?' Love is the reconciliation of man with God in Jesus Christ. The disunion of men with God, with other men, with the world and with themselves, is at an end. Man's origin is given back to him.

Love, therefore, is the name for what God does to man in overcoming the disunion in which man lives. This deed of God is Jesus Christ, is reconciliation. And so love is something which happens to man, something passive, something over which he does not himself dispose, simply because it lies beyond his existence in disunion. Love means the undergoing of the transformation of one's entire existence by God; it means being drawn in into the world as it lives and must live before God and in God. Love, therefore, is not man's choice, but it is the election of man by God.

In what sense, then, is it still possible to speak, as the New Testament does clearly enough, of love as an activity of men, of the love of men for God and for their neighbour? In view of the fact that God is love, what can now be meant by saying that man, too, can love and ought to love? 'We love him, because he first loved us' (I John 4.19). This means that our love for God rests solely upon our being loved by God, in other words that our love can be nothing other than the willing acceptance of the love of God in Jesus Christ. 'If any man love God, the same is known of him' (I Cor. 8.3). 'Known' in the language of the Bible means 'elected' and 'engendered'. To love God means to accept willingly His election and His engendering in Christ. The relation between the divine love and human love is wrongly understood if we say that the divine love precedes the human love, but solely for the purpose of setting human love in motion as a love which, in relation to the divine love is an independent, free and autonomous activity of man. On the contrary, everything which is to be said of human love, too, is governed by the principle that God is love. The love with which man loves God and his neighbour is the love of God and no other; for there is no other love; there is no love which is free or independent from the love of God. In this, then, the love of men remains purely passive. Loving God is simply the other aspect of being loved by God. Being loved by God implies loving God; the two do not stand separately side by side.

In order to make this clearly intelligible a further word of explanation is necessary with regard to the use of the concept of passivity in this context. Here, as always in theology when there is reference to the passivity of men, we are not concerned with a psychological concept but with one which applies to the existence of men before God, that is to say, with a theological concept. Passivity with respect to the love of God does not mean that exclusion of all thoughts, words and deeds which is possible when I seek repose in a love of God that can come to me only in a particular 'quiet hour'. The love of God is not only that haven of refuge in which I take shelter in distress. Being loved by God does not by any means deprive man of his mighty thoughts and his spirited deeds. It is as whole men, as men who think and who act, that we are loved by God and reconciled with God in Christ. And it is as whole men, who think and who act, that we love God and our brothers.[1]

[1] *Editor's note.* This chapter was not finished.

II

THE CHURCH AND THE WORLD

WE will begin this section by referring to one of our most astonishing experiences during the years when everything Christian was sorely oppressed. The deification of the irrational, of blood and instinct, of the beast of prey in man could be countered with the appeal to reason; arbitrary action could be countered with the written law; barbarity with the appeal to culture and humanity; the violent maltreatment of persons with the appeal to freedom, tolerance and the rights of man; the subordination of science, art and the rest to political purposes with the appeal to the autonomy of the various different fields of human activity. In each case this was sufficient to awaken the consciousness of a kind of alliance and comradeship between the defenders of these endangered values and the Christians. Reason, culture, humanity, tolerance and self-determination, all these concepts which until very recently had served as battle slogans against the Church, against Christianity, against Jesus Christ Himself, had now, suddenly and surprisingly, come very near indeed to the Christian standpoint. This took place at a time when everything Christian was more closely hemmed in than ever before and when the cardinal principles of Christian belief were displayed in their hardest and most uncompromising form, in a form which could give the greatest offence to all reason, culture, humanity and tolerance. And indeed it was precisely in inverse proportion to this oppression and to this narrowing of its field of action that Christian thought acquired the alliance of all these concepts and with it an entirely unexpected new wide field of activity. It was clear that it was not the Church that was seeking the protection and the alliance of these concepts; but, on the contrary, it was the concepts that had somehow become homeless and now sought refuge in the Christian sphere, in the shadow of the Christian Church. It would not correspond at all to the real situation if we were to interpret this experience simply as a purely tactical move, as an alliance of expediency which would be dissolved as soon as the struggle was at an end. What is decisive is rather the fact that there took place a return to the origin. The children of the Church, who had become independent and gone their own ways, now in the hour of danger returned to their mother. During the time of their estrangement their appearance and their language had altered a great deal, and yet at the crucial moment the mother and the children once again recognized one another. Reason, justice, culture, humanity and all the kindred concepts sought and found a new purpose and a new power in their origin.

This origin is Jesus Christ. In Soloviev's story of the Antichrist, in the last days before Christ's return the heads of the persecuted churches discuss the question of what is for each of them the most precious thing in Christianity; the decisive answer is that the most precious thing in Christianity is Jesus Christ Himself. That is to say, that in the face of the Antichrist only one thing has force and permanence, and that is Christ Himself. Only he who shares in Him has the power to withstand and to overcome. He is the centre and the strength of the Bible, of the Church, and of theology, but also of humanity, of reason, of justice and of culture. Everything must return to Him; it is only under His protection that it can live. There seems to be a general unconscious knowledge which, in the hour of ultimate peril, leads everything which desires not to fall victim to the Antichrist to take refuge with Christ.

The Total and Exclusive Claim of Christ

'He that is not against us is for us' (Mark 9.40). Christ defines the limits of membership in Himself more widely than His disciples wish Him to do or themselves do. The particular concrete instance to which this saying of Jesus refers is the case of a man who, without himself being a disciple or follower, nevertheless casts out devils in the name of Jesus. Jesus forbids the disciples to hinder him, for 'there is no man which shall do a miracle in my name, that can lightly speak evil of me' (Mark 9.39). Wherever the name of Jesus is still spoken, even though it be in ignorance or in the knowledge only of its objective power but without personal obedience, and even though it be only with hesitation and embarrassment, wherever this name is spoken it creates for itself a space to which the revilement of Jesus has no access, a region which still belongs to the power of Christ, where one must not interfere and hinder but where one must allow the name of Jesus Christ to do its work. It is an experience of our days that the spoken name of Jesus alone exercises an unforeseen power; and the effort which it costs to speak this name is perhaps connected with some faint apprehension of the power which is inherent in it. Wherever the name of Jesus Christ is spoken it is a protection and a claim. This is the case with all those who in their struggle for justice, truth, humanity and freedom have learnt once again to speak the name of Jesus Christ, even though it is often with hesitation and with genuine fear. This name gives protection to them and to the high values for which they stand; and it is at the same time the claim to these men and to these values.

'He that is not with me is against me' (Matt. 12.30). It is the same Jesus who speaks these words. For abstract analysis these two sayings of Jesus are in irreconcilable contradiction; but in reality they necessarily belong together. Here again we have living experience to prove our case; under the pressure of anti-Christian forces there came together groups of men who confessed the faith unequivocally and who were impelled to seek a clear decision for or against Christ in strict discipline of doctrine and of life. In their struggle these confessing congregations could not but perceive that the greatest of all the dangers which threatened the Church with inner disintegration and disruption lay in the neutrality of large numbers of Christians; they saw in this the true hostility to Christ. The exclusive demand for a clear profession of allegiance to Christ caused the band of confessing

40

Christians to become ever smaller; the saying 'he that is not with me is against me' became an actual concrete experience of the Christian Church; and then, precisely through this concentration on the essential, the Church acquired an inward freedom and breadth which preserved her against any timid impulse to draw narrow limits, and there gathered around her men who came from very far away, and men to whom she could not refuse her fellowship and her protection; injured justice, oppressed truth, vilified humanity and violated freedom all sought for her, or rather for her Master, Jesus Christ. So now she had the living experience of that other saying of Jesus: 'He that is not against us is for us.'

These two sayings necessarily belong together as the two claims of Jesus Christ, the claim to exclusiveness and the claim to totality. The greater the exclusiveness, the greater the freedom. But in isolation the claim to exclusiveness leads to fanaticism and to slavery; and in isolation the claim to totality leads to the secularization and self-abandonment of the Church. The more exclusively we acknowledge and confess Christ as our Lord, the more fully the wide range of His dominion will be disclosed to us.

It was not metaphysical speculation, it was not a theologumenon of the *logos spermatikos*, but it was the concrete suffering of injustice, of the organized lie, of hostility to mankind and of violence, it was the persecution of lawfulness, truth, humanity and freedom which impelled the men who held these values dear to seek the protection of Jesus Christ and therefore to become subject to His claim, and it was through this that the Church of Jesus Christ learnt of the wide extent of her responsibility. The relationship of the Church with the world today does not consist, as it did in the Middle Ages, in the calm and steady expansion of the power of the name of Christ, nor yet in an endeavour, such as was undertaken by the apologists of the first centuries of Christianity, to justify and publicize and embellish the name of Jesus Christ before the world by associating it with human names and values, but solely in that recognition of the origin which has been awakened and vouchsafed to men in this suffering, solely in the seeking of refuge from persecution in Christ. It is not Christ who must justify Himself before the world by the acknowledgement of the values of justice, truth and freedom, but it is these values which have come to need justification, and their justification can only be Jesus Christ. It is not that a 'Christian culture' must make the name of Jesus Christ acceptable to the world; but the crucified Christ has become the refuge and the justification, the protection and the claim for the higher values and their defenders that have fallen victim to suffering. It is with the Christ who is persecuted and who suffers in His Church that justice, truth, humanity and freedom now seek refuge; it is with the Christ who found no shelter in the world, the Christ who was cast out from the world, the Christ of the crib and of the cross, under whose protection they now seek sanctuary, and who thereby for the first time displays the full extent of His power. The cross of Christ makes both sayings true: 'He that is not with me is against me' and 'He that is not against us is for us.'

Christ and Good People

'Blessed are they which are persecuted for righteousness' sake: for theirs is the kingdom of heaven' (Matt. 5.10). This does not refer to the righteousness of God; it does not refer to persecution for Jesus Christ's sake. It is the beatification of those who are persecuted for the sake of a just cause, and, as we may now add, for the sake of a true, good and human cause (cf. I Pet. 3.14 and 2.20). This beatitude puts those Christians entirely in the wrong who, in their mistaken anxiety to act rightly, seek to avoid any suffering for the sake of a just, good and true cause, because, as they maintain, they could with a clear conscience suffer only for an explicit profession of faith in Christ; it rebukes them for their ungenerousness and narrowness which looks with suspicion on all suffering for a just cause and keeps its distance from it. Jesus gives His support to those who suffer for the sake of a just cause, even if this cause is not precisely the confession of His name; He takes them under His protection, He accepts responsibility for them, and He lays claim to them. And so the man who is persecuted for the sake of a just cause is led to Christ, so that it happens that in the hour of suffering and of responsibility, perhaps for the first time in his life and in a way which is strange and surprising to him but is neverthe-less an inner necessity, such a man appeals to Christ and professes himself a Christian because at this moment, for the first time, he becomes aware that he belongs to Christ. This, too, is not an abstract deduction, but it is an experience which we ourselves have undergone, an experience in which the power of Jesus Christ became manifest in fields of life where it had previously remained unknown.

In times of established order, when the law rules supreme and the transgressor of the law is disgraced and ostracized, it is in relation to the tax-gatherer and the prostitute that the gospel of Jesus Christ discloses itself most clearly to men. 'The publicans and the harlots go into the kingdom of heaven before you' (Matt. 21.31). In times which are out of joint, in times when lawlessness and wickedness triumph in complete unrestraint, it is rather in relation to the few remaining just, truthful and human men that the gospel will make itself known. It was the experience of other times that the wicked found their way to Christ while the good remained remote from Him. The experience of our own time is that it is the good who find their way back to Christ and that the wicked obstinately remain aloof from Him. Other times could preach that a man must first become a sinner, like the publican and the harlot, before he could know and find Christ, but we in our time must say rather that before a man can know and find Christ he must first become righteous like those who strive and who suffer for the sake of justice, truth and humanity. Both of these principles are alike paradoxical and in themselves impossible; but they make the situation clear. Christ belongs both to the wicked and to the good; He belongs to them both only as sinners, that is to say, as men who in their wickedness and in their goodness have fallen away from the origin. He summons them back to the origin so that they shall no longer be good and evil but justified and sanctified sinners. But

43

before we express this ultimate in which evil and good are one before Christ and in which the difference between all times is annulled before Christ, we must not avoid the question which is set us by our own experience and by our own time, the question of what is meant by saying that the good find Christ, in other words the question of the relationship of Jesus Christ to good people and to goodness.

Over and over again the Church, when she has based herself upon Scripture, has given thought to the relationship of Jesus Christ to the wicked and to wickedness. In the Churches of the Reformation this question has been predominant; and indeed one of the decisive achievements of the Reformation was that in this connexion it spoke the word of the gospel with all the depth and fulness of the New Testament. Yet the question of the relationship of the good man to Christ remained remarkably neglected. The good man here was either the Pharisee and hypocrite who needed to be convinced of his wickedness; or else he was the man who had been converted from his wickedness to Christ and who was now enabled by Him to do good works. Goodness was accordingly either the *splendidum vitium* of the heathen, or else the fruit of the Holy Spirit. This did not, of course, by any means account for the whole of the relationship of Jesus Christ to the good; the neglect of this question had as its consequence that the gospel became merely the call to conversion and the consolation in sin of drunkards, adulterers and vicious men of every kind, and the gospel lost its power over good people. There was now very little to be said about the conversion of the good man to Jesus.[1]

If we now find ourselves obliged to raise precisely this question once again and to think it over afresh, we must first of all make it clear that we are here taking the concept of good in its widest sense, that is to say, simply as the contrary of vicious, lawless and scandalous, as the opposite of public transgression of the moral law, as good in contrast to the

[1] It is one of the greatest merits of A. Schlatter that he raised this question repeatedly, quite apart from the solutions he offers. But he was never understood in this, and that could not very well be otherwise.

publican and harlot. Good, in this sense, contains an extremely wide range of gradations, extending from the purely external observance of good order to the most intimate self-examination and character-formation and to personal self-sacrifice for the most sublime human values. It was very necessary to protest against that bourgeois self-satisfaction which, by a convenient reversal of the gospel, considered being good simply as a preliminary to being Christian and which supposed that the ascent from being good to being Christian could be accomplished more or less without a break. This protest has, however, taken the form of an equally dangerous distortion of the gospel in the opposite sense which was brought forward in the most impassioned terms at various times in the course of the nineteenth century and then especially during the past twenty years. The justification of the good has been replaced by the justification of the wicked; the idealization of good citizenship has given way to the idealization of its opposite, of disorder, chaos, anarchy and catastrophe; the forgiving love of Jesus for the sinful woman, for the adulteress and for the publican, has been misrepresented, for psychological or political reasons, in order to make of it a Christian sanctioning of anti-social 'marginal existences', prostitutes and traitors to their country. In seeking to recover the power of the gospel this protest unintentionally transformed the gospel of the sinner into a commendation of sin. And good, in its citizen-like sense, was held up to ridicule.[1]

[1] *Editor's note.* A preliminary note reads as follows: 'I feel about it more or less like this: the good citizen, too, is humble before God, but the vicious man really lives only by grace.' This chapter was not continued further.

III

ETHICS AS FORMATION

The Theoretical Ethicist and Reality

RARELY perhaps has any generation shown so little interest as ours does in any kind of theoretical or systematic ethics. The academic question of a system of ethics seems to be of all questions the most superfluous. The reason for this is not to be sought in any supposed ethical indifference on the part of our period. On the contrary it arises from the fact that our period, more than any earlier period in the history of the west, is oppressed by a superabounding reality of concrete ethical problems. It was otherwise when the established orders of life were still so stable as to leave room for no more than minor sins of human weakness, sins which generally remained hidden, and when the criminal was removed as abnormal from the horrified or pitying gaze of society. In those conditions ethics could be an interesting theoretical problem.

Today there are once more villains and saints, and they are not hidden from the public view. Instead of the uniform greyness of the rainy day we now have the black storm-cloud and the brilliant lightning-flash. The outlines stand out with exaggerated sharpness. Reality lays itself bare. Shakespeare's characters walk in our midst. But the villain and the saint have little or nothing to do with systematic ethical studies. They emerge from primeval depths and by their appearance they tear open the infernal or the divine abyss from which they come and enable us to see for a moment into mysteries of which we had never dreamed. What is worse than doing evil is being evil. It is worse for a liar to tell the truth than for a lover of truth to lie. It is worse when a misanthropist practises brotherly love than when a philanthropist gives

46

way to hatred. Better than truth in the mouth of the liar is the lie. Better than the act of brotherly love on the part of the misanthrope is hatred. One sin, then, is not like another. They do not all have the same weight. There are heavier sins and lighter sins. A falling away is of infinitely greater weight than a falling down. The most shining virtues of him who has fallen away are as black as night in comparison with the darkest lapses of the steadfast.

If evil appears in the form of light, beneficence, loyalty and renewal, if it conforms with historical necessity and social justice, then this, if it is understood straightforwardly, is a clear additional proof of its abysmal wickedness. But the moral theorist is blinded by it. With the concepts he already has in mind he is unable to grasp what is real and still less able to come seriously to grips with that of which the essence and power are entirely unknown to him. One who is committed to an ethical programme can only waste his forces on the empty air, and even his martyrdom will not be a source of strength for his cause or a serious threat to the wicked. But, remarkably enough, it is not only the adept of an ethical theory or programme who fails to strike his opponent. The wicked adversary himself is scarcely capable of recognizing his rival for what he is. Each falls into the other's trap. It is not by astuteness, by knowing the tricks, but only by simple steadfastness in the truth of God, by training the eye upon this truth until it is simple and wise, that there comes the experience and the knowledge of the ethical reality.

One is distressed by the failure of *reasonable* people to perceive either the depths of evil or the depths of the holy. With the best of intentions they believe that a little reason will suffice them to clamp together the parting timbers of the building. They are so blind that in their desire to see justice done to both sides they are crushed between the two clashing forces and end by achieving nothing. Bitterly disappointed at the unreasonableness of the world, they see that their efforts must remain fruitless and they withdraw resignedly from the scene or yield unresistingly to the stronger party.

Still more distressing is the utter failure of all ethical *fanaticism*. The fanatic believes that he can oppose the power of evil with the purity of his will and of his principle. But since it is part of the nature of fanaticism that it loses sight of the totality of evil and rushes like a bull at the red cloth instead of at the man who holds it, the fanatic inevitably ends by tiring and admitting defeat. He aims wide of the mark. Even if his fanaticism serves the high cause of truth or justice, he will sooner or later become entangled with non-essentials and petty details and fall into the snare set by his more skilful opponent.

The man with a *conscience* fights a lonely battle against the overwhelming forces of inescapable situations which demand decisions. But he is torn apart by the extent of the conflicts in which he has to make his choice with no other aid or counsel than that which his own innermost conscience can furnish. Evil comes upon him in countless respectable and seductive disguises so that his conscience becomes timid and unsure of itself, till in the end he is satisfied if instead of a clear conscience he has a salved one, and lies to his own conscience in order to avoid despair. A man whose only support is his conscience can never understand that a bad conscience may be healthier and stronger than a conscience which is deceived.

It looks as though the way out from the confusing multiplicity of possible decisions is the path of *duty*. What is commanded is seized upon as being surest. Responsibility for the command rests upon the man who gives it and not upon him who executes it. But in this confinement within the limits of duty there can never come the bold stroke of the deed which is done on one's own free responsibility, the only kind of deed which can strike at the heart of evil and overcome it. The man of duty will end by having to fulfil his obligation even to the devil.

But if someone sets out to fight his battles in the world in his own absolute *freedom*, if he values the necessary deed more highly than the spotlessness of his own conscience and reputation, if he is prepared to sacrifice a fruitless principle to a fruitful compromise, or for that matter the fruitless wisdom of the *via media* to a fruitful radicalism, then let him beware lest precisely his supposed freedom may ultimately prove his undoing. He will easily consent to the bad, knowing full well that it is bad, in order to ward off what is worse, and in doing this he will no longer be able to see that precisely the worse which he is trying to avoid may still be the better. This is one of the underlying themes of tragedy.

Some who seek to escape from taking a stand publicly find a place of refuge in a *private virtuousness*. Such a man does not steal. He does not commit murder. He does not commit adultery. Within the limits of his powers he does good. But in his voluntary renunciation of publicity he knows how to remain punctiliously within the permitted bounds which preserve him from involvement in conflict. He must be blind and deaf to the wrongs which surround him. It is only at the price of an act of self-deception that he can safeguard his private blamelessness against contamination through responsible action in the world. Whatever he may do, that which he omits to do will give him no peace. Either this disquiet will destroy him or he will become the most hypocritical of Pharisees.

Who would wish to pour scorn on such failures and frustrations as these? Reason, moral fanaticism, conscience, duty, free responsibility and silent virtue, these are the achievements and attitudes of a noble humanity. It is the best of men who go under in this way, with all that they can do or be. Here is the immortal figure of Don Quixote, the knight of the doleful countenance, who takes a barber's dish for a helmet and a miserable hack for a charger and who rides into endless battles for the love of a lady who does not exist. That is how it looks when an old world ventures to take up arms against a new one and when a world of the past hazards an attack against the superior forces of the commonplace and mean. Even the deep cleft which separates the two halves of the great story is characteristic in that the story-teller himself turns against his hero in the second half, which was not written until many years later than the first, and allies himself with the mean and mocking world. It is all too easy to pour scorn on the weapons which we have inherited from our fathers, the weapons which served them to perform great feats but which in the present struggle can no longer be sufficient. It is a mean-spirited man who can read of what befell Don Quixote and not be stirred to sympathy.

Yet our business now is to replace our rusty swords with sharp ones. A man can hold his own here only if he can combine simplicity with wisdom. But what is simplicity? What is wisdom? And how are the two to be combined? To be simple is to fix one's eye solely on the simple truth of God at a time when all concepts are being confused, distorted and turned upside-down. It is to be single-hearted and not a man of two souls, an ἀνὴρ δίψυχος (Jas. 1.8). Because the simple man knows God, because God is his, he clings to the commandments, the judgements and the mercies which come from God's mouth every day afresh. Not fettered by principles, but bound by love for God, he has been set free from the problems and conflicts of ethical decision. They no longer oppress him. He belongs simply and solely to God and to the will of God. It is precisely because he looks only to God, without any sidelong glance at the world, that he is able to look at the reality of the world freely and without prejudice. And that is how simplicity becomes wisdom. The wise man is the one who sees reality as it is, and who sees into the depths of things. That is why only that man is wise who sees reality in God. To understand reality is not the same as to know about outward events. It is to perceive the essential nature of things. The best informed man is not necessarily the wisest. Indeed there is a danger that precisely in the multiplicity of his knowledge he will lose sight of what is essential. But on the other hand knowledge of an apparently trivial detail quite often makes it possible to see into the depths of things. And so the wise man will seek to acquire the best possible knowledge about events, but always without becoming dependent upon this knowledge. To recognize the significant in the factual is wisdom. The wise man is aware of the limited receptiveness of reality for principles; for he knows that reality is not built upon principles but that it rests upon the living and creating God. He knows too, therefore, that reality cannot be helped by even the purest of principles or by even the best of wills, but only by the living God. Principles are only tools in God's hand, soon to be thrown away as unserviceable. To look in freedom at God and at reality, which rests solely upon Him, this is to combine simplicity with wisdom. There is no true simplicity without wisdom and there is no wisdom without simplicity.

This may sound very theoretical, and it is theoretical until it becomes clear at what point this attitude has its basis in reality so that it can itself become real. 'Be ye wise as serpents and harmless as doves' is a saying of Jesus (Matt. 10.16) and is therefore, like all His sayings, interpreted only by Jesus Himself. No man can look with undivided vision at God and at the world of reality so long as God and the world are torn asunder. Try as he may, he can only let his eyes wander distractedly from one to the other. But there is a place at which God and the cosmic reality are reconciled, a place at which God and man have become one. That and that alone is what enables man to set his eyes upon God and upon the world at the same time. This place does not lie somewhere out beyond reality in the realm of ideas. It lies in the midst of history as a divine miracle. It lies in Jesus Christ, the Reconciler of the world. As an ideal the unity of simplicity and wisdom is doomed to failure, just as is any other attempt to hold one's own against reality. It is an impossible ideal, and an extremely contradictory one. But if it is founded upon the reality of a world which is at one with God in Jesus Christ, the commandment of Jesus·acquires reality and meaning. Whoever sees Jesus Christ does indeed see God and the world in one. He can henceforward no longer see God without the world or the world without God.

Ecce Homo!

Ecce homo!—Behold the man! In Him the world was reconciled with God. It is not by its overthrowing but by its

reconciliation that the world is subdued. It is not by ideals
and programmes or by conscience, duty, responsibility and
virtue that reality can be confronted and overcome, but
simply and solely by the perfect love of God. Here again it is
not by a general idea of love that this is achieved, but by
the really *lived* love of God in Jesus Christ. This love of God
does not withdraw from reality into noble souls secluded from
the world. It experiences and suffers the reality of the world
in all its hardness. The world exhausts its fury against the
body of Christ. But, tormented, He forgives the world its
sin. That is how the reconciliation is accomplished. *Ecce
homo!*

The figure of the Reconciler, of the God-Man Jesus
Christ, comes between God and the world and fills the centre
of all history. In this figure the secret of the world is laid
bare, and in this figure there is revealed the secret of God.
No abyss of evil can remain hidden from Him through whom
the world is reconciled with God. But the abyss of the love
of God encompasses even the most abysmal godlessness of
the world. In a manner which passes all comprehension God
reverses the judgement of justice and piety, declares Himself
guilty towards the world, and thereby wipes out the world's
guilt. God Himself sets out on the path of humiliation and
atonement, and thereby absolves the world. God is willing
to be guilty of our guilt. He takes upon Himself the punishment and the suffering which this guilt has brought on us.
God Himself answers for godlessness, love for hatred, the
saint for the sinner. Now there is no more godlessness, no
more hatred, no more sin which God has not taken upon
Himself, suffered for and expiated. Now there is no more
reality, no more world, but it is reconciled with God and at
peace. God did this in His dear Son Jesus Christ. *Ecce homo!*

The Despiser of Men

Ecce homo!—Behold the God who has become man, the
unfathomable mystery of the love of God for the world. God
loves man. God loves the world. It is not an ideal man that
He loves, but man as he is; not an ideal world, but the real

world. What we find abominable in man's opposition to God, what we shrink back from with pain and hostility, the real man, the real world, this is for God the ground for unfathomable love, and it is with this that He unites Himself utterly. God becomes man, real man. While we are trying to grow out beyond our manhood, to leave the man behind us, God becomes man and we have to recognize that God wishes us men, too, to be real men. While we are distinguishing the pious from the ungodly, the good from the wicked, the noble from the mean, God makes no distinction at all in His love for the real man. He does not permit us to classify men and the world according to our own standards and to set ourselves up as judges over them. He leads us *ad absurdum* by Himself becoming a real man and a companion of sinners and thereby compelling us to become the judges of God. God sides with the real man and with the real world against all their accusers. Together with men and with the world He comes before the judges, so that the judges are now made the accused.

But it is not enough to say that God comes to men's help. This assertion rests upon an infinitely more profound one, and one whose significance is still more impenetrable. This is the assertion that in the conception and birth of Jesus Christ God took on manhood in the flesh. God secures His love against any suggestion that it is not genuine or that it is doubtful or uncertain, for He Himself enters into the life of man as man and takes upon Himself and carries in the flesh the nature, the character, and the guilt and suffering of man. Out of love for man God becomes man. He does not seek out the most perfect man in order to unite Himself with him, but he takes human character upon Himself as it is. Jesus Christ is not the transfiguration of sublime humanity. He is the 'yes' which God addresses to the real man. Not the dispassionate 'yes' of the judge, but the merciful 'yes' of Him who has compassion. In this 'yes' there is comprised the whole life and the whole hope of the world. In the man Jesus Christ sentence is passed on the whole of humanity. Again it is not the indifferent pronouncement of the judge but the merciful decision of Him who Himself bears and suffers to the end the fate of all mankind. Jesus is not *a* man. He is *man*. Whatever happens to Him happens to man. It happens to all men, and therefore it 'happens also to us. The name Jesus contains within itself the whole of humanity and the whole of God.

The news that God has become man strikes at the very heart of an age in which both the good and the wicked regard either scorn for man or the idolization of man as the highest attainable wisdom. The weaknesses of human nature are displayed more clearly in a time of storm than in the smooth course of more peaceful periods. In the face of totally unexpected threats and opportunities it is fear, desire, irresolution and brutality which reveal themselves as the motives for the actions of the overwhelming majority. At such a time as this it is easy for the tyrannical despiser of men to exploit the baseness of the human heart, nurturing it and calling it by other names. Fear he calls responsibility. Desire he calls keenness. Irresolution becomes solidarity. Brutality becomes masterfulness. Human weaknesses are played upon with unchaste seductiveness, so that meanness and baseness are reproduced and multiplied ever anew. The vilest contempt for mankind goes about its sinister business with the holiest of protestations of devotion to the human cause. And, as the base man grows baser, he becomes an ever more willing and adaptable tool in the hand of the tyrant. The small band of the upright are reviled. Their bravery is called insubordination; their self-control is called pharisaism; their independence arbitrariness and their masterfulness arrogance. For the tyrannical despiser of men popularity is the token of the highest love for mankind. His secret profound mistrust for all human beings he conceals behind words stolen from a true community. In the presence of the crowd he professes to be one of their number, and at the same time he sings his own praises with the most revolting vanity and scorns the rights of every individual. He thinks people stupid, and they become stupid. He thinks them weak, and they become weak. He thinks them criminal, and they become criminal. His most sacred earnestness is a frivolous game. His hearty and worthy solicitude is the most impudent cynicism. In his profound contempt for his fellow-men he seeks the favour of those whom he despises, and the more he does so the more certainly he promotes the deification of his own person by the mob. Contempt for man and idolization of man are close neighbours. But the good man too, no less than the wicked, succumbs to the same temptation to be a despiser of mankind if he sees through all this and with-draws in disgust, leaving his fellow-men to their own devices, and if he prefers to mind his own business rather than to debase himself in public life. Of course, his contempt for mankind is more respectable and upright, but it is also more barren and ineffectual. In the face of God's becoming man the good man's contemptuous attitude cannot be maintained, any more than can the tyrant's. The despiser of men despises what God has loved. Indeed he despises even the figure of the God who has become man.

But there is also an honestly intended philanthropism which amounts to the same thing as contempt for mankind. It consists in judging the man according to his latent values, according to his underlying soundness, reasonableness and goodness. This kind of philanthropism will generally arise in peaceful times. But even in great crises when these values shine out on particular occasions they may form the basis for a hard-won and well-meant love for humanity. With forced indulgence evil is interpreted as good. Baseness is overlooked and the reprehensible is excused. For one reason or another one is afraid to give a clear 'no' for an answer, and one ends by acquiescing in everything. One's love is directed to a picture of man of one's own making, a picture which scarcely preserves any resemblance with the reality. And consequently one finishes once again by despising the real man whom God has loved and whose nature He has taken upon Himself.

It is only through God's being made man that it is possible to know the real man and not to despise him. The real man can live before God, and we can allow the real man to live before God side by side with ourselves without either despising or deifying him. That is not to say that this is really a value on its own account. It is simply and solely because God has loved the real man and has taken him to Himself. The ground for God's love towards man does not lie in man but solely in God Himself. And again, the reason why we can live as real men and can love the real man at our side is to be found solely in the incarnation of God, in the unfathomable love of God for man.

The Successful Man

Ecce homo!—Behold the man sentenced by God, the figure of grief and pain. That is how the Reconciler of the world appears. The guilt of mankind has fallen upon Him. It casts Him into shame and death before God's judgement seat. This is the great price which God pays for reconciliation with the world. Only by God's executing judgement upon Himself can there be peace between Him and the world and between man and man. But the secret of this judgement, of this passion and death, is the love of God for the world and for man. What befell Christ befalls every man in Him. It is only as one who is sentenced by God that man can live before God. Only the crucified man is at peace with God. It is in the figure of the Crucified that man recognizes and discovers himself. To be taken up by God, to be executed on the cross and reconciled, that is the reality of manhood.

In a world where success is the measure and justification of all things the figure of Him who was sentenced and crucified remains a stranger and is at best the object of pity. The world will allow itself to be subdued only by success. It is not ideas or opinions which decide, but deeds. Success alone justifies wrongs done. Success heals the wounds of guilt. There is no sense in reproaching the successful man for his unvirtuous behaviour, for this would be to remain in the past while the successful man strides forward from one deed to the next, conquering the future and securing the irrevocability of what has been done. The successful man presents us with accomplished facts which can never again be reversed.

What he destroys cannot be restored. What he constructs will acquire at least a prescriptive right in the next generation. No indictment can make good the guilt which the successful man has left behind him. The indictment falls silent with the passage of time, but the success remains and determines the course of history. The judges of history play a sad rôle in comparison with its protagonists. History rides rough-shod over their heads. With a frankness and off-handedness which no other earthly power could permit itself, history appeals in its own cause to the dictum that the end justifies the means.

So far we have been talking about facts and not about valuations. There are three possible attitudes which men and periods may adopt with regard to these facts.

When a successful figure becomes especially prominent and conspicuous, the majority give way to the idolization of success. They become blind to right and wrong, truth and untruth, fair play and foul play. They have eyes only for the deed, for the successful result. The moral and intellectual critical faculty is blunted. It is dazzled by the brilliance of the successful man and by the longing in some way to share in his success. It is not even seen that success is healing the wounds of guilt, for the guilt itself is no longer recognized. Success is simply identified with good. This attitude is genuine and pardonable only in a state of intoxication. When sobriety returns it can be achieved only at the price of a deep inner untruthfulness and conscious self-deception. This brings with it an inward rottenness from which there is scarcely a possibility of recovery.

The proposition that success is identical with good is followed by another which aims to establish the conditions for the continuance of success. This is the proposition that only good is successful. The competence of the critical faculty to judge success is reaffirmed. Now right remains right and wrong remains wrong. Now one no longer closes one's eye at the crucial moment and opens it only when the deed is done. And now there is a conscious or unconscious recognition of a law of the world, a law which makes right, truth and order more stable in the long run than violence, falsehood and self-will. And yet this optimistic thesis is in the end misleading. Either the historical facts have to be falsified in order to prove that evil has not been successful, which very soon brings one back to the converse proposition that success is identical with goodness, or else one's optimism breaks down in the face of the facts and one ends by finding fault with *all* historical successes.

That is why the arraigners of history never cease to complain that all success comes of wickedness. If one is engaged in fruitless and pharisaical criticism of what is past, one can oneself never find one's way to the present, to action and to success, and precisely in this one sees yet another proof of the wickedness of the successful man. And, if only in a negative sense, even in this one quite involuntarily makes success the measure of all things. And if success is the measure of all things, it makes no essential difference whether it is so in a positive or in a negative sense.

The figure of the Crucified invalidates all thought which takes success for its standard. Such thought is a denial of eternal justice. Neither the triumph of the successful nor the bitter hatred which the successful arouse in the hearts of the unsuccessful can ultimately overcome the world. Jesus is certainly no apologist for the successful men in history, but neither does He head the insurrection of shipwrecked existences against their successful rivals. He is not concerned with success or failure but with the willing acceptance of God's judgement. Only in this judgement is there reconciliation with God and among men. Christ confronts all thinking in terms of success and failure with the man who is under God's sentence, no matter whether he be successful or unsuccessful. It is out of pure love that God is willing to let man stand before Him, and that is why He sentences man. It is a sentence of mercy that God pronounces on mankind in Christ. In the cross of Christ God confronts the successful man with the sanctification of pain, sorrow, humility, failure, poverty, loneliness and despair. That does not mean that all this has a value in itself, but it receives its sanctification from the love of God, the love which takes all this upon itself as its just reward. God's acceptance of the cross is His judgement upon the successful man. But the unsuccessful man must recognize that what enables him to stand before God is not his lack of success as such, not his position as a pariah, but solely the willing acceptance of the sentence passed on him by the divine love. It was precisely the cross of Christ, the failure of Christ in the world, which led to His success in history, but this is a mystery of the divine cosmic order and cannot be regarded as a general rule even though it is repeated from time to time in the sufferings of His Church.

Only in the cross of Christ, that is, as those upon whom sentence has been executed, do men achieve their true form.

The Idolization of Death

Ecce homo!—Behold the man who has been taken to Himself by God, sentenced and executed and awakened by God to a new life. Behold the Risen One. The 'yes' which God addresses to man has achieved its purpose through and beyond judgement and death. God's love for man has proved stronger than death. By God's miracle there has been created a new man, a new life, a new creature. 'Life has secured the victory. It has overcome death.' God's love has become the death of death and the life of man. Humanity has been made new in Jesus Christ, who became man, was crucified and rose again. What befell Christ befell all men, for Christ was man. The new man has been created.

The miracle of Christ's resurrection makes nonsense of that idolization of death which is prevalent among us today. Where death is the last thing, fear of death is combined with defiance. Where death is the last thing, earthly life is all or nothing. Boastful reliance on earthly eternities goes side by side with a frivolous playing with life. A convulsive acceptance and seizing hold of life stands cheek by jowl with indifference and contempt for life. There is no clearer indication of the idolization of death than when a period claims to be building for eternity and yet life has no value in this period, or when big words are spoken of a new man, of a new world and of a new society which is to be ushered in, and yet all that is new is the destruction of life as we have it. The drastic acceptance or rejection of earthly life reveals that only death has any value here. To clutch at everything or to cast away everything is the reaction of one who believes fanatically in death.

But wherever it is recognized that the power of death has been broken, wherever the world of death is illumined by the miracle of the resurrection and of the new life, there no eternities are demanded of life but one takes of life what it offers, not all or nothing but good and evil, the important and the unimportant, joy and sorrow; one neither clings convulsively to life nor casts it frivolously away. One is content with the allotted span and one does not invest earthly things with the title of eternity; one allows to death the limited rights which it still possesses. It is from beyond death that one expects the coming of the new man and of the new world, from the power by which death has been vanquished.

The risen Christ bears the new humanity within Himself, the final glorious 'yes' which God addresses to the new man. It is true that mankind is still living the old life, but it is already beyond the old. It still lives in a world of death, but it is already beyond death. It still lives in a world of sin, but it is already beyond sin. The night is not yet over, but already the dawn is breaking.

The man whom God has taken to himself, sentenced and awakened to a new life, this is Jesus Christ. In Him it is all mankind. It is ourselves. Only the form of Jesus Christ confronts the world and defeats it. And it is from this form alone that there comes the formation of a new world, a world which is reconciled with God.

Conformation

The word 'formation' arouses our suspicion. We are sick and tired of Christian programmes and of the thoughtless and superficial slogan of what is called 'practical' Christianity as distinct from 'dogmatic' Christianity. We have seen that the formative forces in the world do not arise from Christianity at all and that the so-called practical Christianity is at least as unavailing in the world as is the dogmatic kind. The word 'formation', therefore, must be taken in quite a different sense from that to which we are accustomed. And in fact the Holy Scriptures speak of formation in a sense which is at first entirely unfamiliar to us. Their primary concern is not with the forming of a world by means of plans and programmes. Whenever they speak of forming they are concerned only with the one form which has overcome the world, the form of Jesus Christ. Formation can come only from this form. But here again it is not a question of applying directly to the world the teaching of Christ or what are referred to as Christian principles, so that the world might be formed in accordance with these. On the contrary, formation comes only by being drawn in into the form of Jesus Christ. It comes only as formation in His likeness, as *conformation* with the unique form of Him who was made man, was crucified, and rose again.

This is not achieved by dint of efforts 'to become like Jesus', which is the way in which we usually interpret it. It is achieved only when the form of Jesus Christ itself works upon us in such a manner that it moulds our form in its own likeness (Gal. 4.19). Christ remains the only giver of forms. It is not Christian men who shape the world with their ideas, but it is Christ who shapes men in conformity with Himself. But just as we misunderstand the form of Christ if we take Him to be essentially the teacher of a pious and good life, so, too, we should misunderstand the formation of man if we were to regard it as instruction in the way in which a pious and good life is to be attained. Christ is the Incarnate, Crucified and Risen One whom the Christian faith confesses. To be transformed in His image (II Cor. 3.18, Phil. 3.10, Rom. 8.29 and 12.2)—this is what is meant by the formation of which the Bible speaks.

To be conformed with the Incarnate—that is to be a real man. It is man's right and duty that he should be man. The quest for the superman, the endeavour to outgrow the man

61

within the man, the pursuit of the heroic, the cult of the demigod, all this is not the proper concern of man, for it is untrue. The real man is not an object either for contempt or for deification, but an object of the love of God. The rich and manifold variety of God's creation suffers no violence here from false uniformity or from the forcing of men into the pattern of an ideal or a type or a definite picture of the human character. The real man is at liberty to be his Creator's creature. To be conformed with the Incarnate is to have the right to be the man one really is. Now there is no more pretence, no more hypocrisy or self-violence, no more compulsion to be something other, better and more ideal than what one is. God loves the real man. God became a real man.

To be formed in the likeness of the Crucified—this means being a man sentenced by God. In his daily existence man carries with him God's sentence of death, the necessity of dying before God for the sake of sin. With his life he testifies that nothing can stand before God save only under God's sentence and grace. Every day man dies the death of a sinner. Humbly he bears the scars on his body and soul, the marks of the wounds which sin inflicts on him. He cannot raise himself up above any other man or set himself before him as a model, for he knows himself to be the greatest of all sinners. He can excuse the sin of another, but never his own. He bears all the suffering imposed on him, in the knowledge that it serves to enable him to die with his own will and to accept God's judgement upon him. But in surrendering himself to God's judgement upon him and against him he is himself just in the eyes of God. In the words of K. F. Harttmann's poem, 'it is in suffering that the Master imprints upon our minds and hearts his own all-valid image'.

To be conformed with the Risen One—that is to be a new man before God. In the midst of death he is in life. In the midst of sin he is righteous. In the midst of the old he is new. His secret remains hidden from the world. He lives because Christ lives, and lives in Christ alone. 'Christ is my life' (Phil. 1.21). So long as the glory of Christ is hidden, so long, too, does the glory of his new life remain 'hidden with Christ in God' (Col. 3.3). But he who knows espies already here and there a gleam of what is to come. The new man lives in the world like any other man. Often there is little to distinguish him from the rest. Nor does he attach importance to distinguishing himself, but only to distinguishing Christ for the sake of his brethren. Transfigured though he is in the form of the Risen One, here he bears only the sign of the cross and the judgement. By bearing it willingly he shows himself to be the one who has received the Holy Spirit and who is united with Jesus Christ in incomparable love and fellowship.

The form of Jesus Christ takes form in man. Man does not take on an independent form of his own, but what gives him form and what maintains him in the new form is always solely the form of Jesus Christ Himself. It is therefore not a vain imitation or repetition of Christ's form but Christ's form itself which takes form in man. And again, man is not transformed into a form which is alien to him, the form of God, but into his own form, the form which is essentially proper to him. Man becomes man because God became man. But man does not become God. It is not he, therefore, who was or is able to accomplish his own transformation, but it is God who changes his form into the form of man, so that man may become, not indeed God, but, in the eyes of God, man.

In Christ there was re-created the form of man before God. It was not an outcome of the place or the time, of the climate or the race, of the individual or the society, or of religion or of taste, but quite simply of the life of mankind as such, that mankind at this point recognized its image and its hope. What befell Christ had befallen mankind. It is a mystery, for which there is no explanation, that only a part of mankind recognize the form of their Redeemer. The longing of the Incarnate to take form in all men is as yet still unsatisfied. He bore the form of man as a whole, and yet He can take form only in a small band. These are His Church.

'Formation' consequently means in the first place Jesus's taking form in His Church. What takes form here is the form of Jesus Christ Himself. The New Testament states the case

profoundly and clearly when it calls the Church the Body of
Christ. The body is the form. So the Church is not a religious
community of worshippers of Christ but is Christ Himself,
who has taken form among men. The Church can be called
the Body of Christ because in Christ's Body man is really
taken up by Him, and so too, therefore, are all mankind.
The Church, then, bears the form which is in truth the
proper form of all humanity. The image in which she is
formed is the image of man. What takes place in her takes
place as an example and substitute for all men. But it is
impossible to state clearly enough that the Church, too, is
not an independent form by herself, side by side with the
form of Christ, and that she, too, can therefore never lay
claim to an independent character, title, authority or dignity
on her own account and apart from Him. The Church is
nothing but a section of humanity in which Christ has really
taken form. What we have here is utterly and completely the
form of Jesus Christ and not some other form side by side
with Him. The Church is the man in Christ, incarnate,
sentenced and awakened to new life. In the first instance,
therefore, she has essentially nothing whatever to do with
the so-called religious functions of man, but with the whole
man in his existence in the world with all its implications.
What matters in the Church is not religion but the form of
Christ, and its taking form amidst a band of men. If we
allow ourselves to lose sight of this, even for an instant, we
inevitably relapse into that programme-planning for the
ethical or religious shaping of the world, which was where
we set out from.

We have now seen that it is only with reference to the form
that we can speak of formation in a Christian and ethical
sense. Formation is not an independent process or condition
which can in some way or other be detached from this form.
The only formation is formation by and into the form of
Jesus Christ. The point of departure for Christian ethics is
the body of Christ, the form of Christ in the form of the
Church, and the formation of the Church in conformity with
the form of Christ. The concept of formation acquires its

significance, indirectly, for all mankind only if what takes place in the Church does in truth take place for all men. But this again does not mean that the Church is set up, so to speak, as a model for the world. One can speak of formation and of world only if mankind is called by name in its true form, which is its own by right, which it has already received, but which it merely fails to understand and accept, namely, the form of Jesus Christ, which is proper to man, and if in this way, in anticipation as one might say, mankind is drawn in into the Church. This means, then, that even when we speak in terms of the formation of the world we are referring solely to the form of Jesus Christ.

The form of Christ is one and the same at all times and in all places. And the Church of Christ also is one and the same throughout all generations. And yet Christ is not a principle in accordance with which the whole world must be shaped. Christ is not the proclaimer of a system of what would be good today, here and at all times. Christ teaches no abstract ethics such as must at all costs be put into practice. Christ was not essentially a teacher and legislator, but a man, a real man like ourselves. And it is not therefore His will that we should in our time be the adherents, exponents and advocates of a definite doctrine, but that we should be men, real men before God. Christ did not, like a moralist, love a theory of good, but He loved the real man. He was not, like a philosopher, interested in the 'universally valid', but rather in that which is of help to the real and concrete human being. What worried Him was not, like Kant, whether 'the maxim of an action can become a principle of general legislation', but whether my action is at this moment helping my neighbour to become a man before God. For indeed it is not written that God became an idea, a principle, a programme, a universally valid proposition or a law, but that God became man. This means that though the form of Christ certainly is and remains one and the same, yet it is willing to take form in the real man, that is to say, in quite different guises. Christ does not dispense with human reality for the sake of an idea which demands realization at the expense of

65

the real. What Christ does is precisely to give effect to reality. He affirms reality. And indeed He is Himself the real man and consequently the foundation of all human reality. And so formation in conformity with Christ has this double implication. The form of Christ remains one and the same, not as a general idea but in its own unique character as the incarnate, crucified and risen God. And precisely for the sake of Christ's form the form of the real man is preserved, and in this way the real man receives the form of Christ.

The Concrete Place

This leads us away from any kind of abstract ethic and towards an ethic which is entirely concrete. What can and must be said is not what is good once and for all, but the way in which Christ takes form among us here and now. The attempt to define that which is good once and for all has, in the nature of the case, always ended in failure. Either the proposition was asserted in such general and formal terms that it retained no significance as regards its contents, or else one tried to include in it and elaborate the whole immense range of conceivable contents, and thus to say in advance what would be good in every single conceivable case; this led to a casuistic system so unmanageable that it could satisfy the demands neither of general validity nor of concreteness. The concretely Christian ethic is beyond formalism and casuistry. Formalism and casuistry set out from the conflict between the good and the real, but the Christian ethic can take for its point of departure the reconciliation, already accomplished, of the world with God and the man Jesus Christ and the acceptance of the real man by God.

But the question of how Christ takes form among us here and now, or how we are conformed with His form, contains within itself still further difficult questions. What do we mean by 'among us', 'now' and 'here'? If it is impossible to establish for all times and places what is good, then the question still arises for what times and places can any answer at all be given to our enquiry. It must not remain in doubt for a single moment that any one section to which we may now turn our attention is to be regarded precisely as a section, as a part of the whole of humanity. In every section of his history man is simply and entirely the man taken upon Himself by Christ. And for this reason whatever may have to be said about this section will always refer not only to this part but also to the whole. However, we must now answer the question regarding the times and places of which we are thinking when we set out to speak of formation through the form of Christ. These are in the first place quite generally the times and places which in some way concern us, those of which we have experience and which are reality for us. They are the times and places which confront us with concrete problems, set us tasks and charge us with responsibility. The 'among us', the 'now' and 'here' is therefore the region of our decisions and encounters. This region undoubtedly varies very greatly in extent according to the individual, and it might consequently be supposed that these definitions could in the end be interpreted so widely and vaguely as to make room for unrestrained individualism. What prevents this is the fact that by our history we are set objectively in a definite nexus of experiences, responsibilities and decisions from which we cannot free ourselves again except by an abstraction. We live, in fact, within this nexus, whether or not we are in every respect aware of it. Furthermore, this nexus is characterized in a quite peculiar manner by the fact that until our own days its consciously affirmed and recognized underlying basis has been the form of Christ. In our historical identity, therefore, we stand already in the midst of Christ's taking form, in a section of human history which He himself has chosen. It is consequently in this sense that we regard the west as the region for which we wish to speak and must speak, the world of the peoples of Europe and America in so far as it is already united through the form of Jesus Christ. To take a narrower view or to limit our consideration to Germany, for example, would be to lose sight of the fact that the form of Christ is the unity of the western nations and that for this reason no single one of these nations can exist by itself or even be conceived as existing by itself. And to take a wider view would be to overlook the mysterious fact of the self-containedness of the western world.

The purpose of what follows is not indeed to develop a programme for a shaping or formation of the western world. What is intended is rather a discussion of the way in which in this western world the form of Christ takes form. This means that the discussion must be neither abstract nor casuistic, but entirely concrete. It must be insisted that no other form may be placed side by side with the form of Jesus Christ, for He alone is the subduer and reconciler of the world. Only this one form can help. And so whatever concrete assertion may have to be made here and today about the way in which this form takes form amongst us, it must be referred quite strictly to this form of Jesus Christ. Moreover, in the incarnation of Christ the assurance is given us that Christ is willing to take form amongst us here and today.

Ethics as formation, then, means the bold endeavour to speak about the way in which the form of Jesus Christ takes form in our world, in a manner which is neither abstract nor casuistic, neither programmatic nor purely speculative. Concrete judgements and decisions will have to be ventured here. Decision and action can here no longer be delegated to the personal conscience of the individual. Here there are concrete commandments and instructions for which obedience is demanded.

Ethics as formation is possible only upon the foundation of the form of Jesus Christ which is present in His Church. The Church is the place where Jesus Christ's taking form is proclaimed and accomplished. It is this proclamation and this event that Christian ethics is designed to serve.

INHERITANCE AND DECAY

It is only in the Christian west that it is possible to speak of a historical heritage. Certainly there are also traditions in Asia and they are much older than ours, but they share in the timelessness of Asiatic existence, and even in Japan, where the western way of existence has been most fully accepted, history still retains a mythological character. The first article of the present-day [1940] Japanese constitution prescribes belief in the descent of the Emperor or Tenno from the sun-god. The concept of historical inheritance, which is linked with the consciousness of temporality and opposed to all mythologization, is possible only where thought is consciously or unconsciously governed by the entry of God into history at a definite place and a definite point of time, that is to say, by the incarnation of God in Jesus Christ. Here history becomes a serious matter without being canonized. The 'yes' and the 'no' which God addresses to history in the incarnation and crucifixion of Jesus Christ introduces into every historical instant an infinite and unresolvable tension. History does not become a transient vehicle, but through the life and death of Jesus Christ it does for the first time become truly temporal. It is precisely in its temporality that it is history with God's consent. Consequently when we ask about the historical inheritance we are not asking the timeless question about those values of the past of which the validity is eternal. Man himself is set in history and it is for that reason that he now asks himself about the present and about the way in which the present is taken up by God in Christ.

Our forefathers are for us not ancestors who are made the object of worship and veneration. Interest in genealogies can all too easily become mythologization, as was known already to the writers of the New Testament (I Tim. 1.4). Our forefathers are witnesses of the entry of God into history. It is the fact of the appearance of Jesus Christ nineteen hundred years ago, a fact for which no further proof is to be sought, that directs our gaze back to the ancients and raises in our minds the question of our historical inheritance.

The historical Jesus Christ is the continuity of our history. But Jesus Christ was the promised Messiah of the Israelite-Jewish people, and for that reason the line of our forefathers goes back beyond the appearance of Jesus Christ to the people of Israel. Western history is, by God's will, indissolubly linked with the people of Israel, not only genetically but also in a genuine uninterrupted encounter. The Jew keeps open the question of Christ. He is the sign of the free mercy-choice and of the repudiating wrath of God. 'Behold therefore the goodness and severity of God' (Rom. 11.22). An expulsion of the Jews from the west must necessarily bring with it the expulsion of Christ. For Jesus Christ was a Jew.

Greco-Roman antiquity, in quite a different way and very indirectly indeed, is also a part of our historical heritage. And we stand in yet another relation to our own, pre-Christian national past.

Classical antiquity stands in a twofold relation to the appearance of Jesus Christ. It is the time when the time of God was fulfilled, the time when God became man. And it is the world which God took to Himself in the incarnation, the world of which God made use in order to spread far and wide the Christian message. The apostle Paul's appeal to his Roman citizenship and to the authority of the Emperor makes it clear that Rome is placed at the service of Christ. But it is at the same time also in the eyes of antiquity that the holiest token of the presence of God, the cross, appears as the symbol of utter shame and utter remoteness from God. It is in this twofold relation to Christ that antiquity becomes our historical heritage, in its nearness to Christ and in its opposition to Him.

It is the Roman heritage which comes to represent the combination and assimilation of antiquity with the Christian element, and it is the Greek heritage which comes to represent opposition and hostility to Christ. While the peoples of western Europe, France, Holland, England and Italy sought

in antiquity mainly for the Roman heritage, the relation of
the Germans to antiquity has been determined primarily by
Hellenism. And while through the Roman Catholic Church
the Roman heritage persists in an unbroken tradition into
our own time, the Reformation at once brought with it a
return to the Greek sources. The relation of the western
nations to antiquity was positive and fundamental. Antiquity
became a fixed form of life, especially in education and
politics, a form of which the Christian element was the
content. The French, Dutch and English humanists worked
for the reconciliation of antiquity with Christianity. In
Germany the tension, and in some cases the breach, between
antiquity and Christianity was strongly felt in that one-sided
love for Greece which came near to scandalizing the western
humanists. From Winckelmann to Nietzsche there was in
Germany a consciously anti-Christian conjuring up of the
Greek heritage. The reason why Germany's attitude to
the heritage of antiquity differs so profoundly from that of
the West European nations is undoubtedly to be found in the
form assumed in Germany by the gospel as a result of the
Reformation. It was only from the soil of the German Reformation that there could spring a Nietzsche. The revolt of the
natural against grace contrasts sharply here with that reconciliation of nature with grace which is found in the Roman
heritage. It was for this reason that, in a way which for the
West European nations was quite incomprehensible, Nietzsche
could win the positive approval of one school of German
Protestant theology.

It is only in relation to Christ that there is a genuine
inheritance from classical antiquity in the west. Once it is
detached from this relation antiquity is and must be timeless,
a matter fit only for the museum. It is only through Christ
that antiquity becomes a historical heritage in the proper
sense of the term. Wherever the incarnation of Christ, His
becoming man, is more intensely in the foreground of
Christian consciousness, there one will seek for the reconciliation of antiquity with Christianity. And wherever the
cross of Christ dominates the Christian message, there the

breach between Christ and antiquity will be very greatly emphasized. But Christ is both the Incarnate and the Crucified, and He demands to be recognized as both of these alike. For this reason the due acceptance of the historical heritage of antiquity is a task which the Christian west has yet to complete, and with the completion of this task as their common purpose the West European peoples and the Germans will draw more closely together.

Our own Germanic, pre-Christian, ethnic past presents a peculiar contrast with classical antiquity in that it does not confront us as a historical heritage but rather as a continuing process of natural growth. The reason for this is to be found in the fact (which cannot be further accounted for) that German history, and for that matter British and French history, came into being only after the encounter with Christ, or, more specifically, with Roman Christendom. Even the severing of the link with Rome as the Pope's see did not lead in either England or Germany to a return to the native pre-Christian past. In England, indeed, the Roman heritage itself remains essentially intact even now. The new doctrine of the Reformation has left it practically unaltered. In Germany, on the contrary, the breach with Rome struck at the very foundation of the historical Roman heritage. And yet here, too, there was no idea of replacing it by the native German pre-Christian past. This is not because the Germans had irresponsibly forgotten their national heritage, but simply because no genuine historical heritage existed. Recent attempts to restore contact with this indigenous pre-Christian past go hand in hand with a mythologization of history which can now have no prospect of maintaining itself in the western world. And so our own pre-Christian national past does indeed remain with us as a fact of nature, as national character, or, if one prefers it so, as race, but it is not, and never again can be, a historical heritage.

With our own Christian past the case is quite different. It is a historical heritage, a common western heritage. Jesus Christ has made of the west a historical unit. The epoch-making events of history affect the whole of the west. The unity of the west is not an idea but a historical reality, of which the sole foundation is Christ. The great movements in the life of the mind are henceforward the property of the entire western world. Even the wars of the west have the unity of the west as their purpose. They are not wars of extermination and destruction like the wars of pre-Christian times and those which are even today still possible in Asia. So long as they are to be western wars they cannot, therefore ever be total wars. Total war makes use of all conceivable means which may possibly serve the purpose of national self-preservation. Anything which is of advantage to one's own cause is rightful and permissible. Western wars have always distinguished between means of warfare which are permissible and rightful and those which are prohibited and criminal. It was belief in a just, divine government of the world which made it possible to dispense with the perhaps effective but certainly un-Christian practices of killing the innocent—torture, extortion, and the rest. War now always remained a kind of appeal to the arbitration of God, which both sides were willing to accept. It is only when Christian faith is lost that man must himself make use of all means, even criminal ones, in order to secure by force the victory of his cause. And thus, in the place of a chivalrous war between Christian peoples, directed towards the achievement of unity in accordance with God's judgement in history, there comes total war, war of destruction, in which everything, even crime, is justified if it serves to further our own cause, and in which the enemy, whether he be armed or defenceless, is treated as a criminal. Only with the advent of total war is there a threat to the unity of the west.

The unity of the west through the form of Christ is the heritage which we have received from the early periods of our history. Pope and Emperor strove for the formation of this unity. Christ stood uncontestedly as the ultimate unity over them both. In the papacy the supreme Christian authority, the Vicar of Christ on earth, claimed also the supreme political power for himself for the purpose of establishing Christ's kingdom on earth. And from its supreme political

73

power the Empire at the same time derived a claim to the supreme Christian authority. The form of western unity was for the Pope the Roman Church, and for the Emperor it was the Empire. The Emperor and the Pope were not out for each other's blood. They fought, face to face and side by side, for the unity of Church and Empire, for unity in the faith and in the political form of the west. In their most far-reaching claim they must either be victorious together or suffer final defeat together. The western schism brought with it the collapse of the Empire. The Reformation broke asunder the *corpus christianum*, the historical order of the Christian west, which was ruled and held together by Emperor and Pope in the name of Jesus Christ. The heritage of the Middle Ages remains with us in our own time in the form of the Roman Church. But the Roman Church is the papacy. She solemnly asserted this truth in a noble protest precisely at the time of the inward collapse of Germany. She claims, in tones which cannot remain unheard, that there is only one Church and only one faith, and that Christendom has need of a visible head, a supreme pastor, to lead it and to take fatherly care of the faithful. So long as there is a papacy it will always be possible to yearn for the lost western Empire, the *corpus christianum*, in which Emperor and Pope were together the defenders of the unity of the Christian west.

It was the Reformation that broke asunder the unity of the faith. That was not because Luther willed it so. He was indeed wholly concerned for the true unity of the Church. But the word of the Bible forced him to the conclusion that the unity of the Church can lie only in Jesus Christ as He lives in His word and sacrament, and not in any political power. In this way he shattered the whole structure of the Church, which was founded upon the Roman tradition. Only a Pope who submitted unreservedly to the word of the Bible could be the shepherd of a united Christendom. But the Pope, bound as he was by tradition, was incapable of this submission, and that is why the unity of Christendom was destroyed. The *corpus christianum* is resolved into its true constituents, the *corpus Christi* and the world. In His Church

Christ rules not by the sword but solely with His word. Unity of faith exists only in obedience to the true word of Jesus Christ. But the sword is the property of the secular government, which in its own way, in the proper discharge of its office, also serves the same Lord Jesus Christ. There are two kingdoms which, so long as the world continues, must neither be mixed together nor yet be torn asunder. There is the kingdom of the preached word of God, and there is the kingdom of the sword. The kingdom of the Church, and the kingdom of the world. The realm of the spiritual office, and the realm of secular government. The sword can never bring about the unity of the Church and of the faith. Preaching can never govern nations. But the Lord of both kingdoms is the God who is made manifest in Jesus Christ. He rules the world through the office of the word and the office of the sword. It is to Him that those who bear these offices must render account. There is only one Church, and that is the Church of faith, which is governed solely by the word of Jesus Christ. This is the true Catholic Church, which has never been destroyed and which also still lies hidden in the Church of Rome. She is the Body of Christ, the *corpus Christi*. She is the true unity of the western world. The question of the political unity of the west was not an urgent one for Luther. He believed that this unity was still secured by the Emperor. The political disruption became apparent to him only after his friends had with great difficulty persuaded him to recognize the right of the princes to resist the Emperor by force of arms. But if we pursue Luther's line of thought further we may no doubt say that political unity must consist in the proper discharge of the office of government in all places of authority and that a sound government would find the firmest basis for political unity precisely in the acknowledgement of the true unity of the faith. The Thirty Years' War finally laid bare the political disunity of the west which had resulted from the schism of faith. The Peace of Westphalia confirmed and ratified the confessional schism as the fate and inheritance of the western world. The guilt and the distress which this inheritance entails are shared in common by the whole of western Christendom; they cannot be removed by human endeavour. At the same time, however, the fact that they are recognized for what they are marks the beginning of a new awareness of western unity which persists despite and even through this separation. The guilt of western Christendom towards Christ was guilt shared in common, and thus it was not destined to destroy the unity of the west, since this unity lay in the name of Jesus Christ, which was called upon by both sides.

Nevertheless, all along the line there very quickly set in the great process of secularization, at the end of which we are standing today. On the Protestant side Luther's doctrine of the two kingdoms was misinterpreted as implying the emancipation and sanctification of the world and of the natural. Government, reason, economics and culture arrogate to themselves a right of autonomy, but do not in any way understand this autonomy as bringing them into opposition to Christianity. On the contrary, precisely in this they are standing in the true service of God as the Christianity of the Reformation requires it. What has been utterly forgotten here is the original message of the Reformation that there is no holiness of man either in the sacred or in the profane as such, but only that which comes through the merciful and sin-forgiving word of God. The Reformation is celebrated as the emancipation of man in his conscience, his reason and his culture and as the justification of the secular as such. The Reformers' biblical faith in God had radically removed God from the world. The ground was thereby prepared for the efflorescence of the rational and empirical sciences, and while the natural scientists of the seventeenth and eighteenth centuries were still believing Christians, when faith in God was lost all that remained was a rationalized and mechanized world.

On the Catholic side the process of secularization rapidly became anti-clerical in a revolutionary sense, and indeed anti-Christian. That is why the first revolutionary upheaval took place in Catholic France. Even at the present day the French Revolution is still the rallying cry of the modern

76

western world. With a most astonishing concentration of forces, the ideas, demands and aspirations of many successive generations were here suddenly all at once hurled upwards with elemental violence into the daylight of history. The cult of reason, the deification of nature, faith in progress and a critical approach to civilization, the revolt of the bourgeoisie and the revolt of the masses, nationalism and anti-clericalism, the rights of man and dictatorial terror—all this together erupted chaotically as something new in the history of the western world. The French Revolution was the laying bare of the emancipated man in his tremendous power and his most terrible perversity. Emancipated man meant here emancipated reason, an emancipated class and an emancipated people. The French Revolution left behind it throughout the west a profound dread of this representation of the new man and a horror of the abysses of error. There was a faint awareness of what was really new and of all the promise it held in store, but above all there was dread of a repetition of the terror. And yet, willingly or reluctantly, room still had to be made for the new.

Emancipated reason rose to unsuspected heights. The free exercise of reason created an atmosphere of truthfulness, light and clarity. Prejudices, social conceits, hollow forms and insensitive sentimentality were swept clean by the fresh wind of intellectual clarity. Intellectual honesty in all things, including questions of belief, was the great achievement of emancipated reason and it has ever since been one of the indispensable moral requirements of western man. Contempt for the age of rationalism is a suspicious sign of failure to feel the need for truthfulness. If intellectual honesty is not the last word that is to be said about things, and if intellectual clarity is often achieved at the expense of insight into reality, this can still never again exempt us from the inner obligation to make clean and honest use of reason. We cannot now go back to the days before Lessing and Lichtenberg.

Yet it was not so much in the questions of belief and life that emancipated reason displayed its immense power, but rather in the discovery of that mysterious correspondence

77

between the laws of thought and the laws of nature. Reason became a working hypothesis, a heuristic principle, and so led on to the unparalleled rise of technology. This is something essentially new in the history of the world. From the Egyptian pyramids and the Greek temples to the medieval cathedrals and the eighteenth century, technology had always been a matter of artisanship. It stood in the service of religion, of kings, of art, and of the daily needs of men. The technical science of the modern western world has emancipated itself from any kind of subservience. It is in essence not service but mastery, mastery over nature. It was an entirely new spirit that evoked it, and it will continue only so long as this spirit continues. This is the spirit of the forcible subjugation of nature beneath the rule of the thinking and experimenting man. Technology became an end in itself. It has a soul of its own. Its symbol is the machine, the embodiment of the violation and exploitation of nature. It is therefore easy to understand that it is only this modern technology which elicits a protest from the naive believer. Naive faith sees signs here of a human arrogance which tries to set up an anti-world in the face of the world that was created by God. In the conquest of time and space by technical science it sees an undertaking which sets God's will at defiance. The benefits of technology pale into insignificance beside its demoniacal properties.

It cannot be overlooked that technology has arisen only in the west, that is to say, in the world which has been shaped by Christianity and more particularly by the Reformation. When it penetrates to oriental countries it acquires a totally different significance in that it ceases to be an end in itself. Technical development in the Islamic world, for example, continues to stand entirely in the service of belief in God and of the constructive furtherance of Islamic history. In the course of a conversation, Ibn Saud is reported to have said something like this: 'I am not shutting myself off from European civilization, but I make use of it in a way which is consistent with Arabia, with the Arab soul, and with the will of God. I have had machines brought here from Europe, but

78

I want no irreligion. The Moslem nations must wake from their long dream. They need arms, but the most powerful weapon is faith in God and humble obedience to the divine laws. Hatred does not come from God. Europe is full of hatred and will destroy itself with its own weapons.'

Emancipated reason acquired mastery over creation and so led to the triumph of technical science. The age of technology is a genuine heritage of our western history. We must come to grips with it. We cannot return to the pretechnical era.

An outcome of the emancipation of reason was the discovery of the Rights of Man. They were found to lie in the innate title of every man to liberty, in the equality of all men before the law, and in the fraternal bond which links together all those who bear human features. By an eternal right which is implicit in his nature, man broke free from all repressive coercion, from the chaperonage of church and state, and from social and economic oppression. He claimed for himself the right to human dignity, to free cultural development, and to recognition for his achievements. He saw in his neighbour either a brother or else an enemy of the rights of man. Centralist and absolutist despotism, intellectual and social tyranny, class prejudice and class privilege, and the claims to power advanced by the Church—all these were overthrown by the shock of this assault. German humanism and idealism ensued. The underprivileged classes began to stir. 'There is no privilege for any part of the nation or for any individual, nor is any exception made from the general law of the French.' 'The law is the expression of the general will' (*Declaration of the Rights of Man*). First of all the bourgeoisie secured parity of rights for itself as the nobility of achievement side by side with the nobility of birth. Reason secured its titles against blood. Bourgeoisie and reason were henceforward inseparable. But behind the bourgeoisie there loomed the dark menace of the masses, the fourth estate. All it stood for was simply the masses and their misery. The millions who possessed and could possess no other title of nobility than their own undeserved wretchedness now raised their accusation and their claim against both the nobility of blood and the nobility of achievement. The masses have equal contempt for the laws of blood and for the laws of reason. They make their own law, the law of misery. It is a violent law, and short-lived. We today are standing at the culmination and crisis of this uprising.

In strange contrast to the ideas we have so far been considering, which are directed towards the whole of mankind, the French Revolution now becomes also the moment of birth of modern nationalism. Whatever national consciousness existed earlier was essentially dynastic in character. But the Revolution was the liberation of the people from the absolutism of *l'état c'est moi*. The revolutionary concept of the nation arose in opposition to an exaggerated dynastic absolutism. The people deemed that they had now come of age, that they were now capable of taking in hand the direction of their own internal and external history. They asserted their right to freedom and development as a people, the right to a government which should rest on the will of the nation. 'The origin of all sovereignty lies in the nation' (*Declaration of the Rights of Man*). Nation was a revolutionary concept. It sided with the people against the government, with becoming against being, and with the organic against the institutional. It was thought from below, in opposition to thought from above. Consequently it is one of the most grotesque mistakes the historian can make, if Prussia of all countries is declared to be the birthplace and the typical representative of nationalism. No political unit has ever been more alien and indeed hostile to nationalism than was Prussia. Prussia was a state, but not a nation. Prussia stood for established government, being, the institutional. Certainly it differed from Louis XIV in that it understood these things in the sense of Frederick the Great's dictum: 'I am the first servant of the state.' Prussia viewed the German national cause with profound suspicion, a suspicion which repeatedly found expression in genuinely Prussian circles even in and after the time of the founding of the Wilhelmine Empire. Prussia had a sound instinctive sense of the revolutionary implications of the notion of nationhood, and refused to accept them. In nationalism Prussiandom was combating the revolution of the *grande nation* and resisting its encroachment into Germany. Nationalism evokes the countermovement of internationalism. The two are equally revolutionary. To both of these movements Prussia opposed the state. Prussia wished to be neither nationalistic nor international. In this respect its thought was more western than was that of the Revolution.

But the Revolution had its way. Technology, mass movements and nationalism are the inheritance which the Revolution has bequeathed to the western world. The three are closely associated, and yet at the same time they are sharply opposed. Technology produces the masses and the masses demand an intensification of technology, yet at the same time technology itself is a matter for strong and mentally superior personalities. The engineer and the *entrepreneur* are not men of the masses, and the question arises whether perhaps the increasing acceptance of mass standards will in the course of time level down mental achievements to such an extent that technology itself will cease to develop and will therefore cease to exist. Technology and the masses arose and are confined within national communities, but they have an irresistible tendency to break down the frontiers of nationalism. The masses and nationalism are hostile to reason. Technology and the masses are hostile to nationalism. Nationalism and technology are hostile to the masses.

The French Revolution created a new unity of mind in the west. This unity lies in the emancipation of man as reason, as the mass, as the nation. In the struggle for freedom these three are in agreement, but once their freedom is achieved they become deadly foes. Thus the new unity already bears within itself the seeds of decay. Furthermore, there becomes apparent in this an underlying law of history, namely that the demand for absolute liberty brings men to the depths of slavery. The master of the machine becomes its slave. The machine becomes the enemy of men. The creature turns against its creator in a strange re-enactment of the Fall.

The emancipation of the masses leads to the reign of terror of the guillotine. Nationalism leads inevitably to war. The liberation of man as an absolute ideal leads only to man's self-destruction. At the end of the path which was first trodden in the French Revolution there is nihilism.

The new unity which the French Revolution brought to Europe—and what we are experiencing today is the crisis of this unity—is therefore western godlessness. It is totally different from the atheism of certain individual Greek, Indian, Chinese and western thinkers. It is not the theoretical denial of the existence of a God. It is itself a religion, a religion of hostility to God. It is in just this that it is western. It cannot break loose from its past. It cannot but be religious in essence. That is why to the human eye it is so hopelessly godless. Western godlessness ranges from the religion of Bolshevism to the midst of the Christian churches. In Germany especially, but also in the Anglo-Saxon countries, it is a markedly Christian godlessness. In the form of all the possible Christianities, whether they be nationalist, socialist, rationalist or mystical, it turns against the living God of the Bible, against Christ. Its god is the New Man, no matter whether he bears the trade-mark of Bolshevism or of Christianity. This differs fundamentally from all paganism, for in paganism gods are adored in the form of men but here it is man who is adored in the form of God, indeed in the form of Jesus Christ.

Luther's great discovery of the freedom of the Christian man and the Catholic heresy of the essential good in man combined to produce the deification of man. But, rightly understood, the deification of man is the proclamation of nihilism. With the destruction of the biblical faith in God and of all divine commands and ordinances, man destroys himself. There arises an unrestrained vitalism which involves the dissolution of all values and achieves its goal only in final self-destruction, in the void.

Since the French Revolution the west has come to be essentially hostile to the Church. In modern demagogies attacks on the Church are particularly effective. Throughout

Europe there is intense and widespread resentment against the Church. Yet the Churches lose remarkably few of their members, and this points to an important fact, namely, the ambiguous character of the hostility to the Church. It would be quite wrong simply to identify western godlessness with enmity towards the Church. There is the godlessness in religious and Christian clothing, which we have called a hopeless godlessness, but there is also a godlessness which is full of promise, a godlessness which speaks against religion and against the Church. It is the protest against pious godlessness in so far as this has corrupted the Churches, and thus in a certain sense, if only negatively, it defends the heritage of a genuine faith in God and of a genuine Church. There is relevance here in Luther's saying that perhaps God would rather hear the curses of the ungodly than the alleluia of the pious. No less than hopeless godlessness, this promising godlessness, too, is a specifically western phenomenon. In spite of the essentially hostile attitude towards her, the complete breach with the Church has been effected to only a relatively small extent, a fact which must be seen against the following background. Some seek in pious godlessness for a last support to save themselves from falling into the void, but they will not often escape this fall. Others are impelled by their 'promising' godlessness to stop short of a final breach with the centre of a possible genuine faith in God. And in the same way, too, no single conclusion can be drawn from the number of resignations from the Churches. These, too, may be the result either of hopeless or of hopeful godlessness, quite apart from the question whether even genuine faith in God may make it possible, and indeed in some circumstances necessary, to leave the Church.

At this point some thought must be given to the special developments in the Anglo-Saxon countries and particularly in America. The American Revolution was almost contemporary with the French one, and politically the two were not unconnected; yet they were profoundly different in character. The American democracy is not founded upon the emancipated man but, quite on the contrary, upon the kingdom of

God and the limitation of all earthly powers by the sovereignty of God. It is indeed significant when, in contrast to the *Declaration of the Rights of Man*, American historians can say that the federal constitution was written by men who were conscious of original sin and of the wickedness of the human heart. Earthly wielders of authority, and also the people, are directed into their proper bounds, in due consideration of man's innate longing for power and of the fact that power pertains only to God. With these ideas, which derive from Calvinism, there is combined the essentially contrary idea which comes from the spiritualism of the Dissenters who took refuge in America, the idea that the kingdom of God on earth cannot be built by the authority of the state but only by the congregation of the faithful. The Church proclaims the principles of the social and political order, and the state makes available the technical means for putting them into effect. These two quite alien lines of thought converge in the demand for democracy, and it is enthusiastic spiritualism that becomes the determining factor in American thought. This explains the remarkable fact that on the European continent it has never been possible to find a Christian basis for democracy, while in the Anglo-Saxon countries democracy and democracy alone is regarded as the Christian form of the state. The persecution and expulsion of the spiritualists from the Continent has in this respect been fraught with the most far-reaching political consequences. If in spite of this the Anglo-Saxon countries, too, are suffering from severe symptoms of secularization, the cause does not lie in the misinterpretation of the distinction between the two offices or kingdoms, but rather in the reverse of this, in the failure of the enthusiasts to distinguish at all between the office or kingdom of the state and the office or kingdom of the Church. The claim of the congregation of the faithful to build the world with Christian principles ends only with the total capitulation of the Church to the world, as can be seen clearly enough by a glance at the New York church registers. If this does not involve a radical hostility to the Church, that is only because no real distinction has ever been drawn here between the offices of Church and state. Godlessness remains more covert. And indeed in this way it deprives the Church even of the blessing of suffering and of the possible rebirth which suffering may engender.

By the loss of the unity which it possessed through the form of Jesus Christ, the western world is brought to the brink of the void. The forces unleashed exhaust their fury in mutual destruction. Everything established is threatened with annihilation. This is not a crisis among other crises. It is a decisive struggle of the last days. The western world senses the uniqueness of the moment at which it stands, and it throws itself into the arms of the void, while the Christians talk among themselves of the approach of the Day of Judgement. The void towards which the west is drifting is not the natural end, the dying away and decline of a once flourishing history of nations. It is, once again, a specifically western void, a rebellious and outrageous void, and one which is the enemy of both God and man. As an apostasy from all that is established it is the supreme manifestation of all the powers which are opposed to God. It is the void made god. No one knows its goal or its measure. Its dominion is absolute. It is a creative void, which blows its anti-god's breath into the nostrils of all that is established and awakens it to a false semblance of new life while sucking out from it its proper essence, until at last it falls in ruin as a lifeless husk and is cast away. The void engulfs life, history, family, nation, language, faith. The list can be prolonged indefinitely, for the void spares nothing.

In the face of the peril of the void there is no longer any meaning in the question of the historical inheritance which requires of those who receive it that they shall both develop it in the present and hand it on to the future. There is no future and there is no past. There is only the moment which has been rescued from the void, and the desire to snatch from the void the next moment as well. Already what belongs to yesterday is consigned to oblivion, and the affairs of tomorrow are still too far off to impose any obligation today. The burden of yesterday is shaken off by glorifying the misty past, and tomorrow's task is evaded by speaking rather of the coming millennium. Nothing makes a permanent impression and nothing imposes a lasting obligation. A sign of the deep forgetfulness of the present time is the film which is erased from the viewer's memory as soon as it is over. Events which are of profound significance for the history of the world and the most monstrous and unheard-of crimes are alike incapable of leaving any trace in the oblivious soul. The future is made a game of hazard. Lotteries and bets seek in the future only for the improbable chance, swallowing up almost inconceivable sums of money and often the livelihood of the workman. With the loss of past and future, life fluctuates between the most bestial enjoyment of the moment and an adventurous game of chance. An abrupt end is put to any kind of inner self-development and to any gradual attainment of personal or vocational maturity. There is no personal destiny, and consequently there is no personal dignity. Serious tensions and inwardly necessary periods of waiting are not sustained. This is apparent in the field of labour and in the erotic field alike. Slow pain is more feared than death. There is no recognition, there is even contempt, for the value of suffering in giving form to life through the threat of death. The alternative now is health or death. Genuine tensions are not endured. Whatever is silent, constant and consistent is disregarded as being valueless. 'Great convictions' and the quest for a path of one's own are now replaced by the line of least resistance and sailing before the wind. In the political sphere the unscrupulous exploitation of the moment now goes by the false name of Machiavellism. The all-or-nothing gamble is called heroism and unfettered action. Whatever is neither Machiavellian nor heroic can now be explained only as 'hypocrisy', because there is no longer any understanding for the slow, laborious conflict between knowledge of the right and the necessities of the hour, the conflict which was the genuine political life of the west, with all its voluntary concessions and its authentically free responsibility. Strength is disastrously confused with weakness, and historical continuity with decadence. The absence of anything lasting means the collapse of the foundation of historical life, confidence, in all its forms. Since there is no confidence in truth, the place of truth is usurped by sophistic propaganda. Since there is no confidence in justice, whatever is useful is declared to be just. And even the tacit confidence in one's fellow-man, which rests on the certainty of permanence and constancy, is now superseded by suspicion and an hour-to-hour watch on one's neighbour. If we ask what remains, there can be only one answer: fear of the void. The most astonishing observation we can make today is that in the face of the void one is prepared to sacrifice anything and everything: one's own judgement, one's human character, and one's neighbour. If this fear is unscrupulously exploited, there is no limit to what can be achieved.

Two things alone have still the power to avert the final plunge into the void. One is the miracle of a new awakening of faith, and the other is that force which the Bible calls the 'restrainer', κατέχων (II Thess. 2.7), that is to say the force of order, equipped with great physical strength, which effectively blocks the way of those who are about to plunge into the abyss. The miracle is the saving act of God, which intervenes from above, from beyond whatever is historically attainable or probable, and creates new life out of the void. It is a raising of the dead. And the 'restrainer' is the force which takes effect within history through God's governance of the world, and which sets due limits to evil. The 'restrainer' itself is not God; it is not without guilt; but God makes use of it in order to preserve the world from destruction. The place where the miracle of God is proclaimed is the Church. The 'restrainer' is the power of the state to establish and maintain order. The two are entirely different in nature, yet in the face of imminent chaos they are in close alliance, and they are both alike objects of the hatred of the forces of destruction, which see in them their deadliest enemies.

What the west is doing is to refuse to accept its historical inheritance for what it is. The west is becoming hostile towards Christ. This is the peculiar situation of our time, and it is genuine decay. Amid the disruption of the whole established order of things there stand the Christian Churches as guardians of the heritage of the Middle Ages and of the Reformation and especially as witnesses of the miracle of God in Jesus Christ 'yesterday, and today, and for ever' (Heb. 13.8). And at their side there stands the 'restrainer', that is to say the remaining force of order which still opposes effective resistance to the process of decay. The task of the Church is without parallel. The *corpus christianum* is broken asunder. The *corpus Christi* confronts a hostile world. The world has known Christ and has turned its back on Him, and it is to this world that the Church must now prove that Christ is the living Lord. Even while she waits for the last day, the Church, as the bearer of a historical inheritance, is bound by an obligation to the historical future. Her vision of the end of all things must not hinder her in the fulfilment of her historical responsibility. She must leave not only the end to God's decision, but also the possibility of the continuance of history. She must set her mind on both. In devoting herself to her proper task, that is to say to preaching the risen Jesus Christ, the Church strikes a mortal blow at the spirit of destruction. The 'restrainer', the force of order, sees in the Church an ally, and, whatever other elements of order may remain, will seek a place at her side. Justice, truth, science, art, culture, humanity, liberty, patriotism, all at last, after long straying from the path, are once more finding their way back to their fountain-head. The more central the message of the Church, the greater now will be her effectiveness. Her suffering presents an infinitely greater danger to the spirit of destruction than does any political power which may still remain. But through her message of the living Lord Jesus Christ the Church makes it clear that she is not concerned merely for the maintenance and preservation of the past. Even the forces of order she compels to listen and to turn back. Yet she does not reject those who come to her and seek to place themselves at her side. She leaves it to God's governance of the world to decide whether He will permit the success of the forces of order and whether she, the Church, while still preserving the essential distinction between herself and these forces, even though she unreservedly allies herself with them, will be allowed to pass on to the future that historical inheritance which bears within it the blessing and the guilt of past generations.

GUILT, JUSTIFICATION AND RENEWAL

The Confession of Guilt

Our concern is with the taking form among us of the form of Christ. Our concern, therefore, is with the real man, sentenced and made new. The real, sentenced and renewed man exists nowhere else save in the form of Jesus Christ and, therefore, in the likeness of this form, in conformation with Him. Only the man who is taken up in Christ is the real man. Only the man who suffers the cross of Christ is the man under sentence. Only the man who shares in the resurrection of Christ is the man who is made new. Since God became man in Christ all thought about man without Christ has been a barren abstraction. The antitype to the man who is taken up into the form of Christ is the man who is his own creator, his own judge and his own restorer, the man whose life misses the mark of his own human existence, and who, therefore, sooner or later destroys himself. Man's apostasy from Christ is at the same time his apostasy from his own essential nature.

The only way to turn back is through recognition of the guilt incurred towards Christ. What must be recognized as guilt is not the occasional lapse of error, or transgressions against an abstract law, but the defection from Christ, from the form which was ready to take form in us and to lead us to our own true form. True acknowledgement of guilt does not arise from the experience of disruption and decay, but for us, who have encountered the form of Christ, solely from this form. It presupposes, therefore, some measure of communion with this form. For just this reason it is a miracle. For how shall he who has fallen away from Christ still have communion with Christ except through the grace by which

Christ holds the renegade fast and preserves him in communion with Him? There can be recognition of guilt only because of Christ's grace and because He stretches out His hand to save the one who is falling away. In this recognition of guilt there begins the process by which man is conformed with Christ. This recognition of guilt differs from any other such recognition which is self-effected and sterile.

The place where this recognition of guilt becomes real is the Church. But this is not to be understood as meaning that the Church is the place of genuine recognition of guilt as something additional to the other things which she is and does. The Church is precisely that community of human beings which has been led by the grace of Christ to the recognition of guilt towards Christ. To say, therefore, that the Church is the place of the recognition of guilt is nothing but a tautology. If it were otherwise, she would no longer be the Church. The Church today is that community of men which is gripped by the power of the grace of Christ so that, recognizing as guilt towards Jesus Christ both its own personal sin and the apostasy of the western world from Jesus Christ, it confesses this guilt and accepts the burden of it. It is in her that Jesus realizes His form in the midst of the world. That is why the Church alone can be the place of personal and collective rebirth and renewal.

It is a sign of the living presence of Christ that there are men in whom the knowledge of the apostasy from Jesus Christ is kept awake not merely in the sense that this apostasy is observed in others but in the sense that these men themselves confess themselves guilty of this apostasy. They confess their guilt without any sidelong glance at their fellow offenders. Their confession of guilt is strictly exclusive in that it takes all guilt upon itself. Wherever there is still a weighing up and calculation of guilt, there the sterile morality of self-justification usurps the place of the confession of guilt which is made in the presence of the form of Christ. Not the individual misdeeds but the form of Christ is the origin of the confession of guilt, and for that reason the confession is not unconditional and entire; for Christ subdues us in no other way more utterly than by His having taken our guilt upon Himself unconditionally and entirely, declaring Himself guilty of our guilt and freeing us from its burden. The sight of this grace of Christ blots out entirely the sight of the guilt of other men and compels a man to fall upon his knees before Christ and to confess *mea culpa, mea maxima culpa*.

With this confession the entire guilt of the world falls upon the Church, upon the Christians, and since this guilt is not denied here, but is confessed, there arises the possibility of forgiveness. In a way which is totally incomprehensible to the moralist there is no seeking for the actual guilty party; there is no demand for a condign expiation of the guilt, punishment of the wicked and reward of the good. The wicked man is not charged with his wickedness, in the sense of the apocalyptic saying: 'He that is unjust, let him be unjust still' (Rev. 22.11). It is men who take all, really all, guilt upon themselves, not in some heroic resolve of sacrifice, but simply because they are overwhelmed by their own, their very own, guilt towards Christ, so that at this moment they can no longer think of imposing retributive justice on the 'chief offenders' but only of the forgiveness of their own great guilt.

First of all, it is the entirely personal sin of the individual which is recognized here as a source of pollution for the community. Even the most secret sin of the individual is defilement and destruction of the body of Christ (I Cor. 6.15). From the desires that are in our bodily members come murder and envy, strife and war (Jas. 4.1ff.). If my share in this is so small as to seem negligible, that still cannot set my mind at rest; for now it is not a matter of apportioning the blame, but I must acknowledge that precisely my sin is to blame for all. I am guilty of uncontrolled desire. I am guilty of cowardly silence at a time when I ought to have spoken. I am guilty of hypocrisy and untruthfulness in the face of force. I have been lacking in compassion and I have denied the poorest of my brethren. I am guilty of disloyalty and of apostasy from Christ. What does it matter to you whether others are guilty too? I can excuse any sin of another, but my own sin alone remains guilt which I can never excuse.

91

It is not a morbidly egotistical distortion of reality, but it is the essential character of a genuine confession of guilt that it is incapable of apportioning blame and pleading a case, but is rather the acknowledgement of one's own sin of Adam. And it is senseless to try to oppose this acknowledgement with an argument *ad absurdum* by pointing out that there are innumerable individuals each of whom must in this way be conscious of being to blame for the whole. For indeed these innumerable individuals are united in the collective personality of the Church. It is in them and through them that the Church confesses and acknowledges her guilt.

The Church confesses that she has not proclaimed often and clearly enough her message of the one God who has revealed Himself for all times in Jesus Christ and who suffers no other gods beside Himself. She confesses her timidity, her evasiveness, her dangerous concessions. She has often been untrue to her office of guardianship and to her office of comfort. And through this she has often denied to the outcast and to the despised the compassion which she owes them. She was silent when she should have cried out because the blood of the innocent was crying aloud to heaven. She has failed to speak the right word in the right way and at the right time. She has not resisted to the uttermost the apostasy of faith, and she has brought upon herself the guilt of the godlessness of the masses.

The Church confesses that she has taken in vain the name of Jesus Christ, for she has been ashamed of this name before the world and she has not striven forcefully enough against the misuse of this name for an evil purpose. She has stood by while violence and wrong were being committed under cover of this name. And indeed she has left uncontradicted, and has thereby abetted, even open mockery of the most holy name. She knows that God will not leave unpunished one who takes His name in vain as she does.

The Church confesses herself guilty of the loss of the Sabbath day, of the withering away of her public worship, and of the contemptuous neglect of Sunday as a day of rest. She has incurred the guilt of restlessness and disquiet, and also of the exploitation of labour even beyond the working weekday, because her preaching of Jesus Christ has been feeble and her public worship has been lifeless.

The Church confesses herself guilty of the collapse of parental authority. She offered no resistance to contempt for age and idolization of youth, for she was afraid of losing youth, and with it the future. As though her future belonged to youth! She has not dared to proclaim the divine authority and dignity of parenthood in the face of the revolution of youth, and in a very earthly way she has tried 'to keep up with the young'. She has thus rendered herself guilty of the breaking up of countless families, the betrayal of fathers by their children, the self-deification of youth, and the abandonment of youth to the apostasy from Christ.

The Church confesses that she has witnessed the lawless application of brutal force, the physical and spiritual suffering of countless innocent people, oppression, hatred and murder, and that she has not raised her voice on behalf of the victims and has not found ways to hasten to their aid. She is guilty of the deaths of the weakest and most defenceless brothers of Jesus Christ.

The Church confesses that she has found no word of advice and assistance in the face of the dissolution of all order in the relation between the sexes. She has found no strong and effective answer to the contempt for chastity and to the proclamation of sexual libertinism. All she has achieved has been an occasional expression of moral indignation. She has thus rendered herself guilty of the loss of the purity and soundness of youth. She has failed to proclaim with sufficient emphasis that our bodies belong to the Body of Christ.

The Church confesses that she has witnessed in silence the spoliation and exploitation of the poor and the enrichment and corruption of the strong.

The Church confesses herself guilty towards the countless victims of calumny, denunciation and defamation. She has not convicted the slanderer of his wrongdoing, and she has thereby abandoned the slandered to his fate.

The Church confesses that she has desired security, peace

and quiet, possessions and honour, to which she had no right, and that in this way she has not bridled the desires of men but has stimulated them still further.

The Church confesses herself guilty of breaking all ten commandments, and in this she confesses her defection from Christ. She has not borne witness to the truth of God in such a manner that all pursuit of truth, all science, can perceive that it has its origin in this truth. She has not proclaimed the justice of God in such a manner that all true justice must see in it the origin of its own essential nature. She has not succeeded in making the providence of God a matter of such certain belief that all human economy must regard it as the source from which it receives its task. By her own silence she has rendered herself guilty of the decline in responsible action, in bravery in the defence of a cause, and in willingness to suffer for what is known to be right. She bears the guilt of the defection of the governing authority from Christ.

Is this saying too much? Will some entirely blameless people stand up at this point and try to prove that it is not the Church which is guilty but the others? Are there perhaps some churchmen who would reject all this as mere insulting abuse, who set themselves up to be more competent judges of the world, and who weigh up and apportion the guilt this way and that? Was not the Church hindered and tied on all sides? Did not the entire secular force stand against her? Had the Church the right to jeopardize her last remaining asset, her public worship and her parish life, by taking up the struggle against the anti-Christian powers? This is the voice of unbelief, which sees in the confession of guilt only a dangerous moral derogation and which fails to see that the confession of guilt is the re-attainment of the form of Jesus Christ who bore the sin of the world. For indeed the free confession of guilt is not something which can be done or left undone at will. It is the emergence of the form of Jesus Christ in the Church. Either the Church must willingly undergo this transformation, or else she must cease to be the Church of Christ. If anyone stifles or corrupts the Church's confession of guilt, his guilt towards Christ is beyond hope.

94

By her confession of guilt the Church does not exempt men from their own confession of guilt, but she calls them in into the fellowship of the confession of guilt. Apostate humanity can endure before Christ only if it has fallen under the sentence of Christ. It is to this judgement that the Church summons all those who hear her message.

Justification and the Healing of the Wound

The Church and the individual are sentenced in their guilt, and as such they are justified by Him who takes upon Himself all human guilt and forgives it, by Jesus Christ. This justification of the Church and of the individual consists in their becoming partakers of the form of Christ. It is the form of the man who has been sentenced by God and delivered up to the death of a sinner, and who has been awakened by God to new life. It is the form of man as he is in truth before God. The Church, and the individual man within the Church, must share in the shame of the cross, the public death of the sinner, for only through this can they be partakers in the glory of Him who is awakened to new righteousness and new life.

The justification of the western world, which has fallen away from Christ, lies solely in the divine justification of the Church, which leads her to the full confession of guilt and to the form of the cross. The renewal of the western world lies solely in the divine renewal of the Church, which leads her to the fellowship of the risen and living Jesus Christ.

Or must such expressions as 'the justification and renewal of the west' be regarded as unwarrantable hyperboles, since clearly the whole of the western world can never be justified and renewed by faith in Jesus Christ? It should certainly be borne in mind that it must be in a different sense that one speaks of the justification and renewal of the Church and of the justification and renewal of the western world. The Church is justified and renewed through her faith in Christ, that is to say through submission to the form of Christ. The western world, as a historical and political form, can be 'justified and renewed' only indirectly, through

95

the faith of the Church. The Church experiences in faith the forgiveness of all her sins and a new beginning through grace. For the nations there is only a healing of the wound, a cicatrization of guilt, in the return to order, to justice, to peace, and to the granting of free passage to the Church's proclamation of Jesus Christ. Thus the nations bear the inheritance of their guilt. Yet, through God's merciful governance in history, it may happen that what began as a curse may end as a blessing for them; out of power which has been wrongfully seized there may come justice and right; out of turmoil and insurrection there may come order; and out of bloodshed there may come peace. When crowns have been usurped, it has often transpired that, even though the beginning was arbitrary violence, yet the inner force of the crown itself, the power of the divine institution of government, has gradually exercised its healing influence and has cicatrized the wounds. Over and over again, when a policy of imperialistic conquest has been pursued amid contempt for law and justice and brutal mishandling of the weak there has come a gradual turning towards rightful order and peace, and even towards the happiness of those who had been the victims of violence, a change of course which has brought with it the healing of the wounds of guilt. This does not, of course, mean that the guilt is justified, or that it is removed or forgiven. The guilt continues, but the wound which it has inflicted is healed. For the Church and for the individual believer there can be only a complete breach with guilt and a new beginning which is granted through the forgiveness of sin, but in the historical life of the nations there can always be only the gradual process of healing. If he who wears the crown has gained it by wrongful means, but in the course of time has established justice, order and peace, he cannot simply be compelled to renounce it. Nor can the conqueror who has led his subject lands into peace, prosperity and happiness simply be forced to give them up. For through the abdication of the crown or the abandonment of the conquered lands there might now arise still more disorder and still more guilt. In the life of the Church and of the faithful all continuity with past guilt is broken through atonement and forgiveness, but in the historical life of the nations it is maintained. The only question here is whether the wounds of this past guilt are in fact healed, and at this point, even within the history of the internal and external political struggle of the nations, there is something in the nature of forgiveness, though it be only a faint shadow of the forgiveness which Jesus Christ vouchsafes to faith. What happens here is the waiving of the demand that the guilty man shall fully expiate the wrong he has committed. It is recognized that what is past cannot be restored by any human might, and that the wheel of history cannot be turned back. Not all the wounds inflicted can be healed, but what matters is that there shall be no further wounds. The law of retribution, 'an eye for an eye and a tooth for a tooth' (Ex. 21.24), is the prerogative of God, the Judge of the nations. In the hands of men this law could only give rise to new disaster. This forgiveness within history can come only when the wound of guilt is healed, when violence has become justice, lawlessness has become order, and war has become peace. If this is not achieved, if wrong still rules unhindered and still inflicts new wounds, then, of course, there can be no question of this kind of forgiveness and man's first concern must be to resist injustice and to call the offenders to account for their guilt.

The 'justification and renewal' of the west, therefore, will come only when justice, order and peace are in one way or another restored, when past guilt is thereby 'forgiven', when it is no longer imagined that what has been done can be undone by means of punitive measures and reprisals, and when the Church of Jesus Christ, as the fountain-head of all forgiveness, justification and renewal, is given room to do her work among the nations. The guilt of the apostasy from Christ is a guilt which is shared in common by the entire western world, however greatly the degree of the offence may vary. The justification and the renewal must therefore likewise be shared in common by the whole of the west. No attempt can succeed which aims at saving the west while excluding one of the western nations.

IV

THE LAST THINGS AND THE
THINGS BEFORE THE LAST

Justification as the Last Word

THE origin and the essence of all Christian life are comprised in the one process or event which the Reformation called justification of the sinner by grace alone. The nature of the Christian life is disclosed not by what the man is in himself but by what he is in this event. The whole length and breadth of human life is here compressed into a single instant, a single point. The totality of life is encompassed in this event. What event is this? It is something final, something which cannot be grasped by the being or the action or the suffering of any man. The dark pit of human life, inwardly and outwardly barred, sinking ever more hopelessly and inescapably in the abyss, is torn open by main force, and the word of God breaks in. In the rescuing light man for the first time recognizes God and his neighbour. The labyrinth of the life he has so far led falls in ruin. Man is free for God and his brothers. He becomes aware that there is a God who loves him; that a brother is standing at his side, whom God loves as he loves him himself and that there is a future with the triune God, together with His Church. He believes. He loves, He hopes. The past and the future of his whole life are merged in one in the presence of God. The whole of the past is comprised in the word forgiveness. The whole of the future is in safe keeping in the faithfulness of God. Past sin is swallowed up in the abyss of the love of God in Jesus Christ. The future will be without sin, a life which proceeds from God (I John 3.9). Life knows now that it is held in tension between the two poles of eternity, that it extends from the choice made before the time of the world to the everlasting salvation. It knows itself to be a member of a Church and a creation which sings the praise of the triune God. All this takes place when Christ comes to men. In Christ all this is truth and reality, and just because it is not a dream, the life of the man who experiences the presence of Christ is henceforward no longer a lost life, but it has become a justified life, a life justified by grace alone.

Yet not only by grace alone, but also by faith alone. That is the teaching of the Bible and of the Reformation. A life is not justified by love or by hope, but only by faith. For indeed faith alone sets life upon a new foundation, and it is this new foundation alone that justifies my being able to live before God. This foundation is the life, the death and the resurrection of the Lord Jesus Christ. Without this foundation a life is unjustified before God. It is delivered up to death and damnation. To live by the life, the death and the resurrection of Jesus Christ is the justification of a life before God. And faith means the finding and holding fast of this foundation. It means casting anchor upon it and being held fast by it. Faith means founding my life upon a foundation which is outside myself, upon an eternal and holy foundation, upon Christ. Faith means being held captive by the sight of Jesus Christ, no longer seeing anything but Him, being wrested from my imprisonment in my own self, being set free by Jesus Christ. Faith is a passive submission to an action, and in this submission alone it is itself an action; yet these two words are inadequate to express the mystery which this implies. Faith alone is certainty. Everything but faith is subject to doubt. Jesus Christ alone is the certainty of faith. My faith that my life is justified is faith in the Lord Jesus Christ. There is, therefore, no other means of access to the justification of my life than through faith alone.

But faith never is alone. As surely as faith is the true presence of Christ, so surely, too, is it accompanied by love and hope. It would be a false faith, a dissembling faith, a hypocritical and self-invented faith such as can never justify, if it were not accompanied by love and hope. It would be a vain repetition of articles of faith, a dead faith, if it

99

were not accompanied by the works of penitence and love. Not for a moment can faith and evil intention exist side by side. When a man undergoes justification he is given everything, but only faith brings justification. When a man encounters Christ, everything that Christ is and has is made the property of this man; yet my life is justified solely by that which is the property of Christ and never by that which has become my own property. Thus the heaven opens over man's head and the joyful tidings of God's salvation in Jesus Christ come down like a shout of rejoicing from heaven to earth, and man believes, and, in believing, he has already received Christ to himself; he possesses everything. He lives before God.

He never knew before what life is. He did not understand himself. Only by his own potentialities or by his own achievements could he try to understand himself and to justify his life. In this way he could justify himself to himself and to a god of his own imagining, but he could have no means of access to the potentialities and the works of the living God; he could have no conception of a life which should proceed from these potentialities and works of the living God. He could not conceive of a life on a foundation other than himself, sustained by a power other than his own. Yet this is the life that he found when Christ justified him in His way. He lost his own life to Christ, and Christ became his life. 'I live; yet not I, but Christ liveth in me' (Gal. 2.20). Christian life is the life of Christ.

We said at the beginning that the event of the justification of a sinner is something final. This was meant in the strict sense of the word. God's compassion on a sinner must and can be heard only as God's final word; for otherwise it is not heard at all. The word is final in two respects. It is final in a qualitative sense, by the nature of its contents. There is no word of God that goes beyond His mercy. There is nothing that goes beyond a life which is justified before God. This word implies the complete breaking off of everything that precedes it, of everything that is before the last; it is therefore never the natural or necessary end of the way which has been pursued so far, but it is rather the total condemnation and invalidation of this way. It is God's own free word, which is subject to no compulsion; for this reason it is the irreversible final word, an ultimate reality. Consequently it excludes any method of achieving it by a way of one's own. There is no Lutheran method and no Pauline method of attaining to this final word. The final word did not justify the way of Paul, who gloried in the law and thereby became an enemy of Christ. Nor did it justify the way of Luther, the monastery and desperate defeat by the law. Quite the reverse was the case, for both these ways were condemned in the final judgement, and it was the sinner Paul and the sinner Luther, but not their sins, that were justified by the grace of God for Christ's sake. The final word was at the same time the judgement on the ways and the things before the last. The qualitatively final word, therefore, forbids us from the outset to set our eyes on the way of Luther or the way of Paul as though these were ways which we had to pursue again. For they are condemned ways. Strictly speaking, we may no more retread the path which Luther followed than we may go the way of the adulteress, of the thief on the cross, of Peter who denied Christ, and of Paul who was filled with zeal against Christ. The qualitatively final word excludes every kind of method once and for all. For it is the word of forgiveness, and the word which justifies by forgiveness alone. It is senseless and wrong, therefore, if one preaches to a Christian congregation today, as one can quite often hear done, that each and every man must first become like Mary Magdalene, like the beggar Lazarus, like the thief on the cross, like all these dim 'peripheral figures', before he can become capable of hearing the final word of God. By speaking in this way one endeavours to emphasize the finality of God's word, but in reality one undermines it. The purport of the Christian message is not that one should become like one or other of those biblical characters, but that one shall be like Christ Himself. No method leads to this end, but only faith. Otherwise the gospel would lose its value, its great price. Dear mercy would become cheap.

But the justifying word of God is also a final word in the sense of time. It is always preceded by something penultimate, some action, suffering, movement, volition, defeat, uprising, entreaty or hope, that is to say, in a quite genuine sense by a span of time, at the end of which it stands. Only he can be justified who has already become the object of an accusation in time. Justification presupposes that the creature has incurred guilt. The time of mercy is not always here, but now, precisely now, and now once and for all, is the 'day of salvation' (II Cor. 6.2). The time of mercy is the final time in the sense that it can never be assumed that, over and above the word of God which comes to me now, there will be a further, future word. There is a time when God permits, awaits and prepares, and there is a final time which cuts short and passes sentence upon the penultimate. Luther had to pass through the monastery, and Paul through his bigoted zeal for the law; even the thief had to go through guilt to the cross; for only thus could they hear the last word. A way had to be trodden; the whole length of the way of the things before the last had to be traversed; each one had to sink to his knees under the burden of these things, and yet the last word was then not the crowning but the complete breaking off of the penultimate. In the presence of the last word the situation of Luther and Paul was in no way different from that of the thief on the cross. A way must be traversed, even though, in fact, there is no way that leads to this goal; this way must be pursued to the end, that is to say, to the point at which God sets an end to it. The penultimate, therefore, remains, even though the ultimate entirely annuls and invalidates it.

The word of the justifying grace of God never departs from its position as the final word; it never yields itself simply as a result that has been achieved, a result that might just as well be set at the beginning as at the end. The way from the penultimate to the ultimate can never be dispensed with. The word remains irreversibly the last; for otherwise it would be reduced to the quality of what is calculable, a merchandise, and would thereby be robbed of its divine character. Grace would be venal and cheap. It would not be a gift.

The Penultimate

Justification by grace and faith alone remains in every respect the final word and for this reason, when we speak of the things before the last, we must not speak of them as having any value of their own, but we must bring to light their relation to the ultimate. It is for the sake of the ultimate that we must now speak of the penultimate. This must now be made clearly intelligible.

One must ask the question at this point, without answering it, whether man can live by the ultimate alone, whether faith can, so to speak, be extended in time, or whether faith does not rather always become real in life as the ultimate phase of a span of time or of many spans of time. We are not speaking here of the recollection of past faith, or of the repetition of articles of faith, but of the living faith which justifies a life. We are asking whether this faith is and ought to be realizable every day, at every hour, or whether here, too, the length of the penultimate must every time be traversed anew for the sake of the ultimate. We are asking, therefore, about the penultimate in the lives of Christians. We are asking whether to deny it is pious self-deception, or whether to take it seriously in its own way is to incur guilt. This means that we are asking also whether the word, the gospel, can be extended in time, whether it can be spoken at any time in the same way, or whether here, too, there is a difference between the ultimate and the penultimate. So that this may become quite clear, let us ask why it is that precisely in thoroughly grave situations, for instance when I am with someone who has suffered a bereavement, I often decide to adopt a 'penultimate' attitude, particularly when I am dealing with Christians, remaining silent as a sign that I share in the bereaved man's helplessness in the face of such a grievous event, and not speaking the biblical words of comfort which are, in fact, known to me and available to me. Why am I often unable to open my mouth, when I ought to give expression to the ultimate? And why, instead, do I decide on an expression of thoroughly penultimate human solidarity? Is it from mistrust of the power of the ultimate word? Is it from fear of men? Or is there some good positive reason for such an attitude, namely, that my knowledge of the word, my having it at my finger-tips, in other words my being, so to speak, spiritually master of the situation, bears only the appearance of the ultimate, but is in reality itself something entirely penultimate? Does one not in some cases, by remaining deliberately in the penultimate, perhaps point all the more genuinely to the ultimate, which God will speak in His own time (though indeed even then through a human mouth)? Does not this mean that, over and over again, the penultimate will be what commends itself precisely for the sake of the ultimate, and that it will have to be done not with a heavy conscience but with a clear one? Of course, this question is not concerned only with a particular case. Fundamentally it embraces the whole domain of Christian social life, and especially the whole range of Christian pastoral activity. What we have said about this particular case applies in countless instances to the daily life of Christians together, and to the whole activity of the Christian preacher with his flock.

Two extreme solutions can be given to the problem of the relation of the penultimate with the ultimate in Christian life. It may be solved 'radically' or by means of a compromise; and it is to be noted at once that the compromise solution, too, is an extreme solution.

The radical solution sees only the ultimate, and in it only the complete breaking off of the penultimate. Ultimate and penultimate are here mutually exclusive contraries. Christ is the destroyer and enemy of everything penultimate, and everything penultimate is enmity towards Christ. Christ is the sign that the world is ripe for burning. There are no distinctions. Everything must go to the judgement. There are only two categories: for Christ, and against Him. 'He that is not with me is against me' (Matt. 12.30). Everything penultimate in human behaviour is sin and denial. In the face of the approaching end there is for the Christian only the last word and his last conduct. What becomes of the world through this is no longer of any consequence. The Christian bears no responsibility for it, and the world must in any case perish. No matter if the whole order of the world breaks down under the impact of the word of Christ, there must be no holding back. The last word of God, which is a word of mercy, here becomes the icy hardness of the law, which despises and breaks down all resistance.[1]

The other solution is the compromise. Here the last word is on principle set apart from all preceding words. The penultimate retains its right on its own account, and is not threatened or imperilled by the ultimate. The world still stands; the end is not yet here; there are still penultimate things which must be done, in fulfilment of the responsibility for this world which God has created. Account must still be taken of men as they are.[2] The ultimate remains totally on the far side of the everyday; it is thus, in fact, an eternal justification for things as they are; it is the metaphysical purification from the accusation which weighs upon everything that is. The free word of mercy now becomes the law of mercy, which rules over everything penultimate, justifying it and certifying its worth.

The two solutions are equally extreme, and both alike contain elements both of truth and of untruth. They are extreme because they place the penultimate and the ultimate in a relation of mutual exclusiveness. In the one case the penultimate is destroyed by the ultimate; and in the other case the ultimate is excluded from the domain of the penultimate. In the one case the ultimate does not admit the penultimate; and in the other case the penultimate does not admit the ultimate. In both cases thoughts which are in themselves equally right and necessary are in an inadmissible manner made absolute. The radical solution has as its point of departure the end of all things, God the Judge and Redeemer; the compromise solution bases itself upon the Creator and Preserver. On the one side it is the end that is

[1] Ibsen's Brand exemplifies this.   [2] *Cf.* Dostoevsky's Grand Inquisitor.

regarded as absolute, and on the other side it is things as they are. Thus creation and redemption, time and eternity confront one another in a conflict which cannot be resolved; the unity of God Himself is sundered, and faith in God is broken apart. The answer to the exponents of the radical solution is that Christ is not radical in their sense and similarly the answer to the adherents of the compromise solution must also be that Christ does not make compromises. Christian life, therefore, is a matter neither of radicalism nor of compromise. There is no point in debating the relative earnestness of these two conceptions; for there is earnestness only in Jesus Christ, and His earnestness reveals that neither of these solutions is earnest. There is earnestness neither in the idea of a pure Christianity in itself nor in the idea of man as he is in himself; there is earnestness only in the reality of God and the reality of man which became one in Jesus Christ. What is earnest and serious is not some kind of Christianity, but it is Jesus Christ Himself. And in Jesus Christ there is neither radicalism nor compromise, but there is the reality of God and men. There is no Christianity in itself, for this would destroy the world; there is no man in himself, for he would exclude God. Both of these are merely ideas; only the God-Man Jesus Christ is real, and only through Him will the world be preserved until it is ripe for its end.

Radicalism always springs from a conscious or unconscious hatred of what is established. Christian radicalism, no matter whether it consists in withdrawing from the world or in improving the world, arises from hatred of creation. The radical cannot forgive God His creation. He has fallen out with the created world, the Ivan Karamazov, who at the same time makes the figure of the radical Jesus in the legend of the Grand Inquisitor. When evil becomes powerful in the world, it infects the Christian, too, with the poison of radicalism. It is Christ's gift to the Christian that he should be reconciled with the world as it is, but now this reconciliation is accounted a betrayal and denial of Christ. It is replaced by bitterness, suspicion and contempt for men and the world. In the place of the love that believes all, bears all

and hopes all, in the place of the love which loves the world
in its very wickedness with the love of God (John 3.16), there
is now the pharisaical denial of love to evil, and the restriction of love to the closed circle of the devout. Instead of the
open Church of Jesus Christ, which serves the world till the
end, there is now some allegedly primitive Christian ideal of
a Church, which in its turn confuses the reality of the living
Jesus Christ with the realization of a Christian idea. Thus a
world which has become evil succeeds in making the
Christians become evil too. It is the same germ that disintegrates the world and that makes the Christians become
radical. In both cases it is hatred towards the world, no
matter whether the haters are the ungodly or the godly. On
both sides it is a refusal of faith in the creation. But devils are
not cast out through Beelzebub.

Compromise always springs from hatred of the ultimate.
The Christian spirit of compromise arises from hatred of the
justification of the sinner by grace alone. The world and life
within it have to be protected against this encroachment on
their territory. The world must be dealt with solely by
means which are of the world. The ultimate has no voice in
determining the form of life in the world. Even the raising of
the question of the ultimate, even the endeavour to give
effect to God's word in its authority for life in the world, is
now accounted radicalism and apathy or antipathy towards
the established orders of the world and towards the men who
are subject to these orders. That freedom from the world
which Christ has given to the Christians, as well as the
renunciation of the world (I John 2.17), is now denounced as
opposition to creation, as unnatural estrangement from the
world and from men, and even as hostility towards them. In
their place adaptability, even to the point of resignedness,
and mere worldly-wise prudence and discretion are passed
off as genuine openness to the world and as genuine Christian
charity.

Radicalism hates time, and compromise hates eternity.
Radicalism hates patience, and compromise hates decision.
Radicalism hates wisdom, and compromise hates simplicity.

Radicalism hates moderation and measure, and compromise hates the immeasurable. Radicalism hates the real, and compromise hates the word.

To contrast the two attitudes in this way is to make it sufficiently clear that both alike are opposed to Christ. For in Jesus Christ those things which are here ranged in mutual hostility are one. The question of the Christian life will not, therefore, be decided and answered either by radicalism or by compromise, but only by reference to Jesus Christ Himself. In Him alone lies the solution for the problem of the relation between the ultimate and the penultimate.

In Jesus Christ we have faith in the incarnate, crucified and risen God. In the incarnation we learn of the love of God for His creation; in the crucifixion we learn of the judgement of God upon all flesh; and in the resurrection we learn of God's will for a new world. There could be no greater error than to tear these three elements apart; for each of them comprises the whole. It is quite wrong to establish a separate theology of the incarnation, a theology of the cross, or a theology of the resurrection, each in opposition to the others, by a mis-conceived absolutization of one of these parts; it is equally wrong to apply the same procedure to a consideration of the Christian life. A Christian ethic constructed solely on the basis of the incarnation would lead directly to the com-promise solution. An ethic which was based solely on the cross or the resurrection of Jesus would fall victim to radicalism and enthusiasm. Only in the unity is the conflict resolved.

Jesus Christ the man—this means that God enters into created reality. It means that we have the right and the obligation to be men before God. The destruction of man-hood, of man's quality as man (*Menschsein*), is sin, and is therefore a hindrance to God's redemption of man. Yet the manhood (*Menschsein*) of Jesus Christ does not mean simply the corroboration of the established world and of the human character as it is. Jesus was man 'without sin' (Heb. 4.15); that is what is decisive. Yet among men Jesus lived in the most utter poverty, unmarried, and He died as a criminal.

Thus the manhood of Jesus implies already a twofold condemnation of man, the absolute condemnation of sin and the
relative condemnation of the established human orders. But
even under this condemnation Jesus is really man, and it is
His will that we shall be men. He neither renders the human
reality independent nor destroys it, but He allows it to
remain as that which is before the last, as a penultimate which
requires to be taken seriously in its own way, and yet not to
be taken seriously, a penultimate which has become the
outer covering of the ultimate.

Jesus Christ the crucified—this means that God pronounces its final condemnation on the fallen creation. The
rejection of God on the cross of Jesus Christ contains within
itself the rejection of the whole human race without exception. The cross of Jesus is the death sentence upon the world.
Man cannot glory now in his humanity, nor the world in its
divine orders. The glory of men has come now to its last end
in the face of the Crucified, bruised and bloody and spat
upon. Yet the crucifixion of Jesus does not simply mean the
annihilation of the created world, but under this sign of
death, the cross, men are now to continue to live, to their
own condemnation if they despise it, but to their own salvation if they give it its due. The ultimate has become real in
the cross, as the judgement upon all that is penultimate, yet
also as mercy towards that penultimate which bows before
the judgement of the ultimate.

Jesus Christ who rose again—this means that God out of
His love and omnipotence sets an end to death and calls a
new creation into life, imparts new life. 'Old things are
passed away' (II Cor. 5.17). 'Behold, I make all things new'
(Rev. 21.5). Already in the midst of the old world, resurrection has dawned, as a last sign of its end and of its future,
and at the same time as a living reality. Jesus rose again as a
man, and by so doing He gave to men the gift of the resurrection. Thus man remains man, even though he is a new, a
risen man, who in no way resembles the old man. Until he
crosses the frontier of his death, even though he has already
risen again with Christ, he remains in the world of the pen-

ultimate, the world into which Jesus entered and the world in which the cross stands. Thus, so long as the earth continues, even the resurrection does not annul the penultimate, but the eternal life, the new life, breaks in with ever greater power into the earthly life and wins its space for itself within it.

We have tried to make clear the unity and the diversity of the incarnation, the cross and the resurrection. Christian life is life with the incarnate, crucified and risen Christ, whose word confronts us in its entirety in the message of the justification of the sinner by grace alone. Christian life means being a man through the efficacy of the incarnation; it means being sentenced and pardoned through the efficacy of the cross; and it means living a new life through the efficacy of the resurrection. There cannot be one of these without the rest.

As for the question of the things before the last, it follows from what has been said so far that the Christian life means neither a destruction nor a sanctioning of the penultimate. In Christ the reality of God meets the reality of the world and allows us to share in this real encounter. It is an encounter beyond all radicalism and beyond all compromise. Christian life is participation in the encounter of Christ with the world.

It has now become clear that the ultimate—the last things —leaves open a certain amount of room for the penultimate, the things before the last. We must, therefore, consider this penultimate more closely.

The Preparing of the Way

What is this penultimate? It is everything that precedes the ultimate, everything that precedes the justification of the sinner by grace alone, everything which is to be regarded as leading up to the last thing when the last thing has been found. It is at the same time everything which follows the ultimate and yet again precedes it. There is, therefore, no penultimate in itself; as though a thing could justify itself in itself as being a thing before the last thing; a thing becomes penultimate only through the ultimate, that is to say, at the moment when it has already lost its own validity. The penultimate, then, does not determine the ultimate; it is the

ultimate which determines the penultimate. The penultimate
is not a state or condition in itself, but it is a judgement
which the ultimate passes upon that which has preceded it.
Concretely, two things are called penultimate in relation to
the justification of the sinner by grace, namely being man
(*Menschsein*) and being good. Now it would be quite wrong,
it would be robbing the ultimate, if we were to say, for
example, that to be man is a precondition of justification by
grace. On the contrary, it is only on the basis of the ultimate
that we can know what it is to be man, so that manhood can
be determined and established through justification. And
yet the relationship is such that manhood precedes justification, and that from the standpoint of the ultimate it is necessary that it should precede it. The penultimate does not
therefore rob the ultimate of its freedom; but it is the freedom
of the ultimate that validates the penultimate. And so, with
all necessary reservations, it is now possible to speak of
manhood, for example, as a penultimate to justification by
faith. Only man can be justified, precisely because only he
who is justified becomes 'man'.

Now from this there follows something which is of crucial
importance. For the sake of the ultimate the penultimate
must be preserved. Any arbitrary destruction of the penultimate will do serious injury to the ultimate. If, for example, a
human life is deprived of the conditions which are proper to
it, then the justification of such a life by grace and faith, if it
is not rendered impossible, is at least seriously impeded. In
concrete terms, if a slave is so far prevented from making free
use of his time that he can no longer hear the preaching of the
word, then this word of God cannot in any case lead him to
the justifying faith. From this fact it follows that it is necessary
to see to it that the penultimate, too, is provided with the
preaching of the ultimate word of God, the proclamation of
the justification of the sinner by grace alone, lest the destruction of the penultimate should prove a hindrance to the
ultimate. If the proclaimer of the word does not at the same
time take every measure to ensure that the word may be
heard, then he is not satisfying the claim of the word to pass

freely and unhindered. The way must be made ready for the word. It is the word itself that demands it.

Preparing the way for the word: this is the purpose of everything that has been said about the things before the last. 'Prepare ye the way of the Lord, make his paths straight. Every valley shall be filled, and every mountain and hill shall be brought low; and the crooked shall be made straight, and the rough ways shall be made smooth; and all flesh shall see the salvation of God' (Luke 3.4ff.). Christ indeed makes His own way when He comes; He is the 'breaker' of all bonds (Micah 2.13). 'He breaketh the gates of brass, and cutteth the bars of iron in sunder' (Ps. 107.16); 'He putteth down the mighty from their seat, and exalteth the humble and meek' (Luke 1.52). His entry is a triumph over His enemies. But lest the might of his coming should overwhelm mankind in anger, and in order that it may find them humble and expectant, the entry is preceded by the summons to the preparation of the way. Yet this making ready of the way is not merely an inward process; it is a formative activity on the very greatest visible scale. 'The valleys shall be exalted' (Isa. 40.4). That which has been cast down into the depths of human wretchedness, that which has been abased and humbled, is now to be raised up. There is a depth of human bondage, of human poverty, of human ignorance, which impedes the merciful coming of Christ. 'The mountains and hills shall be made low' (Isa. 40.4). If Christ is to come, then all that is proud and haughty must bow down. There is a measure of power, of wealth, of knowledge, which is an impediment to Christ and to His mercy. 'The crooked shall be made straight' (Luke 3.5). The way of Christ is a straight way. There is a measure of entanglement in the lie, in guilt, in one's own labour, in one's own work (Ps. 9.16) and in self-love, which makes the coming of grace particularly difficult. That is why the way had to be made straight on which Christ is to come to man. 'The rough ways shall be made smooth' (Luke 3.5). Defiance, stubbornness and unreceptiveness may have hardened a man so much that Christ can now only destroy him in anger as one who resists Him, and so that Christ can no longer enter into him in mercy, because the door is bolted against Christ's merciful coming and is not opened to Him when He knocks.

Christ comes indeed, and opens up His own way, no matter whether man is ready beforehand or not. No one can hinder His coming, but we can resist His coming in mercy. There are conditions of the heart, of life and of the world which impede the reception of grace in a special way, namely, by rendering faith infinitely difficult. We say that they impede it and render it difficult, but not that they make it impossible. And we are well aware also that even the levelling of the way and the removal of the obstacles cannot compel the imparting of grace. The merciful coming of Christ must still 'break the gates of brass and cut the bars of iron' (Ps. 107.16); grace must in the end itself prepare and make level its own way and grace alone must ever anew render possible the impossible. But all this does not release us from our obligation to prepare the way for the coming of grace, and to remove whatever obstructs it and makes it difficult. The state in which grace finds us is not a matter of indifference, even though it is always by grace alone that grace comes to us. We may, among other things, make it difficult for ourselves to attain to faith. For him who is cast into utter shame, desolation, poverty and helplessness, it is difficult to have faith in the justice and goodness of God. For him whose life has become a prey to disorder and indiscipline, it will be difficult to hear the commandments of God in faith. It is hard for the sated and the mighty to grasp the meaning of God's judgement and God's mercy. And for one who has been disappointed in mistaken belief, and who has become inwardly undisciplined, it is hard to attain to the simplicity of the surrender of the heart to Jesus Christ. That is not said in order either to excuse or to discourage those whom these things have befallen. They must know, on the contrary, that it is precisely to the depths of downfall, of guilt and of misery, that God stoops down in Jesus Christ; that precisely the dispossessed, the humiliated and the exploited, are especially near to the justice and mercy of God; that it is to the undisciplined that Jesus Christ offers His help and His strength; and that the truth is ready to set upon firm ground those who stray and despair.

But all this does not exclude the task of preparing the way. This task is, on the contrary, a charge of immense responsibility for all those who know of the coming of Christ. The hungry man needs bread and the homeless man needs a roof; the dispossessed need justice and the lonely need fellowship; the undisciplined need order and the slave needs freedom. To allow the hungry man to remain hungry would be blasphemy against God and one's neighbour, for what is nearest to God is precisely the need of one's neighbour. It is for the love of Christ, which belongs as much to the hungry man as to myself, that I share my bread with him and that I share my dwelling with the homeless. If the hungry man does not attain to faith, then the guilt falls on those who refused him bread. To provide the hungry man with bread is to prepare the way for the coming of grace.

But what is happening here is a thing before the last. To give bread to the hungry man is not the same as to proclaim the grace of God and justification to him, and to have received bread is not the same as to have faith. Yet for him who does these things for the sake of the ultimate, and in the knowledge of the ultimate, this penultimate does bear a relation to the ultimate. It is a pen*ultimate*. The coming of grace is the ultimate. But we must speak of the preparing of the way, of the penultimate, the things before the last, for the sake of those who with their radicalism, which repudiates the things before the last, have encountered only failure, and who are now in danger of being thrown back even before the things before the last, and for the sake of those who stick fast in the things before the last and are content to remain there, but who must nevertheless now be claimed for the last things. Finally, and perhaps even primarily, we speak of the penultimate things for the sake of those who have not even attained to these penultimate things, those for whom no one performs this service, for whom no one has prepared the way, and who must now be afforded help, so that the word of God, the ultimate, grace, can come to them.

Certainly one would have misunderstood all this if one were to say that before he can become a Christian the slave must have received his liberty, the outcast his rights, and the hungry man his bread; in other words that values must first be set in order. This is refuted by the evidence of the New Testament and of Church history; indeed it has perhaps been precisely at times when the world has seemed to be relatively in order that the estrangement from the faith has been especially deep-seated and alarming. The preparation of the way for Christ cannot, therefore, be simply a matter of the establishment of certain desirable and expedient conditions; it cannot be simply the realization of a programme of social reform. It is quite certain that the preparation of the way is a matter of concrete interventions in the visible world, and it is certain that hunger and the satisfaction of hunger are concrete and visible matters; yet everything depends on this activity being a spiritual reality, precisely because ultimately it is not indeed a question of the reform of earthly conditions, but it is a question of the coming of Christ. Only a spiritual preparation of the way will be followed by the merciful coming of the Lord. And this implies that the visible actions which must be performed in order to prepare men for the reception of Jesus Christ must be acts of humiliation before the coming of the Lord, that is to say, they must be acts of repentance. Preparation of the way means repentance (Matt. 3.1ff.). But repentance means a concrete turning back; repentance demands action. Thus the preparation of the way does indeed also envisage certain definite conditions which are to be established. And when we endeavour to express in positive terms these conditions towards which the preparing of the way is directed, we come to two formulations: to be man and to be good.

Only the triumphal entry of the Lord will bring with it the fulfilment of manhood and goodness. But a light is already shed by the coming Lord upon what is meant by being man and by being good in the way which is required for true preparation and expectation. It is only by reference to the Lord who is to come, and who has come, that we can know what it is to be man and to be good. It is because Christ is coming that we must be men and that we must be good. For Christ is not coming to hell, but to 'His own' (John 1.11); He is coming to His creation, which, in spite of its fall, is His creation still. Christ is not coming to devils but to men, certainly to men who are sinful, lost and damned, but still to men. That the fallen creation is still the creation, and that sinful man still remains man, follows from the fact that Christ is coming to them and that Christ redeems them from sin and from the power of the devil. It is in relation to Christ that the fallen world becomes intelligible as the world which is preserved and sustained by God for the coming of Christ, the world in which we can and should live good lives as men in orders which are established. But wherever man becomes a thing, a merchandise, a machine, wherever the established orders are arbitrarily destroyed, and wherever the distinction is lost between 'good' and 'evil', there the reception of Christ is impeded by an additional obstacle over and above the general sinfulness and forlornness of the world. There the world is destroying itself, so that it is in grave peril of becoming devilish. Even in the midst of the fallen, lost world, it makes a difference in God's sight whether a man observes or violates the order of marriage and whether he acts justly or arbitrarily. Certainly he is still a sinner, even though he is blameless in marriage and a protector of justice, but it still makes a difference whether the penultimate is attended to and taken seriously or not. The preparation of the way requires that the penultimate shall be respected and validated for the sake of the approaching ultimate.

It is an essential characteristic of the divine revelation through the word that I must go to hear it preached if I am to hear this word at all; for 'belief cometh of hearing' (Rom. 10.17). If the word is to be able to come to me, then the last act in the preparation of the way, the last deed of the penultimate, is that I go to the place at which it has pleased God to impart His word. In the observance of the established orders, attendance at church is the extreme limit of what is commanded within the framework of the penultimate. Our fathers, too, could speak in this way. It was assumed that everyone possessed the outward possibility, the physical ability, and the measure of inward self-possession and intelligence necessary for fulfilling this requirement. But if it transpires that this assumption is on some occasion not correct, and that these prerequisites are absent, so that the summons to the preaching can for some quite extraneous reason no longer be obeyed, then the care for the penultimate is transferred elsewhere. Care must be taken in the first place that it is outwardly possible to hear and to obey the call to the preaching. This may mean that man must first become man again before he can be addressed in this way. The preparation of the way for the coming Lord is not being treated seriously if this task has not been undertaken. This action is dictated by compassion for men and by responsibility to Christ, who desires to come to all men.

Yet in spite of all this it is impossible to state too clearly that only the coming Lord Himself can make ready the way for His coming. He will lead man to a wholly new manhood and to goodness. The end of all preparation of the way for Christ must lie precisely in perceiving that we ourselves can never prepare the way. And consequently it is this very obligation to prepare the way that must in every circumstance lead us to repentance. In the words of Valentin Thilo's hymn: 'At this holy time, of Thy goodness and mercy, poor as I am, Lord Jesus, make me ready!' It is precisely in this that preparation of the way for Christ differs from all ways of our own to Christ. As we said at the beginning, there is, in fact, no 'method', no way to attain to the ultimate. Unlike all methods, the preparation of the way sets out from the clear awareness that Christ Himself must go this way: it is not our way to Him but His way to us that has to be prepared and it can be prepared through my knowledge that He Himself must prepare it. Method is a way from the penultimate to the ultimate. Preparation of the way is a way from the ultimate to the penultimate. Christ is coming, of His own will, by His

own strength, and out of His own love; He has the power and
the desire to overcome all obstacles, even the greatest; He is
the preparer of His own way; it is this, and really only this,
that makes us the preparers of His way. How, indeed, should
we do otherwise than desire and be compelled to be the
preparers of the way of such a Master? How should we do
otherwise than allow Him who is coming to make us the
preparers of His way who stand in earnest expectation of His
advent? We await Christ; we know that He is coming; that
alone is why we prepare His way.

Christ alone creates faith. Yet there are situations in which
faith is easier or more difficult.[1] There are different degrees
of impenitence and obduracy. Christ alone brings us the
ultimate, the justification of our lives before God, and yet in
spite of this, or rather just because of this, the penultimate is
not taken from us but is spared. The penultimate is swallowed
up in the ultimate, and yet it is still necessary and it retains
its right so long as the earth continues.

Christian life is the dawning of the ultimate in me; it is the
life of Jesus Christ in me. But it is always also life in the
penultimate which waits for the ultimate. The earnestness of
Christian life lies solely in the ultimate, but the penultimate,
too, has its earnestness, which consists indeed precisely in
never confusing the penultimate with the ultimate and in
regarding the penultimate as an empty jest in comparison
with the ultimate, so that the ultimate and the penultimate
may alike retain their seriousness and validity. This demonstrates once again the impossibility of any radical Christianity
and of any compromising Christianity in the face of the
reality of Jesus Christ and of His coming into the world.

The spiritual situation of western Christendom in relation
to the problem we are discussing displays the following
characteristics. The calling in question of the last things, of
the ultimate, which has been taking place to an ever increasing extent during the past two hundred years, has at the
same time imperilled the stability of the penultimate, which
was closely linked here with the ultimate, and has brought it

1 *Cf. The Cost of Discipleship*, Chapter I.

near to disruption. And in its turn the breaking up of the penultimate has as its consequence an intensified neglect and depreciation of the ultimate. Ultimate and penultimate are closely allied. What must be done, therefore, is to fortify the penultimate with a more emphatic proclamation of the ultimate, and also to protect the ultimate by taking due care for the penultimate. And at the same time there are to be found in western Christendom today large numbers of those who do indeed hold fast to the things before the last, and who are resolved to continue to hold fast to them, but who do not clearly perceive, or at any rate do not resolutely accept, the connexion of the penultimate with the ultimate, even though their attitude to this ultimate is not in any way hostile. In such cases the loss of the ultimate must necessarily lead sooner or later to the collapse of the penultimate as well, unless it is found possible once again to claim this penultimate for the ultimate. Whatever humanity and goodness is found in this fallen world must be on the side of Jesus Christ. It is nothing less than a curtailment of the gospel if the nearness of Jesus Christ is proclaimed only to what is broken and evil and if the father's love for the prodigal son is so emphasized as to appear to diminish his love for the son who remained at home. Certainly the humanity and goodness of which we are speaking are not the humanity and goodness of Jesus Christ; they cannot stand before the judgement; and yet Jesus loved the young man who had kept the commandments (Mark 10.17ff.). Humanity and goodness should not acquire a value on their own account, but they should and shall be claimed for Jesus Christ, especially in cases where they persist as the unconscious residue of a former attachment to the ultimate. It may often seem more in earnest to treat a man in this situation simply as a non-Christian and to urge him to confess his unbelief. But it will be more Christian to claim precisely that man as a Christian who would himself no longer dare to call himself a Christian, and then with much patience to help him to the profession of faith in Christ. It is partly from this point of view that the two following chapters are to be understood.

THE NATURAL

The concept of the natural has fallen into discredit in Protestant ethics. For some it was completely lost to sight in the darkness of general sinfulness, while for others, conversely, it was lighted up by the brilliance of absolute historicity. In both cases this was a disastrous mistake, for its consequence was that the concept of the natural no longer had a place in Protestant thought but was entirely abandoned to Catholic ethics. Now this meant a serious and substantial loss to Protestant thought, for it was now more or less deprived of the means of orientation in dealing with the practical questions of natural life. The significance of the natural for the gospel was obscured, and the Protestant Church was no longer able to return a clear word of direction in answer to the burning questions of natural life. She thus left countless human beings unanswered and unassisted in the midst of vitally important decisions, and confined herself more and more to an (orthodoxly static) apology for the divine grace. Before the light of grace everything human and natural sank into the night of sin, and now no one dared to consider the relative differences within the human and natural, for fear that by their so doing grace as grace might be diminished. It was its treatment of the concept of the natural that demonstrated most clearly that this Protestant thought was no longer conscious of the true relation of the ultimate to the penultimate. The consequences of this loss were grave and far-reaching. If there were no longer any relative distinctions to be made within the fallen creation, then the way was open for every kind of arbitrariness and disorder, and natural life, with its concrete decisions and orders, was no longer subject to responsibility to God. The sole antithesis to the natural was the word of God; the natural was no longer contrasted with the unnatural. For in the presence of the word of God both the natural and the unnatural were equally damned. And this meant complete disruption in the domain of natural life.

The concept of the natural must, therefore, be recovered

on the basis of the gospel. We speak of the natural, as distinct from the creaturely, in order to take into account the fact of the Fall; and we speak of the natural rather than of the sinful so that we may include in it the creaturely. The natural is that which, after the Fall, is directed towards the coming of Christ. The unnatural is that which, after the Fall, closes its doors against the coming of Christ. There is indeed only a relative difference between that which is directed towards Christ and that which closes its doors to Christ; for the natural does not compel the coming of Christ, and the unnatural does not render it impossible. In both cases the real coming is an event of grace. And it is only through the coming of Christ that the natural is confirmed in its character as a penultimate, and that the unnatural is exposed once and for all as destruction of the penultimate. Thus, even in the sight of Christ, there is a distinction between the natural and the unnatural, a distinction which cannot be obliterated without doing grave harm.

The concept of the natural (which is derived from *nasci, natura*) differs from the concept of the creaturely (from *creare, creatura*) in that it implies an element of independence and self-development which is entirely appropriate to what it denotes. Through the Fall the 'creature' becomes 'nature'. The direct dependence of the creature on God is replaced by the relative freedom of natural life. Within this freedom there are the differences between the true and the mistaken use of freedom, and there is therefore the difference between the natural and the unnatural. In other words there is relative openness and relative closedness for Christ. But it is of crucial importance that this relative freedom shall not be confused with an absolute freedom for God and one's neighbour such as only the imparted word of God itself can create and bestow; yet this relative freedom is still important even for him to whom Christ has given the freedom for God and for his neighbour.

Natural life must not be understood simply as a preliminary to life with Christ. It is only from Christ Himself that it receives its validation. Christ Himself entered into the natural life, and it is only through the incarnation of Christ that the natural life becomes the penultimate which is directed towards the ultimate. Only through the incarnation of Christ do we have the right to call others to the natural life and to live the natural life ourselves.

How does one recognize the natural? The natural is the form of life preserved by God for the fallen world and directed towards justification, redemption and renewal through Christ. The natural is, therefore, determined according to its form and according to its contents. Formally the natural is determined through God's will to preserve it and through its being directed towards Christ. In its formal aspect, therefore, the natural can be discerned only in its relation to Jesus Christ Himself. As for its contents, the natural is the form of the preserved life itself, the form which embraces the entire human race. On this side, in relation to its contents, man's 'reason' is the organ of knowledge of the natural. Reason is not a divine principle of knowledge and order in man which is raised above the natural, but it is itself a part of this preserved form of life, namely that part which is adapted to the function of introducing into the consciousness, of 'perceiving',[1] as a unity whatever is entire and general in the real. Reason, then, is wholly embedded in the natural; it is the conscious perception of the natural as it, in fact, presents itself. The natural and reason are related to one another as the form of being and the form of consciousness of the preserved life. The suitability of reason for the grasping of the natural derives, therefore, neither from the spontaneity of reason, as though it were itself to create the natural, nor yet from the divinity of reason, which would enable it to adapt itself to the natural, but rather from the fact of the Fall, in which reason is just as much involved as is the rest of the world. Certainly reason does not now cease to be reason, but it is now fallen reason, perceiving only the datum of the fallen world, and perceiving it only in the aspect of its contents.

[1] *Translator's note.* The noun *Vernunft* (reason) is derived from the verb *vernehmen* (perceive).

Reason perceives the universal in what is given; and thus the given natural, as reason perceives it, is a universal. It embraces the whole of human nature. Reason understands the natural as something that is universally established and independent of the possibility of empirical verification.[1]

From this there follows a conclusion that is of crucial importance, namely, that the natural can never be something that is determined by any single part or any single authority within the fallen world. Neither the individual nor any community or institution within the preserved world establishes and decides what is natural; but it is already established and decided in advance, in the sense that the individual, the community and the institution all receive their allotted share in it. What is natural cannot be determined by any arbitrary decision, and indeed whatever is set up in this arbitrary manner by an individual, a society or an institution will necessarily collapse and destroy itself in the encounter with the natural which is already established. Whoever does injury or violence to the natural will suffer for it.

The reason for this is that the natural is at the same time the true means of protection of the preserved life. And so the natural is not only acknowledged by 'reason' but it commands the assent and approval of the 'underlying will' of the preserved life. Here again it would not be true to say that this 'underlying will' is a residue of the divine in man which has remained untouched by the Fall and which is capable of giving its assent to the divine order; on the contrary, this underlying will is no less embedded and immersed in the Fall and in the preserved world than is reason itself, and consequently it is exclusively directed towards the contents, the non-formal aspect of the natural, and favours this aspect

[1] This view differs from the Catholic theory in that (1) we regard reason as as having been entirely involved in the Fall, while according to Catholic dogmatics reason still retained a certain essential integrity, and (2) according to the Catholic doctrine, reason may also grasp the formal determination of the natural, the second of these principles being connected with the first. Our view differs from the Enlightenment view in that it takes the natural to rest upon what is objectively given and not upon the subjective spontaneity of reason.

because it discerns in it the means of protection of life. The natural is the safeguarding of life against the unnatural. It is in the last analysis life itself that tends towards the natural and keeps turning against the unnatural and bringing about its downfall. This, in the last analysis, is what underlies the maintenance and recovery of physical and mental health. Life is its own physician, whether it be the life of an individual or the life of a community; it wards off the unnatural because the unnatural is a destroyer of life; only when life itself is no longer able to offer the necessary resistance do the destructive forces of the unnatural carry off the victory.[1]

Destruction of the natural means destruction of life. Knowledge and the will to live fall into disorder and confusion and are directed to the wrong objects. The unnatural is the enemy of life.

The fact that it is at all possible to injure the natural is adequately explained by the relative liberty of the preserved life. In the abuse of this relative liberty some given entity within the fallen world posits itself as an absolute, declares itself to be the source of the natural, and thereby disintegrates the natural life. There now begins a struggle between the unnatural and the natural, in which the unnatural may for a time forcibly prevail, for the unnatural consists essentially in organization, and the natural cannot be organized but is simply there. It is possible, for example, to organize the undermining of children's respect for their parents, but respect for parents itself is simply practised and cannot by its very nature be organized. For this reason the natural may be temporarily overcome by the unnatural. But in the long run every organization collapses, and the natural endures and prevails by its own inherent strength; for life itself is on the side of the natural. In the meanwhile, however, there may indeed have occurred serious disturbances and revolutionary changes in the external forms of life. But, so long as life continues, the natural will always reassert itself.

[1] It is in this respect that F. Künkel is correct. Over and over again in his characterological books it is 'life' that appears as the actual final corrective of what is psychically unnatural and diseased.

In this context there is a solid basis for that optimistic view of human history which confines itself within the limits of the fallen world. It has, of course, already been made sufficiently clear that this optimism has nothing to do with the idea of a gradual overcoming of sin. We are referring here to an entirely immanent optimism, one which is entirely rooted in the natural. It is true that, according to the Holy Scripture (Luke 21.16), one of the portents of the approaching end of the world is the destruction of the natural in every respect; here a limit is set to the immanent optimism. Indeed the biblical prophecy extrudes this optimism once and for all from its rôle as a historical principle and as a quietive. It remains a hope which is not altogether without foundation, but which is purely immanent and is therefore never certain.

On the basis of these preliminaries we may now approach the task of describing the natural, the form of life preserved by God after the Fall, with reference to the way in which it is directed towards the coming of Christ.

Natural Life

Natural life is formed life. The natural is form, immanent in life and serving it. If life detaches itself from this form, if it seeks to break free and to assert itself in isolation from this form, if it is unwilling to allow itself to be served by the form of the natural, then it destroys itself to the very roots. Life which posits itself as an absolute, as an end in itself, is its own destroyer. Vitalism cannot but end in nihilism, in the disruption of all that is natural. Life in itself, in the strict sense of the word, is a void, a plunge into the abyss; it is movement without end and without purpose, movement into nothing. It does not rest until it has involved everything in this movement of destruction. This vitalism occurs both in individual and in social life. It arises from the misconceived absolutization of an insight which is in itself correct, namely, that life is not only a means to an end but is also an end in itself; this insight, too, holds true both for individual and for social life. God desires life, and He gives life a form in which it can live, because if it is left to itself it can only destroy itself. But this form at the same time places life in the service of other life and of the world; in a limited sense it makes life a means to an end. Now there is not only an absolutization of life as an end in itself, namely, vitalism, which destroys life, but there is also an absolutization of life as a means to an end, and this has the same result. This, too, applies both to the individual and to the community. We may call this aberration the mechanization of life. Here the individual is understood only in terms of his utilizable value for the whole, and the community is understood only in terms of its utilizable value for some higher institution or organization or idea. The collectivity is the god to whom individual and social life are sacrificed in the process of their total mechanization. Life is extinguished, and the form which exists for the purpose of serving life now assumes unrestricted mastery over life. Life is no longer in any sense an end in itself, and it is swallowed up in the void, for mechanization draws its strength only from life and when it has killed all life it must itself collapse.

Natural life stands between the extremes of vitalism and mechanization. It is at the same time life as an end in itself and life as a means to an end. Both vitalism and mechanization, in the sense in which we have described them, are expressions of an attitude of—perhaps unconscious—despair towards natural life; they express a certain hostility to life, tiredness of life and incapacity for life. The taste for the natural has yielded to the attractions of the unnatural. In relation to Jesus Christ the status of life as an end in itself is understood as creaturehood, and its status as a means to an end is understood as participation in the kingdom of God; while, within the framework of the natural life, the fact that life is an end in itself finds expression in the rights with which life is endowed, and the fact that life is a means to an end finds expression in the duties which are imposed on it. Thus, for the sake of Christ and His coming, natural life must be lived within the framework of certain definite rights and certain definite duties. To repudiate or annul or destroy these rights and duties is to place a serious obstacle in the way of the coming of Christ and to strike at the roots of the gratitude which reverently preserves the life that has been received and which at the same time commits this life to the service of the Creator.

To idealistic thinkers it may seem out of place for a Christian ethic to speak first of rights and only later of duties. But our authority is not Kant; it is the Holy Scripture, and it is precisely for that reason that we must speak first of the rights of natural life, in other words of what is given to life, and only later of what is demanded of life. God gives before He demands. And indeed in the rights of natural life it is not to the creature that honour is given, but to the Creator. It is the abundance of His gifts that is acknowledged. There is no right before God, but the natural, purely as what is given, becomes the right in relation to man. The rights of natural life are in the midst of the fallen world the reflected splendour of the glory of God's creation. They are not primarily something that man can sue for in his own interest, but they are something that is guaranteed by God Himself. The duties, on the other hand, derive from the rights themselves, as tasks are implied by gifts. They are implicit in the rights. Within the framework of the natural life, therefore, we in every case speak first of the rights and then of the duties, for by so doing, in the natural life too, we are allowing the gospel to have its way.

Suum cuique

The most general formulation of the rights which are given with the natural is the Roman law dictum: *suum cuique*, to each his own. This principle expresses not only the multiplicity of the natural and of the rights that pertain to it but also the unity which the right retains even in this multiplicity. The principle is misapplied whenever there is a violation of either the multiplicity or the unity of the rights which are given with the natural. This is the case if 'his own' is taken to mean 'the same', so that the manifoldness of the natural is destroyed in favour of an abstract law, and it is also the case if 'his own' is defined arbitrarily and subjectively so that the unity of rights is nullified in the interests of free self-will. In both these cases violence is done to the natural itself. The 'his own' which belongs to each and every man is at the same time different and unequal in every case (though not indeed arbitrarily so); yet it is based upon what is naturally given and is therefore universal (but not abstractedly formal).

If there is a right that is rooted in what is naturally given, an 'innate right', then this must not be rendered ineffective or destroyed by any right that comes from without, for otherwise the natural itself will be driven to revolution against an unnatural right. The principle of *suum cuique* recognizes the priority of the rights which are implied in the natural over all other rights. But at the same time it preserves the natural from arbitrary and revolutionary outbursts by pointing to the right which is due to the other man and which is just as much a natural right as is my own. One can have a natural right of one's own only if one respects the natural rights of others. But here already the principle of *suum cuique* reaches the limits of its applicability; for it rests on the assumption that the given natural rights can be made to accord with one another, in other words that there are no natural rights which fundamentally conflict. On this basis any actual events of this kind, that is to say, conflicts between rights which are rooted in the natural, must be ascribed to imperfections, misunderstandings or inadequate concepts of right, but they are not ascribed to the actual structure of the world as it is; in other words they are not seen to arise from sin, which operates in the natural. *Suum cuique*, as the supreme principle for the determination of rights, does not take into account the conflict of rights which is inherent in the natural itself, and when the conflict arises it demands the intervention of positive rights, rights which are introduced from outside nature, and these positive rights are to be both divine and secular.[1]

Yet the fact that the principle of *suum cuique* is of such limited

1 *Editor's note.* The MS. contains the following pencil comment: 'Must be developed later! At the end of the chapter on natural rights or in the next chapter on good.'

application does not deprive it of its relative correctness. If right is sought for in what is naturally given, then due honour is being rendered to the will and to the gift of the Creator, even in a world which is involved in conflict; and attention is being drawn also to the fulfilment of all rights when Jesus Christ through the Holy Ghost shall give to each his own. And so respect for this principle may in the true sense be regarded as penultimate, a thing before the last, which is determined by the last thing.

However, *suum cuique* implies yet another decisive pre-supposition, and one which has not remained uncontested, though the contesting of it has over and over again shaken the natural foundations of life. What is presupposed here is that 'each man', in other words the individual, comes into the world with a natural right of his own. This assertion is contradicted by those who concede a natural right only to the community and not to the individual. For them the individual is only a means to an end in the service of the community. The happiness of the community takes precedence over the natural right of the individual. This means in principle the proclamation of social eudemonism and the curtailment of all the rights of individuals. But this constitutes an attack on natural life itself, and the destruction of the rights of the individual paves the way for the destruction of all rights without exception; this is the way to chaos. It is, therefore, not at all by chance that the consequence of social eudemonism has repeatedly been the annihilation by despotism of the rights even of the community. The right of the individual is the power which upholds the right of the community, just as, conversely, it is the community that upholds and defends the right of the individual. The existence of a natural right of the individual follows from the fact that it is God's will to create the individual and to endow him with eternal life. Whether it be recognized or not, it is this fact that ever anew finds expression in natural life and opposes triumphantly effective resistance to the unnatural principle of social eudemonism. God's having created the individual, and His having called him to eternal life, is a reality which is operative in natural life, and a reality which it is extremely dangerous to neglect. Within natural life, therefore, it is incumbent upon reason to take account of the right of the individual, even though the divine origin of this right is not recognized. Consequently the natural enemy of social eudemonism has always been reason, the organ which 'perceives' and introduces into consciousness the reality of the fallen world. Social eudemonism, for its part, allies itself with a blind voluntarism in an 'irrational', inconceivable overestimation of the power of the will in its encounter with the reality of natural life itself. It is a truth which lies beyond the reach of this voluntarism that reason is closer to reality than is the blind will, even though this blind will may claim to be closer to reality than anything else can be. The principle of *suum cuique* is the highest possible attainment of a reason which is in accord with reality and which, within the natural life, discerns the right which is given to the individual by God (of whom reason knows nothing).

In our discussion of the rights of natural life from the point of view of their contents the question of the guarantor of these rights will repeatedly demand an answer. Who is it that supports the rights of natural life with an effective guarantee? Here we must repeat what we have said already. It is in the first place God Himself who guarantees these rights. But for this purpose He continually makes use of life itself, which sooner or later gains the upper hand in spite of every violation of the natural. We have to reckon here with periods of time which may extend beyond the life span of the individual. The reason for this is that in the domain of natural life what matters is not so much the individual as the preservation of the life of man as a species. Natural life necessarily often rides rough-shod over the individual. If the right of the individual is destroyed, and perhaps not restored, this will augment the power of resistance of natural life and enable it to reassert itself in the next or next but one generation. It is the problem of a theodicy that presents itself here, but the solution of this problem must await a later occasion. If it is God, and through Him life itself, that intervenes effectively on behalf of the rights that are inherent in life, then any action of which the individual is capable in defence of his natural rights can only be of extremely restricted significance. What the individual does, in fact, do will depend on a large number of considerations which at present lie beyond the scope of our enquiry. But in any case he will always have to bear in mind that his most powerful ally is life itself. If one asks whether the individual is entitled to defend his natural rights, then the answer must clearly be yes. But in all circumstances he must defend the right in such a manner as to carry the conviction that it is not the individual but God who guarantees it.

The Right to Bodily Life

Bodily life, which we receive without any action on our own part, carries within itself the right to its own preservation. This is not a right that we have justly or unjustly appropriated to ourselves, but it is in the strictest sense an 'innate' right, one which we have passively received and which pre-exists our will, a right which rests upon the nature of things as they are. Since it is God's will that there should be human life on earth only in the form of bodily life, it follows that it is for the sake of the whole man that the body possesses the right to be preserved. And since all rights are extinguished at death, it follows that the preservation of the life of the body is the foundation of all natural rights without exception and is, therefore, invested with a particular importance. The underlying right of natural life is the safeguarding of nature against intentional injury, violation and killing. That may sound very jejune and unheroic. But the body does not exist primarily in order to be sacrificed, but in order that it may be preserved. Different and more exalted considerations may give rise to the right or the duty of sacrificing the body, but this in itself presupposes the underlying right to the conservation of bodily life.

The life of the body, like life in general, is both a means to an end and an end in itself. To regard the body exclusively as a means to an end is idealistic but not Christian; for a means is discarded as soon as the end is achieved. It is from this point of view that the body is conceived as the prison from which the immortal soul is released for ever by death. According to the Christian doctrine, the body possesses a higher dignity. Man is a bodily being, and remains so in eternity as well. Bodiliness and human life belong inseparably together. And thus the bodiliness which is willed by God to be the form of existence of man is entitled to be called an end in itself. This does not exclude the fact that the body at the same time continues to be subordinated to a higher purpose. But what is important is that as one of the rights of bodily life its preservation is not only a means to an end but also an end in itself. It is in the joys of the body that it becomes apparent that the body is an end in itself within the natural life. If the body were only a means to an end man would have no right to bodily joys. It would then not be permissible to exceed an expedient minimum of bodily enjoyment. This would have very far-reaching consequences for the Christian appraisal of all the problems that have to do with the life of the body, housing, food, clothing, recreation, play and sex. But if the body is rightly to be regarded as an end in itself, then there is a right to bodily joys, even though these are not necessarily subordinated to some higher purpose. It is inherent in the nature of joy itself that it is spoilt by any thought of purpose. We shall have to return to this later on when we come to deal with the right to happiness. Within the natural life the joys of the body are reminders of the eternal joy which has been promised to men by God. If a man is deprived of the possibility of bodily joys through his body being used exclusively as a means to an end, this is an infringement of the original right of bodily life. 'There is nothing better for a man, than that he should eat and drink, and that he should make his soul enjoy good in his labour. This also I saw, that it was from the hand of God' (Eccl. 2.24). 'I know that there is no good in them, but for a man to rejoice, and to do good[1] in his life' (Eccl. 3.12). 'Eat thy

[1] *Translator's note.* Luther's strong colloquial expression *sich gütlich tun* conveys the sense more clearly. An early German-English dictionary renders it as 'to take one's ease and conveniency, to cocker, pamper, or make much of one's self'.

bread with joy, and drink thy wine with a merry heart; for God now accepteth thy works. Let thy garments be always white; and let thy head lack no ointment. Live joyfully with the wife whom thou lovest all the days of the life of thy vanity, which he hath given thee under the sun, all the days of thy vanity; for that is thy portion in this life, and in thy labour which thou takest under the sun' (Eccl. 9.7ff.). 'Rejoice, O young man, in thy youth; and let thy heart cheer thee in the days of thy youth, and walk in the ways of thine heart, and in the sight of thine eyes: but know thou, that for all these things God will bring thee into judgement' (Eccl. 11.9). 'Who can eat gladly and have enjoyment without him?' (Eccl. 2.25)[1], [2].

The homes of men are not, like the shelters of animals, merely the means of protection against bad weather and the night or merely places for rearing the young; they are places in which a man may relish the joys of his personal life in the intimacy and security of his family and of his property. Eating and drinking do not merely serve the purpose of keeping the body in good health, but they afford natural joy in bodily living. Clothing is not intended merely as a mean covering for the body, but also as an adornment of the body. Recreation is not designed solely to increase working efficiency, but it provides the body with its due measure of repose and enjoyment. Play is by its nature remote from all subordination to purpose, and it thus demonstrates most clearly that the life of the body is an end in itself. Sex is not only the means of reproduction, but, independently of this defined purpose, it brings with it its own joy, in married life, in the love of two human beings for one another. From all this it emerges that the meaning of bodily life never lies solely in its subordination to its final purpose. The life of the body assumes its full significance only with the fulfilment of its inherent claim to joy.

[1] Luther's version.

[2] *Editor's note.* Among Bonhoeffer's preparatory notes there is the following sentence: 'There is a measure of psychical selflessness which is worse than undisguised egoism. And precisely those who are really "spiritually" selfless display an admirable freedom in the expression of their own wishes.'

The intensity of the predisposition of bodily life to joy is perhaps most clearly illustrated by the fact that, even when the body is in due manner subjected to severe strain in order to achieve some necessary purpose, it experiences joy in being put to service in this way. Yet this will be the case only so long as due account is taken not only of the serviceability of the body for a given purpose, but also of its rights as an end in itself.

The body is in each individual case always 'my body'. It can never, even in marriage, belong to another in the same sense as it belongs to me. It is my body that separates me in space from other men and that presents me as a man to other men. Any hurt done to my body is an injury to my personal existence. The deference which I owe to another is expressed in my keeping my distance from his bodily life. Corporal punishment is rightful only if the person punished is not yet to be regarded as possessing an independent existence, or rather if the purpose of the punishment is precisely to demonstrate this lack of independence in order that the necessary independence may be developed. It is not possible to establish a definite rule for deciding who is to be regarded as possessing independent existence, but the limit of childhood will in general determine this, and an adult who has become conscious of his natural rights must quite certainly be regarded as possessing independent existence. Corporal punishment for criminals is a different matter. There may be good grounds for it in cases where a deliberate deprivation of honour is intended in view of the vileness and heinousness of the offence or in cases where criminal injury to the bodily lives of others calls for the infliction of punishment on the body of the offender.

Among free independent persons any conscious injury to the body of another constitutes the destruction of the first natural right of man; it means that he is in principle deprived of all his rights and that natural life is destroyed.

The first right of natural life consists in the safeguarding of the life of the body against arbitrary killing. One must speak of arbitrary killing wherever innocent life is deliberately destroyed. But in this context any life is innocent which does not engage in a conscious attack upon the life of another and which cannot be convicted of any criminal deed that is worthy of death. This means that the killing of the enemy in war is not arbitrary killing. For even if he is not personally guilty, he is nevertheless consciously participating in the attack of his people against the life of my people and he must share in bearing the consequences of the collective guilt. And, of course, there is nothing arbitrary about the killing of a criminal who has done injury to the life of another; nor yet about the killing of civilians in war, so long as it is not directly intended but is only an unfortunate consequence of a measure which is necessary on military grounds. But it would be arbitrary to kill defenceless prisoners or wounded men who can no longer render themselves guilty of an attack on my life. It is arbitrary to kill an innocent man out of passion or for the sake of some advantage. All deliberate killing of innocent life is arbitrary.

This last principle has not remained uncontradicted. The problem which arises here is the problem of euthanasia. The question of principle is this: Is it permissible to destroy painlessly an innocent life which is no longer worth living? Two kinds of motive lie behind this question, consideration for the sick and consideration for the healthy. But before any particular aspects of the problem can be examined, it is necessary to state, as a matter of principle, that the decision about the right to destroy human life can never be based upon the concurrence of a number of different contributory factors. Either an argument is cogent enough in itself to bring about this decision, or else it is not cogent at all, and if this is the case, no number of good additional reasons can ever justify such a decision. The destruction of the life of another may be undertaken only on the basis of an unconditional necessity; when this necessity is present, then the killing must be performed, no matter how numerous or how good the reasons which weigh against it. But the taking of the life of another must never be merely one possibility among other possibilities, even though it may be an extremely well-founded possibility. If there is even the slightest responsible possibility of allowing others to remain alive, then the destruction of their lives would be arbitrary killing, murder. Killing and keeping alive are never of equal value in the taking of this decision; the sparing of life has an incomparably higher claim than killing can have. Life may invoke all possible reasons in its cause; but only one single reason can be a valid reason for killing. To fail to bear this in mind is to undo the work of the Creator and Preserver of life Himself. It follows from this that to support the rightfulness of euthanasia with a number of essentially different arguments is to put oneself in the wrong from the outset by admitting indirectly that no single absolutely cogent argument exists.

In dealing with this question, therefore, we must consider the various particular arguments separately, and examine whether any one of them is in itself decisive. We must never attempt to compensate the weakness of any one argument by adducing some different argument. Is it the case that consideration for the man who is incurably sick and for the grievousness of his suffering demands the deliberate termination of his life by some humane form of death? It goes without saying, when this question is asked, that it must presuppose the assent or the wish of the patient. If this wish is not explicitly uttered, or if, as in the case of mental defectives, it cannot be explicitly uttered, or if indeed there is expressed an unmistakable demand to remain alive, then we cannot honestly say any longer that it is the patient who is being considered. And who can judge how intensely even a man who is incurably insane may cling to life in spite of his suffering? Who can tell how great a sense of happiness he may still derive even from this life of misery? There is indeed much to suggest that in such cases the positive attitude to life is particularly intense and uninhibited; so that consideration for the patient in such circumstances cannot (should not?) in any case be adduced as the reason for destroying his life. And, on the other hand, when a person who suffers from acute depression asks for his life to be ended, ought we then to overlook the fact that we are concerned here with a request made by a patient who is not his own master? To reply that precisely the same thing is also true of the mental defective who clings to life is to leave out of account the principle that the right to life takes precedence over the right to kill. But let us now consider the case when an incurably diseased person in full possession of his senses gives his assent to the termination of his life, and indeed asks for it. Can a wish of this kind carry with it a valid demand for the application of euthanasia? Undoubtedly one cannot speak of a valid demand so long as the patient's life still raises demands on its own account, in other words so long as the doctor is under an obligation not only towards the will but also towards the actual life of the patient. The question of destroying the life of another is now replaced by the question of the admissibility of terminating one's own life in a case of extremely severe illness, or of assisting in so doing. We shall be discussing this matter in connexion with the problem of suicide. An important point is raised if it is objected that there are certain cases in which a doctor will no longer do everything possible in order to prolong a life artificially; he may for example refrain from sending a tubercular mental defective to a sanatorium and it may appear that no distinction can be drawn between this and the deliberate ending of the patient's life. Yet there is a difference, which it is always important to bear in mind, between allowing to die and killing. It is in any case not always possible in life to give effect to all conceivable means for the postponement of death, and yet this is still fundamentally different from intentional killing. It follows from all this that consideration for the patient cannot be regarded as adequate ground for the necessity of destroying human life.

Now let us ask whether consideration for the healthy can render necessary the destruction of innocent life. This question can be answered affirmatively only if it is assumed that every life must possess a certain utilizable value for the community and that when this utility ceases the life in question no longer possesses any right of its own and may therefore, if occasion arises, be destroyed. Even when this radical form of the idea is avoided, what we have here is still at least a different rating of the right to life of the socially valuable and of the socially valueless, even though in the latter case as well we may here be concerned exclusively with innocent life. But this discriminatory valuation is obviously not practicable in life, for it would lead to impossible consequences. It would, for example, rule out the employment and exposure of socially valuable life in war and in other situations where there is danger of death and where it is sacrificed as a matter of course for the benefit of life which may well be socially less valuable. This fact in itself proves that precisely the socially valuable man makes no discrimination in assessing the rights of life. It is precisely this man who will be ready to risk his life for a lesser man, the strong for the weak and the sound for the sick. It is precisely the strong man who will not enquire about the usefulness to himself of the weak man. If anyone does this it will be the weak man. But the weak man's need will lead the strong man towards new tasks; it will lead him to develop his own social value. The strong man will see in the weak man not a diminution of his strength but a stimulus to loftier achievements. The idea of destroying a life which has lost its social usefulness is one which springs from weakness, not from strength.

But, above all, this idea springs from the false assumption that life consists only in its own usefulness to society. It is not perceived that life, created and preserved by God, possesses an inherent right which is wholly independent of its social utility. The right to live is a matter of the essence and not of any values. In the sight of God there is no life that is not worth living; for life itself is valued by God. The fact that God is the Creator, Preserver and Redeemer of life makes even the most wretched life worth living before God. The beggar Lazarus, a leper, lay at the rich man's gate and the dogs licked his sores; he was devoid of any social usefulness and a victim of those who judge life according to its social usefulness; yet God held him to be worthy of eternal life. And where if not in God should there lie the criterion for the ultimate value of a life? In the subjective will to live?

On this rating many a genius is excelled by half-wits. In the judgement of society? If so it would soon be found that opinion as to which lives were socially valuable or valueless would be determined by the requirements of the moment and therefore by arbitrary decisions; one group of human beings after another would in this way be condemned to extermination. The distinction between life that is worth living and life that is not worth living must sooner or later destroy life itself. Now that we have made this principle clear, we must still say a word about the purely social utility of the seemingly useless and meaningless life. We cannot indeed ignore the fact that precisely the supposedly worthless life of the incurably sick evokes from the healthy, from doctors, nurses and relatives, the very highest measure of social self-sacrifice and even genuine heroism; this devoted service which is rendered by sound life to sick life has given rise to real values which are of the highest utility for the community.

Now it cannot be denied that serious incurable hereditary diseases constitute a grave problem and a certain danger for society. The only question is whether this danger can be obviated only by means of destroying this life. The answer to this question is quite clearly no. From the point of view of health it is sufficient to isolate patients of this kind. From the economic point of view a people's standard of living will never be seriously impaired by providing for these sufferers. A people's expenditure for the care of patients of this kind has never come near to equalling the sums spent on articles of luxury. And indeed precisely the healthy man will always be ready to make certain limited sacrifices for the sake of the sick, if only because of uncertainty about his own personal future, in other words for quite natural reasons.

But must one not regard incurable hereditary disease as an attack against the safety of the community, just as much as for example an enemy attack in war? Here two distinctions must be observed. First of all, this attack can be warded off by other means than the destruction of life. And secondly, in the case of sufferers from hereditary disease we are dealing with innocent life. If we can speak of guilt at all here, then certainly it does not in any case rest with the patient, but rather with society itself. It would therefore be intolerably pharisaical if society were to treat the sick man as though he were a guilty man in order to put itself in the right at his expense. To kill the innocent would be, in the extreme sense, arbitrary.

The question whether in cases of congenital mental deficiency one is dealing with human life at all is so naïve as scarcely to require an answer. It is sick life, born of men, and even though it must be extremely unhappy life, it cannot but be human life. And indeed the very fact that human life can appear so horribly deformed should give food for thought to the healthy.

A borderline case involving all these considerations would arise if, for example, on a ship, where there was no possibility of isolating the sick, there should be an outbreak of plague, and if, so far as human judgement could foretell, it was only through the death of the sick that the healthy could be saved. In this case the decision would have to remain open.

Fundamentally, however, the thesis that innocent sick life may properly be destroyed in the interest of healthy life does not rest on social or economic or hygienic grounds, but it is rooted in a certain philosophical outlook on the world. It springs from the superhuman endeavour to free human society from what appears to be meaningless disease. Men are to enter into a struggle against fate, or, as we may also say, against the essential character of the fallen world itself. It is supposed that by rational means a new and healthy humanity can be created. And meanwhile health is regarded as the highest value, the one to which all other values ought to be sacrificed. The rationalization and the biologization of human life are allied in this vain enterprise whereby the right of all created beings is destroyed and with it in the end the right to life of all society.

Our conclusion must, therefore, be that consideration for the healthy also establishes no right to the deliberate destruction of innocent life, and from this it follows that the question regarding euthanasia must be answered in the negative. The

Bible sums up this judgement in the sentence: 'The innocent
. . . slay thou not' (Ex. 23.7).

Suicide

Man, unlike the beasts, does not carry his life as a compulsion which he cannot throw off. He is free either to accept
his life or to destroy it. Unlike the beasts man can put himself
to death of his own free will. An animal is one with the life
of its body, but man can distinguish himself from the life of
his body. The freedom in which man possesses his bodily life
requires him to accept this life freely, and at the same time it
directs his attention to what lies beyond this bodily life and
impels him to regard the life of his body as a gift that is to be
preserved and as a sacrifice that is to be offered. Only because
a man is free to choose death can he lay down the life of his
body for the sake of some higher good. Without freedom to
sacrifice one's life in death, there can be no freedom towards
God, there can be no human life.

In man the right to live must be safeguarded through
freedom. It is therefore not an absolute right, but a right
which is conditional upon freedom. The right to live has as
its counterpart the freedom to offer and to give one's life in
sacrifice. In the sense of sacrifice, therefore, man possesses
the liberty and the right to death, but only so long as his
purpose in risking and surrendering his life is not the destruction of his life but the good for the sake of which he offers
this sacrifice.

In this liberty to die man is given a unique power which
can easily lead to abuse. Man can indeed by its means become
the master of his earthly destiny, for he can by his own free
decision seek death in order to avoid defeat and he may thus
rob fate of its victory. Seneça's *patet exitus* is the proclamation
of man's freedom in relation to life. If in the struggle with
destiny a man has lost his honour, his work and the only
human being whom he loves, if in this sense his life is
destroyed, it will be difficult to persuade him not to make
use of this opportunity of escape, provided that he still retains
courage enough to secure his freedom and his victory in this

way. And indeed it cannot be contested that through this deed a man is once again asserting his manhood, even though he may be misunderstanding its significance, and that he is opposing it effectively to the blind inhuman force of destiny. Suicide is a specifically human action, and it is not surprising if it has on this account repeatedly been applauded and justified by noble human minds. If this action is performed in freedom it is raised high above any petty moralizing accusation of cowardice and weakness. Suicide is the ultimate and extreme self-justification of man as man, and it is therefore, from the purely human standpoint, in a certain sense even the self-accomplished expiation for a life that has failed. This deed will usually take place in a state of despair, yet it is not the despair itself that is the actual originator of suicide, but rather a man's freedom to perform his supreme act of self-justification even in the midst of this despair. If a man cannot justify himself in his happiness and his success, he can still justify himself in his despair. If he cannot make good his right to a human life in the life of his body, he can still do so by destroying his body. If he cannot compel the world to acknowledge his right, yet he can still assert this right, himself, in his last solitude. Suicide is a man's attempt to give a final human meaning to a life which has become humanly meaningless. The involuntary sense of horror which seizes us when we are faced with the fact of a suicide is not to be attributed to the iniquity of such a deed but to the terrible loneliness and freedom in which this deed is performed, a deed in which the positive attitude to life is reflected only in the destruction of life.

If suicide must nevertheless be declared wrongful, it is to be arraigned not before the forum of morality or of men but solely before the forum of God. A man who takes his own life incurs guilt solely towards God, the Maker and Master of his life. It is because there is a living God that suicide is wrongful as a sin of lack of faith. Lack of faith is not a moral fault, for it is compatible with both noble and base motives and actions, but, both in good and in evil, lack of faith takes no account of the living God. That is the sin. It is through lack of faith that a man seeks his own justification, and has recourse to suicide as the last possible means of his own justification, because he does not believe in a divine justification. Lack of faith is disastrous in that it conceals from a man the fact that even suicide cannot release him from the hand of God, who has prepared his destiny for him. Lack of faith does not perceive, beyond the gift of bodily life, the Creator and Lord who alone has the right to dispose of His creation. And here we are confronted with the fact that natural life does not possess its right in itself, but only in God. The freedom to die, which is given to human life in natural life, is abused if it is used otherwise than in faith in God.

God has reserved to Himself the right to determine the end of life, because He alone knows the goal to which it is His will to lead it. It is for Him alone to justify a life or to cast it away. Before God self-justification is quite simply sin, and suicide is therefore also sin. There is no other cogent reason for the wrongfulness of suicide, but only the fact that over men there is a God. Suicide implies denial of this fact.

It is not the baseness of the motive that makes suicide wrongful. One may remain alive for base motives, and one may give up one's life for noble motives. It is not bodily life itself that possesses an ultimate right over man. Man is free in relation to his bodily life, and, in Schiller's phrase, 'life is not the highest of possessions'. Nor can human society, as Aristotle supposes, establish an ultimate right over the bodily life of the individual. For any such right is negatived by the ultimate right to dispose of himself which is conferred on a man by nature. The community may impose penalties on suicide,[1] but it will not be able to convince the offender himself that it possesses a valid right over his life. Insufficient, too, is the argument which is widely used in the Christian Church to the effect that suicide rules out the possibility of repentance and, therefore, also of forgiveness. Many Christians have died sudden deaths without having repented of all their sins. This is setting too much store by the last moment of life. All the arguments we have mentioned so far

[1] As it does in England. *Cf.* also Aristotle on *atimia* in the *Nicom. Ethics* III 2.

are incomplete; they are correct up to a point, but they do not state the decisive reason and are therefore not cogent.

God, the Creator and Lord of life, Himself exercises the right over life. Man does not need to lay hands upon himself in order to justify his life. And because he does not need to do this it follows that it is not rightful for him to do it. It is a remarkable fact that the Bible nowhere expressly forbids suicide, but that suicide appears there very often (though not always) as the consequence of extremely grave sin, so, for example, in the case of the traitors Ahithophel and Judas. The reason for this is not that the Bible sanctions suicide, but that, instead of prohibiting it, it desires to call the despairing to repentance and to mercy. A man who is on the brink of suicide no longer has ears for commands or prohibitions; all he can hear now is God's merciful summons to faith, to deliverance and to conversion. A man who is desperate cannot be saved by a law that appeals to his own strength; such a law will only drive him to even more hopeless despair. One who despairs of life can be helped only by the saving deed of another, the offer of a new life which is to be lived not by his own strength but by the grace of God. A man who can no longer live is not helped by any command that he should live, but only by a new spirit.

God maintains the right of life, even against the man who has grown tired of his life. He gives man freedom to pledge his life for something greater, but it is not His will that man should turn this freedom arbitrarily against his own life. Man must not lay hands upon himself, even though he must sacrifice his life for others. Even if his earthly life has become a torment for him, he must commit it intact into God's hand, from which it came, and he must not try to break free by his own efforts, for in dying he falls again into the hand of God, which he found too severe while he lived.

Far more difficult than the determining of this general principle is the judgement of particular cases. Since suicide is an act of solitude, the ultimate decisive motives almost always remain hidden. Even when some outward catastrophe in life has gone before, the deepest inward reason for the deed is still concealed from the eye of the stranger. The human eye can often scarcely discern the borderline between the freedom of the sacrifice of life and the abuse of this freedom for the purpose of self-murder, and in such cases there is no basis for forming a judgement. Certainly the taking of one's own life is as a matter of plain fact different from risking one's life in a necessary undertaking. But it would be very short-sighted simply to equate every form of self-killing with murder. For, in cases where a man who kills himself is deliberately sacrificing his own life for other men, judgement must at least be suspended because here we have reached the limits of human knowledge. It is only if the action is undertaken exclusively and consciously out of consideration for one's own person that self-killing becomes self-murder. But who would venture to assess with certainty the degree of consciousness and exclusiveness of such a motive? If a prisoner takes his life for fear that under torture he might betray his country, his family or his friend, or if the enemy threaten reprisals unless a certain statesman is surrendered to them and it is only by his own free death that this statesman can spare his country grievous harm, then the self-killing is so strongly subject to the motive of sacrifice that it will be impossible to condemn the deed. If a sufferer from incurable disease cannot fail to see that his care must bring about the material and psychological ruin of his family, and if he therefore by his own decision frees them from this burden, then no doubt there are many objections to such an unauthorized action, and yet here, too, a condemnation will be impossible. In view of such cases as these the prohibition of suicide can scarcely be made absolute to the exclusion of the freedom of sacrificing one's life. Even the early Church Fathers held that self-destruction was permissible for Christians in certain circumstances, for example when chastity was threatened by force; though certainly already St Augustine contested this and asserted the absolute prohibition of suicide. Yet it seems scarcely possible to draw any distinction of principle between the cases we have just considered and the unquestioned duty of the Christian which requires, for example, that when a ship is sinking he shall leave the last place in the lifeboat to another in the full awareness that he is thereby going to his death, or again which requires that a friend shall with his own body shield his friend's body from the bullet. A man's own decision here becomes the cause of his death, even though one may still distinguish between direct self-destruction and this surrendering of life into the hand of God. Clearly the case is different if suicide is motivated by purely personal matters such as wounded honour, erotic passion, financial ruin, gambling debts or serious personal lapses, in other words if a man kills himself not in order to protect the lives of others but solely in order that his own life may be justified. Even here indeed, in concrete instances, the thought of sacrifice will not be entirely absent, but nevertheless all other motives will be outweighed by the desire to rescue one's own person from shame and despair, and the ultimate ground for the action will therefore be lack of faith. Such a man does not believe that God can again give a meaning and a right even to a ruined life, and indeed that it may be precisely through ruin that a life attains to its true fulfilment. Because he does not believe this, the termination of his life remains to him as the only possible means whereby he himself can impart a meaning and a right to his life, even though it be only at the moment of its destruction. Here again it becomes quite clear that a purely moral judgement on suicide is impossible, and indeed that suicide has nothing to fear from an atheistic ethic. The right to suicide is nullified only by the living God.

But quite apart from all external motivations there is a temptation to suicide to which the believer is especially exposed, a temptation to abuse the freedom which is given by God by turning it against his own life. Hatred for the imperfection of his own life, experience of the headstrong resistance which earthly life in general opposes to its own fulfilment by God, the grief which arises from this and the doubt as to whether life has any meaning at all, all these may lead him into great danger. Luther was able to say a great deal about this from his own experience. In such hours of trial no human or divine law can prevent the deed. Help can come only from the comfort of grace and from the power of brotherly prayer. It is not the right to life that can overcome this temptation to suicide, but only the grace which allows a man to continue to live in the knowledge of God's forgiveness. But who would venture to say that God's grace and mercy cannot embrace and sustain even a man's failure to resist this hardest of all temptations?

Reproduction and Nascent Life

The right of propagation is implied in the right to the preservation of bodily life. But man, unlike the beasts, is not merely dominated by the dark unconscious impulse towards the preservation of the species in general; in man the impulse to reproduce appears rather as a conscious will to have a child of his own. Consequently, with man, reproduction is not simply a necessity of the species, but it is a personal decision and from this it follows that man as a person is entitled to the personal choice of his companion in marriage. This does not at all mean that only individual wishes are to be taken into account in making this choice, but it does at least presuppose the assent of the individual to the marriage, and that implies a free decision on his part. The demand for a child of one's own carries with it the right of choosing the woman or the man who is to be the mother or the father of this child. The making of this personal choice is at the same time the fulfilment of the collective function of propagating the human race. In marriage the most intensely individual aspect of human life is combined with its most general aspect, to the exclusion of all that lies between. Marriage is the union of two human beings as human beings, on the basis of the free decision of the individual. So long as human nature continues, it will continue to lay claim to this right. The denial of this right for any reason which lies neither on the entirely individual plane nor on the general human plane will sooner or later always prove ineffectual in the face of the power of natural life. The right of men and women to a child of their own, which implies the right to the choice of a partner in marriage, can never, in the long run, be overruled by considerations of class or of religious outlook or on economic or biological grounds. The human will to reproduce can never be interpreted as a purely social, economic, religious or biological obligation. All these factors may, and indeed must, be considered in making one's own choice, but they cannot replace the free decision. In marriage an individual unites himself with an individual, a human being with a human being. Economic, denominational, social and national ties all contribute to determining the decision of the individual, but they can neither obviate nor anticipate this decision. The reason for this lies in the fact that the desire for a child of one's own and the free choice of a mate which this implies, in other words human marriage, is the oldest of all human institutions and cannot therefore be conditional upon these secondary factors.

Human marriage existed before the development of any of the other bonds of human society. Marriage was given already with the creation of the first man. Its right is founded in the beginnings of mankind.

To restrict the right of marriage by demanding that both partners shall be members of a particular religious denomination, and to describe as concubinage all marriages which have not been solemnized according to the requirements of a particular religion, as is the case with the Roman Catholic doctrine of marriage, is to deprive marriage of its essential natural character and of its natural right and to transmute what had been an institution of nature into an institution of grace or salvation in a way which exactly resembles that racial and national restriction of the right of marriage by which marriage is robbed of its universal human title and declared to be a purely racial and national institution. In both of these cases there is an arbitrary diminution of the abundance of marriage and consequently also of the propagation of the human race which God desires. Alien authorities assert a claim to direct and shape the coming generation, and they thereby impoverish the abundance of God's creation which seeks to develop through the desire of individuals for children of their own and not through the compulsory breeding of a particular human type. This constitutes a disastrous interference in the natural order of the world. Concerned as they are for the securing of new blood for their church or nation, and possessing very little confidence in natural inhibitions and natural choice, they deliberately deprive themselves of unsuspected human forces.

Marriages are not concluded either by the Church or by the state, and it is not solely from these institutions that they derive their title. Marriage is concluded rather by the two partners. The fact that a marriage is performed publicly in the presence of the state and in the presence of the Church signifies no more than the civil and ecclesiastical public recognition of marriage and its inherent rights. That is the Lutheran doctrine.

In cases where there, in fact, exist such ecclesiastical and civil restrictions of the right to contract a marriage, there arises, without in any way affecting the validity of what has just been said, the general question of the duty of obedience towards the authority of church and state, a question which in the present context cannot yet be discussed. Nevertheless, the fact that the state finds it necessary to impose restrictions in this field, assuming that these do not arise from arbitrary decisions, makes it quite clear that the natural inhibitions and the natural choice have not afforded adequate guarantees against aberrations and lapses which do grave injury to the community. Nature is here subjected to what must occasionally be necessary limitation and regulation by the positive law of the state.

Marriage involves acknowledgement of the right of life that is to come into being, a right which is not subject to the disposal of the married couple. Unless this right is acknowledged as a matter of principle, marriage ceases to be marriage and becomes a mere liaison. Acknowledgement of this right means making way for the free creative power of God which can cause new life to proceed from this marriage according to His will. Destruction of the embryo in the mother's womb is a violation of the right to live which God has bestowed upon this nascent life. To raise the question whether we are here concerned already with a human being or not is merely to confuse the issue. The simple fact is that God certainly intended to create a human being and that this nascent human being has been deliberately deprived of his life. And that is nothing but murder. A great many different motives may lead to an action of this kind; indeed in cases where it is an act of despair, performed in circumstances of extreme human or economic destitution and misery, the guilt may often lie rather with the community than with the individual. Precisely in this connexion money may conceal many a wanton deed, while the poor man's more reluctant lapse may far more easily be disclosed. All these considerations must no doubt have a quite decisive influence on our personal and pastoral attitude towards the person concerned, but they cannot in any way alter the fact of murder.[1]

The right of nascent life is violated also in the case of a marriage in which the emergence of new life is consistently prevented, a marriage in which the desire for a child is consistently excluded. Such an attitude is in contradiction to the meaning of marriage itself and to the blessing which God has bestowed upon marriage through the birth of the child. Certainly a distinction is to be drawn between the consistent refusal to allow children to come of a marriage and the concrete responsible control of births.[2] Human reproduction is a matter of the will to have a child of one's own, and for precisely this reason it would not be right for blind impulse simply to run its course as it pleases and then to go on to

[1] In view of the general practice serious thought must be provoked by the strong disapproval which the Roman Catholic Church expresses with regard to the killing of the foetus in cases where the mother is in danger of losing her life. If the child has its right to life from God, and is perhaps already capable of life, then the killing of the child, as an alternative to the presumed natural death of the mother, is surely a highly questionable action. The life of the mother is in the hand of God, but the life of the child is arbitrarily extinguished. The question whether the life of the mother or the life of the child is of greater value can hardly be a matter for a human decision.

[2] In contradiction to this, *Cat. Rom.*, 2.8.13, went so far as to equate contraception with abortion and to characterize both of these as murder.

claim to be particularly pleasing in the eyes of God; responsible reason must have a share in this decision. There can, in fact, be weighty reasons which in a particular concrete instance will call for a limitation of the number of children. If precisely during the past hundred years birth control has become such a burning question, and if very wide circles of men of all religious denominations have expressed agreement with the principle of birth control, this is not to be interpreted simply as a falling away from the faith or as a lack of trust in God. It is undoubtedly connected with the increasing mastery over nature which has been achieved by technology in all fields of life and with the incontestable triumphs of technical science in the widest sense over the facts of nature, for example in the reduction of infant mortality and in the considerable raising of the average age of the population. In spite of the steady decline in the birth-rate, the absolute total population of Europe has more than doubled in the course of the past century. The decline in the rate of infantile mortality means that fewer births are necessary in order to ensure the preservation of the species (looking at the question strictly from this point of view). Consequently, if one complains that technology has spoilt and demoralized man to such an extent that he is no longer willing to bear the burden of a large family, one must still not overlook the fact that it is precisely this technical progress which has made it possible for the human population of Europe to increase with such overwhelming rapidity. This consideration might well lead one to regard the widespread practice of birth control today as a kind of natural reaction against the scarcely supportable growth of the European peoples, in other words as a kind of natural pause for breath on the part of human nature. But certainly this general view of the matter does not release us from the obligation of enquiring into the rightfulness of birth control itself. The right to practise birth control is denied in principle in Catholic moral theology and consequently also in Catholic instruction in the confessional. But the following difficulties arise in this connexion. Catholic moral theology, too, admits the possibility that in certain circumstances it

151

may be undesirable for further children to be born of a marriage, although, quite rightly, it restricts the validity of this argument to extremely rare cases. It would therefore be wrong to accuse Catholic moral theology of giving free rein to blind natural impulse in these matters, and to say that it excludes human responsibility and reason from playing any part in them. But as a matter of principle Catholic morality recognizes only one means for the achievement of this purpose, namely total abstention.[1] But in this way it undermines the physical basis of marriage and threatens marriage itself with nullification and destruction by robbing it of its fundamental right. Moreover, this is a demand which most people cannot satisfy, and it is hard to imagine that repentance at the confessional for an offence of this kind can quite honestly be accompanied by the intention to renounce this sin for ever. Catholic moral theology bases its rigorism on the unnatural character of an action which deliberately frustrates the natural purpose of marriage, namely reproduction. It does not indeed, as is often asserted, maintain that reproduction is the only purpose of marriage. No one did that before Kant! But it seeks to prevent the second purpose of marriage, the partnership of the sexes, from asserting itself in opposition to the first purpose, reproduction. This argument may sound entirely convincing, and yet it leads to insoluble complications. It certainly eliminates the unnatural act of preventing conception, but this is replaced by the unnatural state of a marriage without bodily union. Furthermore, the naturalness of the action is not in principle affected by the question of whether the intervention of responsible reason takes place in the decision to refrain from further cohabitation or within

[1] Various casuistic solutions have been devised, mainly in order to deal with difficulties arising in the course of the practice of the confessional. Methods are permitted which, if they do not actually prevent conception, nevertheless consciously place obstacles in its way. But these solutions so endanger the Catholic principle that in the end they can no longer ease or cleanse anyone's conscience, and for this reason they have been deliberately rejected by many serious confessors. It would be better if moral theology could be rid of these 'concessions' to the weakness of human nature which fundamentally abandon the principle and which differ from what is technically contraception only in the choice of the means to be employed.

cohabitation itself. The problem which has to be faced here can be solved neither by giving free rein to the natural impulse, nor by marital abstinence, nor yet by the use of contraceptives, and no one of these three possible courses has in principle any higher claim than the others. In this situation it is of the highest importance that men's consciences should not be wrongly weighed down and oppressed. Certainly, for the sake of God's commandment, it may be necessary to impose extremely hard requirements. But in the present case the facts are not so clear. Scope must therefore be allowed for the free action of a conscience which renders account to God. In this sphere, more than in any other, a false rigorism of any kind may entail the most disastrous consequences, ranging from pharisaism to a complete turning away from God.[1]

In approaching this question it is indispensable, for the sake of marriage as a whole, that one should acknowledge a right to full bodily union[2] as a right which is quite distinct from the right of reproduction, even though essentially it can never be entirely separated from it, the two being closely allied; it is a right that is founded upon the mutual love of the married pair. At the same time one must concede that this right of nature nevertheless requires to be exercised rationally, precisely because it is a human right.[3] The relation between

[1] There can be no doubt that the insistence of Catholic morality on this principle has driven incalculable numbers of men away from the confessional altogether. If the Roman Catholic Church accepts this situation with her eyes open, that certainly demonstrates the strength of her conviction, but it can nevertheless lead to unforseeable consequences.

[2] This is in accordance with the biblical conception of marriage. Marriage is not founded upon the purpose of reproduction but on the union of man and woman. Woman is given to man as 'an help meet for him' (Gen. 2.18). The two shall be 'one flesh' (Gen. 2.23). But the fruitfulness of this union is not something that is commanded. (For biblical thought this would have been impossible; it was only in the age of rationalism and technology that it could come to be understood in this way.) It is a blessing from God (Gen. 1.28). St Paul, too, allows sex a right of its own in marriage, independently of the purpose of reproduction (I Cor. 7.3ff.; cf. Ex. 21.10). The sin of Genesis 38 does not therefore consist, as Catholic moral theology assumes, in the abuse of marriage, but in the unlawful refusal of a brother to provide his brother with the progeniture which he owes to him.

[3] I Pet. 3.7.

nature and reason in particular instances is a matter which can be decided and answered for only as the individual case arises. But it must be frankly admitted that in principle there is no difference between the various methods which reason may choose to apply. It quickly becomes clear that it is a great good fortune, and many inward conflicts may also be avoided, if nature and reason can accord in such a way that the many problematic tensions which underly a marriage remain undisturbed. In the present generation this good fortune is granted to relatively few, and that is a burden which we must bear with a due sense of responsibility. But in cases where this good fortune is, in fact, granted, there can be no excuse for mistrustfully throwing it to the winds. Finally, it must be said that Christian faith can win this good fortune by grace, but that is a matter which must be discussed later.

The most radical way in which unwanted births can be prevented is by sterilization, which may be either voluntary or enforced by the law of the state. In order to assess this problem justly, one must above all not conceal from oneself the gravity and the seriousness of this interference with personal life.[1] The human body possesses an inherent right of inviolability. Neither I nor anyone else can lay claim to an absolute right of free disposal over the bodily members that have been given to me by God. This, then, is the limit of the inviolability of the body. It is certainly permissible for me to allow a diseased limb of my body to be amputated for the sake of preserving my body as a whole. And, in fact, the question of sterilization, too, arises only in connexion with disease. But it must be borne in mind that sterilization is not indeed performed for the purpose of preserving the life of the body as a whole, but rather in order to make possible the continuance of certain bodily functions while eliminating the risk of dangerous consequences. If the patient were to forgo

[1] We cannot examine here whether sterilization can achieve its desired results at all; nor can we consider which particular diseases might properly warrant it. That is a question for medical science. We have based our argument here on the assumption that in certain cases sterilization is, in fact, medically advantageous and expedient.

154

the exercise of these functions sterilization would be un-necessary. So the question now arises whether the inviolability of his body is to be forfeited in order to render possible certain bodily functions which are subject to a powerful physical urge. No unequivocal answer can be given to this question. It may be that the physical impulse is so intense that, according to the conscientious self-judgement of the individual concerned, it would constitute a danger to his own life and to the lives of others, and in such cases, for the sake of preserving the patient's life as a whole, sterilization will be the lesser evil. In cases where self-control is known as a matter of experience to be possible, voluntary sterilization is not permissible. In either case there is an infringement of the natural right of reproduction and of the natural right of nascent life. But in the latter case the ground for this lies in the destruction of nature by disease.

Sterilization which is enforced by the state bases its right upon the necessity of safeguarding the general life of the nation and upon mistrust (which from the state's point of view is quite proper) of the possibility of a life of abstention. Undoubtedly it constitutes a grave violation of a man's right to possess his life intact, and there is an overwhelming danger that once this boundary has been crossed (perhaps, in the last analysis, in a manner which can be answered for) all other barriers will soon be broken down as well. The state also lays claim to a man's body in war, for example, and this indicates that there are limits to the inviolability of the body; this case is different from that of sterilization, because in war there is no direct interference with a man's bodily life and a certain element of self-defence is always involved.

On the other hand, the prevention of unwanted births can also be achieved in other ways which avoid the necessity of any direct interference with the body. The patients may, for example, be interned. The fact that this course involves greater economic sacrifices will perhaps be accepted without demur by those who clearly envisage the dangers which the crossing of this boundary must involve, both for the indi-vidual and for the community. Of course, in cases where sterilization is prescribed by the law of the state, the attitude of the patient and of the doctor will be dependent on their duty of obedience towards the governing authority, and in this connexion, too, that is a problem which cannot yet be discussed.[1] All these considerations must be made subordinate to the saying of Jesus: 'If thy right eye offend thee, pluck it out, and cast it from thee: for it is profitable for thee that one of thy members should perish, and not that thy whole body should be cast into hell' (Matt. 5.29). We shall have to speak later of this proclamation of the annulment of all natural rights in the faith in the kingdom of heaven.

The Freedom of Bodily Life

The preservation of bodily life involves protection against arbitrary infringement of the liberty of the body. The human body must never become a thing, an object, such as might fall under the unrestricted power of another man and be used by him solely as a means to his own ends. The living human body is always the man himself. Rape, exploitation, torture and arbitrary confinement of the human body are serious violations of the right which is given with the creation of man, and what is more, like all violations of natural life, they must sooner or later entail their own punishment.

Rape is the use of the body of another for one's own purposes, enforced by the application of a power which is not rightful. In opposition to it there stands the right of the human being to give or to refuse his body in freedom. In

[1] The Roman Catholic Church rejects sterilization entirely (*cf.* the papal encyclical *casti connubii* of 3rd December 1930 and moral theology), and also prohibits the doctor from performing this operation. The objection is based, first, upon the relation of man to his body, which he 'may use only in accordance with its natural purposes', and, secondly, on the limited character of the authority of the government over the body of the individual. Nevertheless, in the first case the Church concedes the right to an operation which is performed for the sake of preserving life, and in the second case she sanctions the compulsory internment of the patient. Ruland, in his handbook on the practical cure of souls (*Handbuch der praktischen Seelsorge*, p. 359), goes so far as to discuss castration as a permissible possibility in a case of severe psychopathic derangement. In these circumstances it is difficult to see how sterilization can be regarded as something which is different in principle.

special circumstances the bodily strength of the individual may rightfully be set to work for the sake of the common good even under compulsion, but human sexuality remains exempt from any such constraint. Any attempt to bring about particular marriages or other sexual relationships by coercion, whatever the reasons may be, is quite clearly an infringement of the bodily liberty of the human being, and it conflicts with that underlying fact of sexual life which, as a natural mode of defence, marks the limit beyond which no alien interference may pass, namely the sense of shame. In the natural feeling of shame expression is given to the essential freedom of the human body in its sexual aspect. The destruction of the sense of shame means the dissolution of all sexual and conjugal order, and indeed of all social order in the widest sense. Certainly the sense of shame assumes various forms and can be cultivated in various ways. But its unchanging essence, which is founded in nature, is the safeguarding• of the freedom of the human body against any sort of violation. This freedom watches over the mystery of human corporeality.

We speak of exploitation of the human body in cases where a man's bodily forces are made the unrestricted property of another man or of an institution. We call this state of affairs slavery. But this does not refer simply to the system of slavery in antiquity. There have been historical forms of slavery which have preserved the essential liberty of man more effectively than do certain social systems in which the concept of slavery is itself rejected but the men who are said to be free are in fact totally enslaved. To this extent there is good reason for the attitude of many of the Church Fathers, including St Thomas Aquinas, who condemn not the name but the fact of slavery. And this fact exists wherever a man has, in fact, become a thing in the power of another man, wherever a man has become exclusively a means to another man's end. This danger is always present in cases where a man has neither freedom to choose his place of work nor the possibility of exchanging his place of work for another, or even of determining the amount of work that he is to perform.

157

This means that in the end the bodily forces of the workman are utilized without restriction; at best this utilization is limited by the need for conserving the man's usefulness, but on occasion even this limit may for some particular reason be overstepped and the consequence is total exhaustion. A man is thus robbed of his bodily strength; his body becomes wholly the object of the stronger man's exploitation. The freedom of the human body is destroyed.[1]

Torture of the body is to be distinguished from that corporal chastisement of which the purpose is to educate the mentally immature to a state of independence. It is also to be distinguished from that retributive punishment[2] through which one who is guilty of a base crime against the body of another has his dishonour brought home to him by the injury done to his own body. By torture of the body we mean in general the arbitrary and brutal infliction of physical pain while taking advantage of a relative superiority of strength, and in particular the extortion by this means of some desired admission or statement. In such cases the body is misused, and therefore dishonoured, exclusively as a means to the achievement of another man's purpose, whether it be for the satisfaction of his lust for power or for the sake of acquiring some particular information. The innocent body's sensitiveness to pain is cruelly exploited. Torture is, in any case, generally an ineffectual means for discovering the truth; though, of course, this argument can have force only in cases where it is really the truth that is being sought for. But, quite apart from that, any physical torture inflicts the most extreme dishonour on the human being, and consequently engenders an intense hatred and the natural bodily impulse to restore this wounded honour by the application of bodily force. Bodily dishonour seeks to avenge itself on the body of the infamous tormentor. In this way the violation of man's bodily freedom once again destroys the foundations of society.

[1] This subject is treated more fully in the chapter entitled *Labour*. (*Editor's note*. This chapter has not been found.)
[2] *vide supra*.

Arbitrary deprivation of liberty, such as the seizure of defenceless and innocent people (for example when African negroes were hunted, captured and transported as slaves to America) and other forms of arbitrary imprisonment, constitutes a violation of the liberty which is given with the human body. When a man is forcibly and wrongfully separated from his home, his work and his family, and is prevented from exercising all his bodily rights and treated as though he were guilty of some crime, then he is being deprived of the honour which is associated with bodily liberty. And if the innocent man is robbed of his freedom and his honour, then the guilty man must remain exempt from punishment and from public dishonour, and that means that the whole order of society will be undermined and that a restoration of the rights of natural life must sooner or later necessarily ensue.

The Natural Rights of the Life of the Mind

There are three fundamental attitudes which the life of the mind assumes with regard to reality: judgement, action and enjoyment (play and delight). In these attitudes man confronts in freedom the reality of which he himself forms part, and he thereby shows that he is man.[1]

[1] *Editor's note.* This section remained unfinished. The preparatory notes include, among other things, the following list of proposed paragraph topics:

'The natural rights of bodily life. The natural rights of the life of the mind. The natural right to work and property.' (Another note contains the following sentence on this subject: 'I myself can voluntarily surrender my property, life, etc. But the property, etc., of my family, my country, etc., does not belong to me and I therefore cannot surrender it. That is not because it has a greater right in itself but because I am called upon to protect the property of others in order to secure the individual his freedom of disposal over his life, property, etc.') 'The natural right to fellowship. The natural right to piety. The natural right to happiness. The right of mental and bodily self-defence.'

The last section to be begun contains a note on the question of what is meant by culture:

'Not the expert or specialist. Not the pious or kindly heart. Nor the possessor of encyclopaedic knowledge as such. Not the development of one's own capabilities on their own account. Not social capabilities on their own account. Not from the point of view of expediency.

Knowledge of the personal and human conventions of the world.

Relation to the *whole* of natural and mental existence (without specialization).

Ability to find one's way in the whole. Sovereignty always. Assimilating the world as a whole and carrying it within oneself.

The humanitarian element.

Freedom, not expediency.

Modesty (limits of knowledge) and breadth of understanding.

Mastery of languages!

An open mind, even for what is new.

It is uncultured to laugh at a film when negro dances are performed.

It is uncultured to regard any kind of work as too trifling.

It is uncultured to bring particular social classes into contempt.

It is uncultured to take advantage of moments of weakness.

It is uncultured to be ignorant of elementary facts and processes of nature or of the life of the mind.

It is uncultured to ridicule something merely because it is different from oneself.

It is uncultured to parade one's 'culture'.

Self-assertiveness and excess of zeal are uncultured. (Tact!)

Culture a matter of course.

What one has learnt and forgotten again. What is no longer present before one's mind but is at one's disposal in a case of concrete real-life necessity.

Concern with things that are not directly useful (classical education).

Culture through the family, friendship and small groups.

Culture is grown (not 'acquired').'

V

CHRIST, REALITY AND GOOD

(Christ, the Church and the World)

The Concept of Reality

WHOEVER wishes to take up the problem of a Christian ethic must be confronted at once with a demand which is quite without parallel. He must from the outset discard as irrelevant the two questions which alone impel him to concern himself with the problem of ethics, 'How can I be good?' and 'How can I do good?', and instead of these he must ask the utterly and totally different question 'What is the will of God?' This requirement is so immensely far-reaching because it presupposes a decision with regard to the ultimate reality; it presupposes a decision of faith. If the ethical problem presents itself essentially in the form of enquiries about one's own being good and doing good, this means that it has already been decided that it is the self and the world which are the ultimate reality. The aim of all ethical reflection is, then, that I myself shall be good and that the world shall become good through my action. But the problem of ethics at once assumes a new aspect if it becomes apparent that these realities, myself and the world, themselves lie embedded in a quite different ultimate reality, namely, the reality of God, the Creator, Reconciler and Redeemer. What is of ultimate importance is now no longer that I should become good, or that the condition of the world should be made better by my action, but that the reality of God should show itself everywhere to be the ultimate reality. Where there is faith in God as the ultimate reality, all concern with ethics will have as its starting-point that God shows Himself to be good, even if this involves the risk that I myself and the world

161

are not good but thoroughly bad. All things appear distorted if they are not seen and recognized in God. All so-called data, all laws and standards, are mere abstractions so long as there is no belief in God as the ultimate reality. But when we say that God is the ultimate reality, this is not an idea, through which the world as we have it is to be sublimated. It is not the religious rounding-off of a profane conception of the universe. It is the acceptance in faith of God's showing forth of Himself, the acceptance of His revelation. If God were merely a religious idea there would be nothing to prevent us from discerning, behind this allegedly 'ultimate' reality, a still more final reality, the twilight of the gods and the death of the gods. The claim of this ultimate reality is satisfied only in so far as it is revelation, that is to say, the self-witness of the living God. When this is so, the relation to this reality determines the whole of life. The apprehension of this reality is not merely a gradual advance towards the discovery of ever more profound realities; it is the crucial turning-point in the apprehension of reality as a whole. The ultimate reality now shows itself to be at the same time the initial reality, the first and last, alpha and omega. Any perception or apprehension of things or laws without Him is now abstraction, detachment from the origin and goal. Any enquiry about one's own goodness, or the goodness of the world, is now impossible unless enquiry has first been made about the goodness of God. For without God what meaning could there be in a goodness of man and a goodness of the world? But God as the ultimate reality is no other than He who shows forth, manifests and reveals Himself, that is to say, God in Jesus Christ, and from this it follows that the question of good can find its answer only in Christ.

The point of departure for Christian ethics is not the reality of one's own self, or the reality of the world; nor is it the reality of standards and values. It is the reality of God as He reveals Himself in Jesus Christ. It is fair to begin by demanding assent to this proposition of anyone who wishes to concern himself with the problem of a Christian ethic. It poses the ultimate and crucial question of the reality which we mean to reckon with in our lives, whether it is to be the reality of the revelational word of God or earthly imperfections, whether it is to be resurrection or death. No man can decide this question by himself, by his own choice, without deciding it wrongly, for it presupposes the answer given, namely that, whatever our decision may be, God has already spoken His word of revelation, and even in the false reality we cannot live otherwise than through the true reality of the word of God. Thus when we ask about the ultimate reality we are thereby at once inescapably bound by the answer to our question. For the question conveys us into the midst of its origin, the reality of the revelation of God in Jesus Christ.

The problem of Christian ethics is the realization among God's creatures of the revelational reality of God in Christ, just as the problem of dogmatics is the truth of the revelational reality of God in Christ. The place which in all other ethics is occupied by the antithesis of 'should be' and 'is', idea and accomplishment, motive and performance, is occupied in Christian ethics by the relation of reality and realization, past and present, history and event (faith), or, to replace the equivocal concept with the unambiguous name, the relation of Jesus Christ and the Holy Spirit. The question of good becomes the question of participation in the divine reality which is revealed in Christ. Good is now no longer a valuation of what is, a valuation, for example, of my own being, my outlook or my actions, or of some condition or state in the world. It is no longer a predicate that is assigned to something which is in itself in being. Good is the real itself. It is not the real in the abstract, the real which is detached from the reality of God, but the real which possesses reality only in God. There is no good without the real, for the good is not a general formula, and the real is impossible without the good. The wish to be good consists solely in the longing for what is real in God. A desire to be good for its own sake, as an end in itself, so to speak, or as a vocation in life, falls victim to the irony of unreality. The genuine striving for good now becomes the self-assertiveness of the prig. Good is not in itself an independent theme for life; if it were so it would be the craziest kind of quixotry. Only if we share in reality can we share in 'good.

It is a fundamentally mistaken formulation of the question that gives rise to the old dispute about whether it is only the will, the mental act or the person that can be good, or whether goodness may also be predicated of performance, achievement or success, and, if so, which of these two precedes the other and which is more important. This dispute has found its way even into theology, and there, as elsewhere, it has been the source of serious errors. It tears asunder what by its origin and essence forms a unity, namely, the good and the real, man and his work. To object that Christ, too, had this distinction between person and work in view in His saying about the good tree that brings forth good fruit (Matt. 7.17) is to distort the meaning of this saying of Jesus into its exact opposite. What is meant by this saying is not that first the person and then the work is good, but that only the two together are good or bad, in other words that the two together are to be understood as a single unit. The same holds true of the distinction which has been drawn by Reinhold Niebuhr, the American philosopher of religion, in his use of the two concepts 'moral man' and 'immoral society'. The distinction which is intended here between individual and society is a purely abstract one, just as is that between the person and work. In such a case one is tearing asunder things which are inseparable and examining separately parts which in isolation from each other, are dead. The consequence is that complete ethical aporia which nowadays goes by the name of 'social ethics'. Naturally, if good is supposed to lie in the conformity of something that is with something that should be, then the relatively more massive resistance which is offered by society to that which should be must necessarily lead to an ethical favouring of the individual at the expense of society. (And conversely it is precisely this circumstance which suggests that this concept of the ethical has its socio-logical origin in the age of individualism.) The question of good must not be reduced to an examination of the motives or consequences of actions by applying to them some ready-made ethical yardstick. An ethic of motives or of mental attitudes is as superficial as an ethic of practical consequences. For what right have we to stop short at the immediate motive and to regard this as the ultimate ethical phenomenon, refusing to take into account the fact that a 'good' motive may spring from a very dark background of human consciousness and unconsciousness and that a 'good attitude' may often be the source of the worst of actions? And just as the question of the motivation of action is in the end lost in the inextricable complexities of the past, so, too, does the question of its consequences finally disappear from view in the mists of the future. On both sides there are no fixed frontiers and nothing justifies us in calling a halt at some point which we ourselves have arbitrarily determined so that we may at last form a definitive judgement. Whether one pursues the line of the ethic of motives or that of the ethic of consequences, it is a matter of sheer expediency, dependent on the conjunctures of the times, that in practice one always ends with some such arbitrary setting of limits. In principle neither of these has anything to commend it in preference to the other, for in both of them the question of good is posed in abstract terms and in isolation from reality. Good is not the correspondence between a criterion which is placed at our disposal by nature or grace and whatever entity I may designate as reality. Good is reality itself, reality seen and recognized in God. The question of good embraces man with his motives and purposes, with his fellow-men and with the entire creation around him; it embraces reality as a whole, as it is held in being by God. The divine words 'Behold, it was very good' (Gen. 1.31) refer to the whole of creation. The good demands the whole, not only the whole of a man's outlook but his whole work, the whole man, together with the fellow-men who are given to him. What sense would it have if only a part were to be called good, a motive perhaps, while the action is bad, or if the reverse were the case? Man is an indivisible whole, not only as an individual in his person and work but also as a member of the community of men and creatures in which he stands. This indivisible whole, this reality which is founded on God and apprehended in Him, is what the question of good has in view. With respect to its origin this indivisible whole is called 'creation'. With respect to its goal it is called the 'kingdom of God'. Both of these are equally remote from us and equally close to us, for God's creation and God's kingdom are present with us solely in God's self-revelation in Jesus Christ.

Participation in the indivisible whole of the divine reality —this is the sense and the purpose of the Christian enquiry concerning good. For the sake of avoiding a misunderstanding, there is need at this point of some further clarification of what is meant here by reality.

There is a way of basing ethics upon the concept of reality which differs entirely from the Christian way. This is the positive and empirical approach, which aims at the entire elimination from ethics of the concept of norms and standards because it regards this concept as being merely the idealization of factual and practically expedient attitudes. Fundamentally, according to this view, the good is no more than what is expedient, useful and advantageous to reality. From this it follows that there is no universal good but only an infinitely varying good which is determined in each case on the basis of 'reality'. This conception is undoubtedly superior to the idealist conception in that it is 'closer to reality'. Good does not consist here in an impossible 'realization' of what is unreal, the realization of ethical ideas. It is reality itself that teaches what is good. The only question is whether the reality that is intended here is capable of satisfying this demand. It now transpires that the concept of reality which underlies the positivistic ethic is the meretricious concept of the empirically verifiable, which implies denial of the origin of this reality in the ultimate reality, in God. Reality, understood in this inadequate sense, cannot be the source of good, because all it demands is complete surrender to the contingent, the casual, the adventitious and the momentarily expedient, because it fails to recognize the ultimate reality and because in this way it destroys and abandons the unity of good.

The Christian ethic speaks in a quite different sense of the reality which is the origin of good, for it speaks of the reality of God as the ultimate reality without and within everything that is. It speaks of the reality of the world as it is, which possesses reality solely through the reality of God. Christian belief deduces that the reality of God is not in itself merely an idea from the fact that this reality of God has manifested and revealed itself in the midst of the real world. In Jesus Christ the reality of God entered into the reality of this world. The place where the answer is given, both to the question concerning the reality of God and to the question concerning the reality of the world, is designated solely and alone by the name Jesus Christ. God and the world are comprised in this name. In Him all things consist (Col. 1.17). Henceforward one can speak neither of God nor of the world without speaking of Jesus Christ. All concepts of reality which do not take account of Him are abstractions. When good has become reality in Jesus Christ, there is no more force in any discussion of good which plays off what should be against what is and what is against what should be. Jesus Christ cannot be identified either with an ideal or standard or with things as they are. The hostility of the ideal towards things as they are, the fanatical putting into effect of an idea in the face of a resisting actuality, may be as remote from good as is the sacrifice of what should be to what is expedient. Both what should be and what is expedient acquire in Christ an entirely new meaning. The irreconcilable conflict between what is and what should be is reconciled in Christ, that is to say, in the ultimate reality. Participation in this reality is the true sense and purpose of the enquiry concerning good.

In Christ we are offered the possibility of partaking in the reality of God and in the reality of the world, but not in the one without the other. The reality of God discloses itself only by setting me entirely in the reality of the world, and when I encounter the reality of the world it is always already sustained, accepted and reconciled in the reality of God. This is the inner meaning of the revelation of God in the man Jesus Christ. Christian ethics enquires about the realization in our world of this divine and cosmic reality which is given in Christ. This does not mean that 'our world' is something outside the divine and cosmic reality which is in Christ, or that it is not already part of the world which is sustained, accepted and reconciled in Him. It does not mean that one must still begin by applying some kind of 'principle' to our situation and our time. The enquiry is directed rather towards the way in which the reality in Christ, which for a long time already has comprised us and our world within itself, is taking effect as something now present, and towards the way in which life may be conducted in this reality. Its purpose is, therefore, participation in the reality of God and of the world in Jesus Christ today, and this participation must be such that I never experience the reality of God without the reality of the world or the reality of the world without the reality of God.

Thinking in Terms of Two Spheres

As soon as we try to advance along this path, our way is blocked by the colossal obstacle of a large part of traditional Christian ethical thought. Since the beginnings of Christian ethics after the times of the New Testament the main under-lying conception in ethical thought, and the one which consciously or unconsciously has determined its whole course, has been the conception of a juxtaposition and conflict of two spheres, the one divine, holy, supernatural and Christian, and the other worldly, profane, natural and un-Christian. This view becomes dominant for the first time in the Middle Ages, and for the second time in the pseudo-Protestant thought of the period after the Reformation. Reality as a whole now falls into two parts, and the concern of ethics is with the proper relation of these two parts to each other. In the scholastic scheme of things the realm of the natural is made subordinate to the realm of grace; in the pseudo-Lutheran scheme the autonomy of the orders of this world is proclaimed in opposition to the law of Christ, and in the scheme of the Enthusiasts the congregation of the Elect takes up the struggle with a hostile world for the establishment of God's kingdom on earth. In all these schemes the cause of Christ becomes a partial and provincial matter within the limits of reality. It is assumed that there are realities which lie outside the reality that is in Christ. It follows that these realities are accessible by some way of their own, and otherwise than through Christ. However great the importance which is attached to the reality in Christ, it still always remains a partial reality amid other realities. The division of the total reality into a sacred and a profane sphere, a Christian and a secular sphere, creates the possibility of existence in a single one of these spheres, a spiritual existence which has no part in secular existence, and a secular existence which can claim autonomy for itself and can exercise this right of autonomy in its dealings with the spiritual sphere. The monk and the nineteenth-century Protestant secularist typify these two possibilities. The whole of medieval history is centred upon the theme of the predominance of the spiritual sphere over the secular sphere, the predominance of the *regnum gratiae* over the *regnum naturae*; and the modern age is characterized by an ever increasing independence of the secular in its relations with the spiritual. So long as Christ and the world are conceived as two opposing and mutually repellent spheres, man will be left in the following dilemma: he abandons reality as a whole, and places himself in one or other of the two spheres. He seeks Christ without the world, or he seeks the world without Christ. In either case he is deceiving himself. Or else he tries to stand in both spaces at once and thereby becomes the man of eternal conflict, the kind of man who emerged in the period after the Reformation and who has repeatedly set himself up as representing the only form of Christian existence which is in accord with reality.

It may be difficult to break the spell of this thinking in terms of two spheres, but it is nevertheless quite certain that it is in profound contradiction to the thought of the Bible and to the thought of the Reformation, and that consequently it aims wide of reality. There are not two realities, but only one reality, and that is the reality of God, which has become manifest in Christ in the reality of the world. Sharing in Christ we stand at once in both the reality of God and the reality of the world. The reality of Christ comprises the reality of the world within itself. The world has no reality of its own, independently of the revelation of God in Christ. One is denying the revelation of God in Jesus Christ if one tries to be 'Christian' without seeing and recognizing the world in Christ. There are, therefore, not two spheres, but only the one sphere of the realization of Christ, in which the reality of God and the reality of the world are united. Thus the theme of the two spheres, which has repeatedly become the dominant factor in the history of the Church, is foreign to the New Testament. The New Testament is concerned solely with the manner in which the reality of Christ assumes reality in the present world, which it has already encompassed, seized and possessed. There are not two spheres, standing side by side, competing with each other and attacking each other's frontiers. If that were so, this frontier dispute would always be the decisive problem of history. But the whole reality of the world is already drawn in into Christ and bound together in Him, and the movement of history consists solely in divergence and convergence in relation to this centre.

Thought which is conducted in terms of two spheres regards such pairs of concepts as secular and Christian, natural and supernatural, profane and sacred, and rational and revelational, as though they were ultimate static antitheses, serving to designate certain mutually exclusive entities. It fails to recognize the original unity of these opposites in the reality of Christ, and in the place of this true unity it sets the forced unity of some sacred or profane system in which these contradictory concepts are combined. In such a system the static antagonism persists. But these things assume quite a different form with the recognition of the divine and cosmic reality in Christ. The world, the natural, the profane and reason are now all taken up into God from the outset. They do not exist 'in themselves' and 'on their own account'. They have their reality nowhere save

in the reality of God, in Christ. It is now essential to the real
concept of the secular that it shall always be seen in the
movement of being accepted and becoming accepted by God
in Christ. Just as in Christ the reality of God entered into the
reality of the world, so, too, is that which is Christian to be
found only in that which is of the world, the 'supernatural'
only in the natural, the holy only in the profane, and the
revelational only in the rational. The unity of the reality of
God and of the world, which has been accomplished in
Christ, is repeated, or, more exactly, is realized, ever afresh
in the life of men. And yet what is Christian is not identical
with what is of the world. The natural is not identical with
the supernatural or the revelational with the rational. But
between the two there is in each case a unity which derives
solely from the reality of Christ, that is to say solely from
faith in this ultimate reality. This unity is seen in the way
in which the secular and the Christian elements prevent one
another from assuming any kind of static independence in
their mutual relations. They adopt a polemical attitude
towards each other and bear witness precisely in this to their
shared reality and to their unity in the reality which is in
Christ. Just as Luther engaged in polemics on behalf of the
secular authority against the extension of ecclesiastical power
by the Roman Church, so, too, must there be a Christian or
'spiritual' polemical reply to the secular element when there
is a danger that this element may make itself independent,
as was the case soon after the Reformation and especially in
nineteenth-century German secularist Protestantism. In both
of these polemical protests the process is the same: men's
attention is called to the divine and cosmic reality—Jesus
Christ. Luther was protesting against a Christianity which
was striving for independence and detaching itself from the
reality in Christ. He protested with the help of the secular
and in the name of a better Christianity. So, too, today,
when Christianity is employed as a polemical weapon against
the secular, this must be done in the name of a better
secularity and above all it must not lead back to a static
predominance of the spiritual sphere as an end in itself.

It is only in this sense, as a polemical unity, that Luther's doctrine of the two kingdoms is to be accepted, and it was no doubt in this sense that it was originally intended.

To think in terms of spheres is to think statically and is therefore, theologically speaking, to think in terms of laws. That is easy to demonstrate. If the secular becomes an independent realm by itself, then the fact of the world having been taken up into Christ is denied. It is denied that the reality of the world has its basis in the reality of the revelation, and this in turn implies denial of the gospel which is addressed to the whole world. The world is not apprehended as being reconciled by God in Christ, but rather it is seen either as a region which is still entirely subject to the claims of the Christian sector or else as one which opposes the law of Christ with a law of its own. If the Christian sector presents itself as an independent entity, then the world is denied that fellowship into which God entered with the world in Jesus Christ. A Christian law is established which condemns the law of the world and is maintained in an irreconcilable struggle against the world which God has reconciled with Himself. Law always engenders lawlessness; nomism leads to antinomism; perfectionism to libertinism. The present case is no exception. A world which stands by itself, in isolation from the law of Christ, falls victim to licence and self-will. A Christianity which withdraws from the world falls victim to the unnatural and the irrational, to presumption and self-will.

Ethical thinking in terms of spheres, then, is invalidated by faith in the revelation of the ultimate reality in Jesus Christ, and this means that there is no real possibility of being a Christian outside the reality of the world and that there is no real worldly existence outside the reality of Jesus Christ. There is no place to which the Christian can withdraw from the world, whether it be outwardly or in the sphere of the inner life. Any attempt to escape from the world must sooner or later be paid for with a sinful surrender to the world. It is after all a matter of experience that when the gross sins of sex have been overcome they are succeeded by covetousness and avarice, which are equally gross sins even though the world may treat them less severely. The cultivation of a Christian inner life, untouched by the world, will generally present a somewhat tragicomical appearance to the worldly observer. For the sharp-sighted world recognizes itself most distinctly at the very point where the Christian inner life deceives itself in the belief that the world is most remote. Whoever professes to believe in the reality of Jesus Christ, as the revelation of God, must in the same breath profess his faith in both the reality of God and the reality of the world; for in Christ he finds God and the world reconciled. And for just this reason the Christian is no longer the man of eternal conflict, but, just as the reality in Christ is one, so he, too, since he shares in this reality in Christ, is himself an undivided whole. His wordliness does not divide him from Christ, and his Christianity does not divide him from the world. Belonging wholly to Christ, he stands at the same time wholly in the world.

Even when we have appealed to the reality in Christ in order to overcome this thinking in terms of spheres, we are still confronted with another important question. Are there really no ultimate static contraries, no spaces which are separated from one another once and for all? Is not the Church of Jesus Christ such a space, a space which is cut off from the space of the world? And, finally, is not the kingdom of the devil a space of this kind, and one which will never enter into the kingdom of Christ?

Undoubtedly the New Testament contains statements about the Church which fit in with the conception of a space. One may think, for example, of the representation of the Church as a temple, a building, a house, and even as a body. And one may conclude from this that, when it is a question of describing the Church as the visible congregation of God on earth, it is impossible to avoid the notion of space. The Church does indeed occupy a definite space in the world, a space which is delimited by her public worship, her organizations and her parish life,[1] and it is this fact that has given rise

[1] Cf. Bonhoeffer, *The Cost of Discipleship*.

to the whole of the thinking in terms of spheres. It would be very dangerous to overlook this, to deny the visible nature of the Church, and to reduce her to the status of a purely spiritual force. For this would be to render ineffective the fact of the revelation of God in the world, and to transform Christ Himself into a spirit. It is essential to the revelation of God in Jesus Christ that it occupies space within the world. But, of course, it would be entirely wrong to interpret this space in a purely empirical sense. If God in Jesus Christ claims space in the world, even though it be only a stable 'because there was no room in the inn' (Luke 2.7), then in this narrow space He comprises together the whole reality of the world at once and reveals the ultimate basis of this reality. And so, too, the Church of Jesus Christ is the place, in other words the space in the world, at which the reign of Jesus Christ over the whole world is evidenced and proclaimed. This space of the Church, then, is not something which exists on its own account. It is from the outset something which reaches out far beyond itself, for indeed it is not the space of some kind of cultural association such as would have to fight for its own survival in the world, but it is the place where testimony is given to the foundation of all reality in Jesus Christ. The Church is the place where testimony and serious thought are given to God's reconciliation of the world with Himself in Christ, to His having so loved the world that He gave His Son for its sake. The space of the Church is not there in order to try to deprive the world of a piece of its territory, but precisely in order to prove to the world that it is still the world, the world which is loved by God and reconciled with Him. The Church has neither the wish nor the obligation to extend her space to cover the space of the world. She asks for no more space than she needs for the purpose of serving the world by bearing witness to Jesus Christ and to the reconciliation of the world with God through Him. The only way in which the Church can defend her own territory is by fighting not for it but for the salvation of the world. Otherwise the Church becomes a 'religious society' which fights in its own interest and thereby ceases at once to be

the Church of God and of the world. And so the first demand
which is made of those who belong to God's Church is not
that they should be something in themselves, not that they
should, for example, set up some religious organization or
that they should lead lives of piety, but that they shall be
witnesses to Jesus Christ before the world. It is for this task
that the Holy Spirit equips those to whom He gives Himself.
It is, of course, to be assumed that this testimony before the
world can be delivered in the right way only if it springs
from a hallowed life in the congregation of God. But a
genuine hallowed life in the congregation of God differs from
any pious imitation of it in that it at the same time impels a
man to testify before the world. If this testimony ceases to
be given, that is a sign of the inner corruption of the congregation, just as the absence of fruit is the sign of the decay of
the tree.

If one wishes to speak, then, of the space or sphere of the
Church, one must bear in mind that the confines of this space
are at every moment being overrun and broken down by the
testimony of the Church to Jesus Christ. And this means
that all mistaken thinking in terms of spheres must be
excluded, since it is deleterious to the proper understanding
of the Church.

So far we have been speaking of the world only in the
sense of the world which is reconciled with God in Christ. We
have spoken of reality always in the sense of the reality which
is taken up, maintained and reconciled in God. And it is in
this sense that we have had to reject all thinking that is
conducted in terms of two spheres. But this still leaves open
the question whether the 'world', if by this we understand
the 'disordered' world which has fallen under the power of
the devil, and whether sinful reality ought perhaps to be
conceived as a space or realm which is established in opposition to the Church or to the kingdom of Christ. Is perhaps
the final static antinomy which justifies this thinking in terms
of two spheres the antinomy of the kingdom of Christ and the
kingdom of the devil? At first sight this question appears to
demand an affirmative answer, yet when it is examined more

closely it is in itself by no means conclusive. Christ and His adversary, the devil, are mutually exclusive contraries; yet the devil must serve Christ even against his will; he desires evil, but over and over again he is compelled to do good; so that the realm or space of the devil is always only beneath the feet of Jesus Christ. But if the kingdom of the devil is taken to mean that world which 'lies in disorder', the world which has fallen under the devil's authority, then here, especially, there is a limit to the possibility of thinking in terms of spheres. For it is precisely this 'disordered' world that in Christ is reconciled with God and that now possesses its final and true reality not in the devil but in Christ. The world is not divided between Christ and the devil, but, whether it recognizes it or not, it is solely and entirely the world of Christ. The world is to be called to this, its reality in Christ, and in this way the false reality will be destroyed which it believes that it possesses in itself as in the devil. The dark and evil world must not be abandoned to the devil. It must be claimed for Him who has won it by His incarnation, His death and His resurrection. Christ gives up nothing of what He has won. He holds it fast in His hands. It is Christ, therefore, who renders inadmissible the dichotomy of a bedevilled and a Christian world. Any static delimitation of a region which belongs to the devil and a region which belongs to Christ is a denial of the reality of God's having reconciled the whole world with Himself in Christ.

That God loved the world and reconciled it with Himself in Christ is the central message proclaimed in the New Testament. It is assumed there that the world stands in need of reconciliation with God but that it is not capable of achieving it by itself. The acceptance of the world by God is a miracle of the divine compassion. For this reason the relation of the Church to the world is determined entirely by the relation of God to the world. There is a love for the world which is enmity towards God (Jas. 4.4) because it springs from the nature of the world as such and not from the love of God for the world. The world 'as such' is the world as it understands itself, the world which resists and even rejects the reality of the love of God which is bestowed upon it in Jesus Christ. This world has fallen under the sentence which God passes on all enmity to Christ. It is engaged in a life-and-death struggle with the Church. And yet it is the task and the essential character of the Church that she shall impart to precisely this world its reconciliation with God and that she shall open its eyes to the reality of the love of God, against which it is blindly raging. In this way it is also, and indeed especially, the lost and sentenced world that is incessantly drawn in into the event of Christ.

It is hard to abandon a picture which one has grown accustomed to using for the ordering of one's ideas and concepts. And yet we must leave behind us the picture of the two spheres, and the question now is whether we can replace it with another picture which is equally simple and obvious.

We shall need above all to direct our gaze to the picture of the body of Christ Himself, who became man, was crucified and rose again. In the body of Jesus Christ God is united with humanity, the whole of humanity is accepted by God, and the world is reconciled with God. In the body of Jesus Christ God took upon himself the sin of the whole world and bore it. There is no part of the world, be it never so forlorn and never so godless, which is not accepted by God and reconciled with God in Jesus Christ. Whoever sets eyes on the body of Jesus Christ in faith can never again speak of the world as though it were lost, as though it were separated from Christ; he can never again with clerical arrogance set himself apart from the world. The world belongs to Christ, and it is only in Christ that the world is what it is. It has need, therefore, of nothing less than Christ Himself. Everything would be ruined if one were to try to reserve Christ for the Church and to allow the world only some kind of law, even if it were a Christian law. Christ died for the world, and it is only in the midst of the world that Christ is Christ. Only unbelief can wish to give the world something less than Christ. Certainly it may have well-intentioned pedagogical motives for this course, but these motives always have a certain flavour of clerical exclusiveness. Such a course implies failure to take seriously the incarnation, the crucifixion and the bodily resurrection. It is a denial of the body of Christ.

If we now follow the New Testament in applying to the Church the concept of the body of Christ, this is not by any means intended primarily as representing the separation of the Church from the world. On the contrary, it is implicit in the New Testament statement concerning the incarnation of God in Christ that all men are taken up, enclosed and borne within the body of Christ and that this is just what the congregation of the faithful are to make known to the world by their words and by their lives. What is intended here is not separation from the world but the summoning of the world into the fellowship of this body of Christ, to which in truth it already belongs. This testimony of the Church is foreign to the world; the Church herself, in bearing this testimony, finds herself to be foreign to the world. Yet even this is always only an ever-renewed consequence of that fellowship with the world which is given in the body of Christ. The Church is divided from the world solely by the fact that she affirms in faith the reality of God's acceptance of man, a reality which is the property of the whole world. By allowing this reality to take effect within herself, she testifies that it is effectual for the whole world.

The body of Jesus Christ, especially as it appears to us on the cross, shows to the eyes of faith the world in its sin, and how it is loved by God, no less than it shows the Church, as the congregation of those who acknowledge their sin and submit to the love of God.

God and the world are thus at one in Christ in a way which means that although the Church and the world are different from each other, yet there cannot be a static, spatial borderline between them. The question now is how one is to conceive this distinction between Church and world without relapsing into these spatial terms. Here one must go to the Bible itself for advice, and the Bible has its answer ready.

The Four Mandates

The world, like all created things, is created through Christ and with Christ as its end, and consists in Christ alone (John 1.10; Col. 1.16). To speak of the world without speaking of Christ is empty and abstract. The world is relative to Christ, no matter whether it knows it or not. This relativeness of the world to Christ assumes concrete form in certain mandates of God in the world. The Scriptures name four such mandates: labour, marriage, government and the Church. We speak of divine mandates rather than of divine orders because the word mandate refers more clearly to a divinely imposed task rather than to a determination of being. It is God's will that there shall be labour, marriage, government and church in the world; and it is His will that all these, each in its own way, shall be through Christ, directed towards Christ, and in Christ. God has imposed all these mandates on all men. He has not merely imposed one of these mandates on each individual, but He has imposed all four on all men. This means that there can be no retreating from a 'secular' into a 'spiritual' sphere. There can be only the practice, the learning, of the Christian life under these four mandates of God. And it will not do to regard the first three mandates as 'secular', in contradistinction to the fourth. For even in the midst of the world these are divine mandates, no matter whether their topic be labour, marriage, government or the Church. These mandates are, indeed, divine only by virtue of their original and final relation to Christ. In detachment from this relation, 'in themselves', they are no more divine than the world 'in itself' is divine. Labour 'in itself' is not divine, but labour for the sake of Jesus Christ, for the fulfilment of the divine task and purpose, is divine. Labour is divine only because God has enjoined labour upon man for the sake of Christ, and has given this labour a promise. The divine character of labour cannot be ascribed to its general usefulness or its intrinsic values, but only to its origin, its continuance and its goal in Jesus Christ. It is the same with the other mandates. They are divine only

179

because they are mandates of God, and not already by virtue of their factual presence in this or that concrete form. It is not because labour, marriage, government and church *are* that they are commanded by God, but it is because they are commanded by God that they *are*. And they are divine mandates only in so far as their being is consciously or unconsciously subordinated to the divinely imposed task. If a concrete form of labour, marriage, government or church persistently and arbitrarily violates the assigned task, then the divine mandate lapses in this particular concrete instance. And yet, through the divine mandate, what has concrete being acquires a relative justification. Not every offence against the divine task must in itself on principle deprive of their divine mandate the concrete forms of labour, marriage, government and church. Marriage, government, etc., which are actually in being, have always a relative precedence over those which are not yet in being. Single offences do not confer the right to eliminate or destroy what is established. What is required here is rather a return to a genuine subordination to the divine mandate and a restoration of genuine responsibility towards the divinely assigned task. This genuine responsibility consists in the adaptation of the concrete form of the divine mandates to their origin, their continuance and their goal in Jesus Christ.

The mandate of labour confronts us, according to the Bible, already with the first man. Adam is 'to dress and to keep' the Garden of Eden (Gen. 2.15). Even after the Fall labour remains a mandate of divine discipline and grace (Gen. 3.17–19). In the sweat of his brow man wrests his nourishment from the soil, and the range of human labour soon embraces everything from agriculture and economy to science and art (Gen. 4.17ff.). The labour which is instituted in Paradise is a participation by man in the action of creation. By its means there is created a world of things and values which is designed for the glorification and service of Jesus Christ. This is not a creation out of nothing, like God's creation; it is a making of new things on the basis of the creation by God. No man can evade this mandate. From the labour which man performs here in fulfilment of the divinely imposed task there arises that likeness of the celestial world by which the man who recognizes Jesus Christ is reminded of the lost Paradise. The first creation of Cain was the city, the earthly counterpart of the eternal city of God. There follows the invention of fiddles and flutes, which afford to us on earth a foretaste of the music of heaven. Next there is the extraction and processing of the metallic treasures from the mines of the earth, partly for the decoration of earthly houses, just as the heavenly city is resplendent with gold and precious stones, and partly for the manufacture of the swords of avenging justice. Through the divine mandate of labour there is to come into being a world which, knowingly or not, is waiting for Christ, is designed for Christ, is open to Christ, serves Him and glorifies Him. But it is the race of Cain that is to fulfil this mandate, and that is what casts the darkest shadow over all human labour.

Like the mandate of labour, the mandate of marriage also confronts us after the creation already with the first man. In marriage man and woman become one in the sight of God, just as Christ becomes one with His Church. 'This is a great mystery' (Eph. 5.32f.). God bestows on this union the blessing of fruitfulness, the generation of new life. Man enters into the will of the Creator in sharing in the process of creation. Through marriage men are brought into being for the glorification and the service of Jesus Christ and for the increase of His kingdom. This means that marriage is not only a matter of producing children, but also of educating them to be obedient to Jesus Christ. The parents are for the child the representatives of God, for they have brought him into the world and are his educators by God's commission. Just as is the case with the new values created by labour, so, too, in marriage it is for the service of Jesus Christ that new men are created. But the first son of the first man, Cain, was born far from Paradise and he became the murderer of his brother; it is for this reason that here, too, a dark shadow falls from the very outset on marriage and the family in this our world.

The divine mandate of government presupposes the divine mandates of labour and marriage. In the world which it rules, the governing authority finds already present the two mandates through which God the Creator exercises his creative power, and is therefore dependent on these. Government cannot itself produce life or values. It is not creative. It preserves what has been created, maintaining it in the order which is assigned to it through the task which is imposed by God. It protects it by making law to consist in the acknowledgement of the divine mandates and by securing respect for this law by the force of the sword. Thus the governing authority is not the performer but the witness and guarantor of marriage. The wide domains of labour are not administered by the governing authority itself, but they are subject to its inspection and supervision, and, within certain limits which will be defined later, to its direction. The governing authority must never itself try to become the subject, the driving force, in this domain of labour; for this would be to imperil gravely both the divine mandate of labour and its own divine mandate. By the establishment of law and by the force of the sword the governing authority preserves the world for the reality of Jesus Christ. Everyone owes obedience to this governing authority—for Christ's sake.

The divine mandate of the Church is different from these three. This mandate is the task of enabling the reality of Jesus Christ to become real in the preaching and organization of the Church and the Christian life. It is concerned, therefore, with the eternal salvation of the whole world. The mandate of the Church extends to all mankind, and it does so within all the other mandates. Man is at the same time a labourer, a partner in marriage, and the subject of a government, so that there is an overlapping of the three mandates in man and all three must be fulfilled simultaneously; and the mandate of the Church impinges on all these mandates, for now it is the Christian who is at once labourer, partner in marriage, and subject of a government. No division into separate spheres or spaces is permissible here. The whole man stands before the whole earthly and eternal reality, the reality which God has prepared for him in Jesus Christ. Man can live up to this reality only if he responds fully to the totality of the offer and the claim. The first three mandates are not designed to divide man up, to tear him asunder; they are concerned with the whole man before God, the Creator, Reconciler and Redeemer; reality, therefore, in all its multiplicity is ultimately one; it is one in the incarnate God Jesus Christ, and precisely this is the testimony which the Church must give. The divine mandates in the world are not intended to consume man in endless conflicts; on the contrary, they are directed toward the whole man, as he stands in reality before God. Man is not the place at which the incompatibility of these divine mandates is to make itself apparent; on the contrary, man, with his concrete life and action, is the first and only centre at which there is achieved the unity of what is 'in itself', that is to say, theoretically, incompatible. But this unity is achieved only when man allows himself to be confronted in Jesus Christ with the accomplished reality of the incarnation of God and of the reconciliation of the world with God in the crib, the cross and the resurrection of Jesus Christ. In the form of a theory of 'estates' the doctrine of the divine mandates threatens to lead to a perilous disintegration of man and of reality; yet it is precisely this doctrine which serves to confront man with the one and entire reality which is manifested to us in Jesus Christ. Thus here again all the lines converge in the reality of the body of Jesus Christ, in which God and man became one.

We began by saying that, instead of asking how one can be good and do good, one must ask what is the will of God. But the will of God is nothing other than the becoming real of the reality of Christ with us and in our world. The will of God, therefore, is not an idea, still demanding to become real; it is itself a reality already in the self-revelation of God in Jesus Christ. Nor is the will of God simply identical with what is in being, which would mean that it would be fulfilled by submissive acquiescence in things as they are. It is, on the contrary, a reality whose purpose is to become real ever anew in what is in being and against what is in being. The

will of God is already fulfilled by God Himself, by His reconciliation of the world with Himself in Christ. It would be a
most hazardous relapse into abstract thought if one were to
wish to disregard the reality of this fulfilment and to replace
it with a fulfilment of one's own. After Christ has appeared,
ethics can have but one purpose, namely, the achievement
of participation in the reality of the fulfilled will of God. But
this participation, too, is possible only in virtue of the fact
that I myself am already included in the fulfilment of the
will of God in Christ, which means that I am reconciled
with God. To ask about the will of God is not to ask about
something hidden and unfulfilled; it is to ask about what has
become manifest and is indeed fulfilled. But the question is
still a genuine question in that I myself and the world which
surrounds me are implicated in this question through the
manifestation and the fulfilment.

The will of God, which became manifest and was fulfilled
in Jesus Christ, embraces the whole of reality. One can gain
access to this whole, without being torn asunder by its
manifold variety, only in faith in Jesus Christ, 'in whom
dwelleth all the fulness of the Godhead bodily' (Col. 2.9 and
1.19), 'by whom all things are reconciled, whether they be
things in earth or things in heaven' (Col. 1.20), and whose
body, the Church, is 'the fulness of him that filleth all in all'
(Eph. 1.23). Faith in this Jesus Christ is the sole fountain-
head of all good.

VI

HISTORY AND GOOD

Good and Life

THE question of good always finds us already in a situation
which can no longer be reversed: we are alive. This means in
any case that we can no longer raise and answer the question
of good as though we had first of all to create life, beautiful
and good, from the outset. It is as creatures and not as
creators that we enquire about good. We are not concerned
with what would be good if we did not live, that is to say in
some quite imaginary circumstances, and indeed, being alive,
we cannot even seriously ask this question; for even to
abstract from life is possible for us only because we are bound
to life, and therefore not in complete freedom. We are not
asking what is good in itself; but we are asking what, on the
assumption that life is given, is good for us as living men.
We are enquiring about good, not at all by abstracting from
life, but by looking deeply into life. The enquiry into good is
itself a part of our life, just as our life pertains to the enquiry
into good. The question of good is posed and is decided in
the midst of each definite, yet unconcluded, unique and
transient situation of our lives, in the midst of our living
relationships with men, things, institutions and powers, in
other words in the midst of our historical existence. The
question of good cannot now be separated from the question
of life, the question of history.

Ethical thought is still largely dominated by the abstract
notion of an isolated individual man who applies the
absolute criterion of a good which is good in itself and has to
make his decision incessantly and exclusively between this
clearly recognized good and an equally clearly recognized
evil. Already, with what we have said previously, we have

left this notion behind us. These isolated individuals do not exist and we do not dispose over any such absolute criterion of a good which is good in itself; nor do good and evil display themselves in history in their pure form. And indeed every detail of the underlying plan of this abstraction fails to make contact with the specifically ethical problem. It is, to say the least, very questionable whether one can at all regard as ethically relevant the notion of an isolated individual in detachment from his historical situation and from historical influences; such a notion is unreal and is therefore, in any case, a theoretical and peripheral matter which is entirely lacking in interest. The absolute criterion of a good which is good in itself, assuming that a notion of this kind can be conceived in the first place without an inherent contradiction, makes good into a dead law, a Moloch to which all life and all liberty are sacrificed, and which fails even to impose a genuine obligation, simply because it is a metaphysical and self-contained construction which bears no essential relation to life itself. The decision between the clearly-known good and the clearly-known evil excludes human knowledge itself from the decision; it transposes the ethical into the struggle between the knowledge, which is already oriented towards the good, and the will, which still offers resistance, and it thereby fails to bring about that authentic decision in which the whole man, complete with his knowledge and his will, seeks and finds the good in the equivocal complexity of a historical situation solely through the venture of the deed. In this abstraction from life the ethical is reduced to a static basic formula which forcibly detaches man from the historicity of his existence and transposes him into the vacuum of the purely private and the purely ideal. The ethical task is now conceived as consisting in the realization of certain definite principles, quite irrespectively of their relation to life. This may mean that life is made a purely private concern; only the man's own loyalty to his principles is represented as being good, without any consideration of other men; and, according as these principles are more or less radical, the appropriate form of life may vary from a retreat into the private sphere of civil existence to a withdrawal to the monastery. Or, alternatively, the abstract interpretation of the ethical leads to enthusiasm; here again the appropriate form of life may vary, according to the principles adopted, from that of the great political fanatics and ideologists down to that of all the various shades of stupidly importunate reformers of life. All these endeavours have failed in the face of life, and they always will fail; when we say this we do not mean simply that they fail in the sense in which the life of Jesus Christ ends in failure, for He was not a private saint or an enthusiast. Theirs is an idealizing failure; it is a failure already in its momentary triumph; it is a failure ultimately because here no true encounter has taken place at all with life, with man; it is rather that something alien, false, factitious, imaginary and at the same time completely tyrannical has been super-imposed on man without really and essentially affecting him, changing him and forcing him to a decision. Ideologies vent their fury on man and then leave him as a bad dream leaves the waking dreamer. The memory of them is bitter. They have not made the man stronger or more mature; they have only made him poorer and more mistrustful. In the hour of this unhappy awakening, if God reveals Himself to men as the Creator before whom man can live only as the creature, that is grace and the blessing of poverty.

When we say that the abstract concept of good fails to make contact with life, we do not mean that good is here set up in opposition to life, but rather that there is no genuine opposition at all, but a complete failure to come to grips with life. Life is here made a *quantité négligeable*, which it is unnecessary to take into account. At best life is understood as that part of 'nature' which owes its origin and its deliverance to mind or spirit, to the idea. But if good and life are to stand towards one another in the relation of nature and mind or spirit, then there is still no real overcoming of life but only the affirmation of an antithesis which is given the status of a law and which cannot be reconciled; the most that is possible is that the one will subdue the other by violence. Such is the essential sterility of a concept of good which does not take

life into account, that is to say, which itself implies a concept
of life which does not correspond to the reality and which is
not capable of overcoming the antithesis between good and
life. This brings us to the question of life itself, and demands
that the answer to this question should also afford some
guidance towards the proper understanding of good.

Jesus Christ said of Himself: 'I am the life' (John 14.6 and
11.25), and this claim, and the reality which it contains,
cannot be disregarded by any Christian thinking, or indeed
by any philosophical thinking at all. This self-affirmation of
Jesus is a declaration that any attempt to express the essence
of life simply as life is foredoomed to failure and has indeed
already failed. So long as we live, so long as we do not know
the boundary of life, death, how can we possibly say what
life is in itself? We can only live life; we cannot define it.
Jesus's saying binds every thought of life to His person. 'I am
the life.' No question about life can go further back than
this 'I am'. The question of what is life gives place to the
answer who is life. Life is not a thing, an entity or concept; it
is a person, a particular and unique person, and it is this
particular and unique person, not in respect of what this
person has in common with other persons, but in the I of this
person; it is the I of Jesus. Jesus sets this I in sharp contrast
with all the thoughts, concepts and ways which claim to
constitute the essence of life. He does not say 'I have the life'
but 'I am the life.' Consequently life can never again be
separated from the I, the person, of Jesus. In proclaiming this,
Jesus does not merely say that He is life, in other words
simply some metaphysical spirit which might possibly light
upon me as well as upon others; He says that He is precisely
my life, our life; St Paul describes this state of affairs very
accurately, though also very paradoxically, in the words 'To
me to live is Christ' (Phil. 1.21) and 'Christ who is our life'
(Col. 3.4). My life is outside myself, outside the range of my
disposal; my life is another than myself; it is Jesus Christ.
This is not intended figuratively, as conveying that my life
would not be worth living without this other, or that Christ
invests my life with a particular quality or a particular value

188

while allowing it to retain its own independent existence, but my life itself is Jesus Christ. That is true of my life, and it is true of all created things. 'In all things that were made —He was the life' (John 1.4).[1]

'I am the life.' This is the word, the revelation, the proclamation of Jesus Christ. Our life is outside ourselves and in Jesus Christ; this is not at all a conclusion which we derive from our knowledge of ourselves; it is a claim which comes to us from without, a claim which we may either believe or contradict. This word is addressed to us, and when we hear it we recognize that we have fallen away from life, from our life, and that we are living in contradiction to life, to our life. In this saying of Jesus Christ, therefore, we hear the condemnation, the negation, of our life; for our life is not life; or, if it is life, it is life only by virtue of the fact that, even though in contradiction to it, we still live through the life which is called Jesus Christ, the origin, the essence and the goal of all life and of our life. This negation of our apostate life means that between it and the life which is Jesus Christ there stands the end, annihilation, death. This negation, the 'no' that we hear, itself brings us this death. But in bringing us death this 'no' becomes a mysterious 'yes', the affirmation of a new life, the life which is Jesus Christ. This is the life that we cannot give to ourselves, the life that comes to us entirely from without, entirely from beyond; and yet it is not a remote or alien life, of no concern to ourselves, but it is our own real daily life. This life lies hidden only behind the symbol of death, the symbol of negation.[2]

We live now in tension between the negation and the affirmation. Our life can be spoken of now only in this relation to Jesus Christ. If we leave Him out of the reckoning, as the origin, the essence and the goal of life, of our life, if we fail to consider that we are creatures, reconciled and redeemed, then we shall achieve no more than mere biological and ideological abstractions. Our life is created, reconciled and redeemed; it finds in Jesus Christ its origin, its essence and its

[1] Cf. Bultmann, Das Evangelium des Johannes, p. 21ff.
[2] Ibid., p.308.

goal; it is in tension between the 'yes' and the 'no'. It is only in this 'yes' and this 'no' that we can recognize Christ as our life. It is the 'yes' of creation, atonement and redemption, and the 'no' of the condemnation and death of the life which has fallen away from its origin, its essence and its goal. But no one who knows Christ can hear the 'yes' without the 'no' or the 'no' without the 'yes'.

It is the 'yes' to what is created, to becoming and to growth, to the flower and to the fruit, to health, happiness, ability, achievement, worth, success, greatness and honour; in short, it is the 'yes' to the development of the power of life. And it is the 'no' to that defection from the origin, the essence and the goal of life which is inherent in all this existence from the outset. This 'no' means dying, suffering, poverty, renunciation, resignation, humility, degradation, self-denial, and in this again it already implies the 'yes' to the new life, a life which does not fall apart into a juxtaposition of 'yes' and 'no', a life in which there is not to be found, for example, an unrestrained expansion of vitality side by side with a wholly separate ascetic and spiritual attitude, or 'creaturely' conduct side by side with 'Christian' conduct. If that were so, the 'yes' and the 'no' would lose their unity in Jesus Christ, but this new life is one in Jesus Christ; it is in tension between the 'yes' and the 'no' in the sense that in every 'yes' the 'no' is already heard and in every 'no' there is heard also the 'yes'. Development of the vital force and self-denial, growing and dying, health and suffering, happiness and renunciation, achievement and humility, honour and self-abasement, all these belong together in irreconcilable contradiction and yet in living unity.

The unity of life is irreparably destroyed if any attempt is made to render the one independent of the other, to play off the one against the other, or to appeal to the authority of the one against the other. This leads only to the abstractions of an ethic of vitality and of a supposed ethic of Jesus; it leads to those well-known theories of the autonomous domains of life which are entirely at variance with the sermon on the mount; it leads to that forcible disruption of the unity of

life which presents itself with all the solemnity of a particularly penetrating perception of reality because it imparts to
life the dark radiance of the tragic and the heroic but which,
nevertheless, entirely fails to make contact with the reality
of life as it is made known in Jesus Christ. In consequence of
false abstractions one is now held fast in conflicts which must
eternally remain unresolved; practical action cannot pass
beyond these conflicts and it is wasted and worn away by
them. There is no need of further proof that all this is entirely
remote from the New Testament and from the words of
Jesus. The actions of the Christian do not spring from bitter
acquiescence in the irreconcilable cleavage between vitality
and self-denial, between 'secular' and 'Christian' or between
'autonomous ethics' and the 'ethic of Jesus', but they spring
from joy in the accomplishment of the reconciliation of the
world with God; they spring from the peace which comes
with the completion of the work of salvation in Jesus Christ;
they spring from the all-embracing life which is Jesus Christ.
In Jesus Christ God and man became one, and therefore
through Him in the actions of the Christians 'secular' and
'Christian' become one also. They are not opposed, as
eternally hostile principles, but the actions of the Christians
spring from the unity which is created in Christ, the unity of
God and world, the unity of life. In Christ life finds its unity
again; the contradiction of 'yes' and 'no' is indeed still
present, but it is continually overcome in the concrete action
of the man who believes in Christ.

If we now return to the question of good, we may say pro-
visionally that we are, in any case, dealing here with life
itself and not with an abstraction from life, with the realization, for example, of certain definite ideals and values which
are independent of life. Good is life as it is in reality, that is
to say, in its origin, essence and goal; it is life in the sense of
the saying 'Christ is my life' (Phil. 1.21). Good is not a
quality of life. It is 'life' itself. To be good is to 'live'.

This life assumes concrete form in the contradictory unity
of 'yes' and 'no' which life finds outside itself in Jesus Christ.
But Jesus Christ is man and is God in one. In Him there takes

place the original and essential encounter with man and with God. Henceforward man cannot be conceived and known otherwise than in Jesus Christ, and God cannot be conceived and known otherwise than in the human form of Jesus Christ. In Him we see humanity as that which God has accepted, borne and loved, and as that which is reconciled with God. In Him we see God in the form of the poorest of our brothers. There is no man 'in himself', just as there is no God 'in Himself'; both of these are empty abstractions. Man is the man who was accepted in the incarnation of Christ, who was loved, condemned and reconciled in Christ; and God is God become man. There is no relation to men without a relation to God, and no relation to God without a relation to men, and it is only our relation to Jesus Christ which provides the basis for our relation to men and to God. Jesus Christ is our life, and so now, from the standpoint of Jesus Christ, we may say that our fellow-man is our life and that God is our life. This means, of course, that our encounter with our fellow-men and our encounter with God are subject to the same 'yes' and 'no' as is our encounter with Jesus Christ.

We 'live' when, in our encounter with men and with God, the 'yes' and the 'no' are combined in a unity of contradictions, in selfless self-assertion, in self-assertion in the sacrifice of ourselves to God and to men.

We live by responding to the word of God which is addressed to us in Jesus Christ. Since this word is addressed to our entire life, the response, too, can only be an entire one; it must be given with our entire life as it is realized in all our several actions. The life which confronts us in Jesus Christ, as a 'yes' and a 'no' to our life, requires the response of a life which assimilates and unites this 'yes' and this 'no'.

We give the name responsibility to this life in its aspect as a response to the life of Jesus Christ as the 'yes' and the 'no' to our life. This concept of responsibility is intended as referring to the concentrated totality and unity of the response to the reality which is given to us in Jesus Christ, as distinct from the partial responses which might arise, for example, from a consideration of utility or from particular

principles. In the face of the life which confronts us in Jesus
Christ these partial responses are not enough and nothing
less can suffice than the entire and single response of our
life. Responsibility means, therefore, that the totality of life
is pledged and that our action becomes a matter of life and
death.

In this way we invest the concept of responsibility with a
fulness of meaning which it does not acquire in everyday
usage, even when it is placed extremely high on the scale of
ethical values, as it was, for example, by Bismarck and Max
Weber. Even in the Bible we scarcely find such great promi-
nence given to this concept, though when it does appear it
displays quite decisive characteristics. Responsibility in the
biblical sense is, in the first place, a verbal response given
at the risk of a man's life to the question asked by another
man with regard to the event of Christ (II Tim. 4.16; I Pet.
3.15; Phil. 1.7 and 17). I answer with words at the risk of my
life for that which has taken place through Jesus Christ. I
do not therefore answer primarily for myself, for my own
action; I do not justify myself (II Cor. 12.19); I answer for
Jesus Christ and thereby also indeed for the commission
which has been encharged to me by Him (I Cor. 9.3). Job
presumptuously desires to answer for his own ways before
God (Job 13.15), and God's words to Job put an end to any
such temerity: 'He that reproveth God, let him answer it.
Then Job answered the Lord, and said, Behold, I am vile;
what shall I answer thee? I will lay mine hand upon my
mouth' (Job 40.2–4). We are continuing along the lines of the
Bible if we say that in answering for Christ, for life, before
men, and only thus, I am at the same time accepting responsibility for men before Christ; I stand for Christ before men
and for men before Christ. The responsibility which I assume
for Christ in speaking to men is also my responsibility for
men in speaking to Christ. My answering to men for Christ
is my answering to Christ for men, and only in this is it my
answering for myself to God and to men. When I am called
to account by men and by God I can answer only through
the witness of Jesus Christ who interceded for God with men

and for men with God. There is responsibility to God and for God, to men and for men; it is always responsibility for the sake of Jesus Christ, and in this alone it is responsibility for my own life. A man can answer for himself only in confessing Jesus Christ with his lips and with his life.

In ethics, as in dogmatics, we cannot simply reproduce the terminology of the Bible. The altered problems of ethics demand an altered terminology. But it must be remembered that an extension of the terminology involves the risk of slipping away from what is essential, and also that the use of the biblical terminology is not without its dangers.

THE STRUCTURE OF RESPONSIBLE LIFE

The structure of responsible life is conditioned by two factors; life is bound to man and to God and a man's own life is free. It is the fact that life is bound to man and to God which sets life in the freedom of a man's own life. Without this bond and without this freedom there is no responsibility. Only when it has become selfless in this obligation does a life stand in the freedom of a man's truly own life and action. The obligation assumes the form of deputyship and of correspondence with reality; freedom displays itself in the self-examination of life and of action and in the venture of a concrete decision. This gives us the arrangement for our discussion of the structure of responsible life.

Deputyship

The fact that responsibility is fundamentally a matter of deputyship is demonstrated most clearly in those circumstances in which a man is directly obliged to act in the place of other men, for example as a father, as a statesman or as a teacher. The father acts for the children, working for them, caring for them, interceding, fighting and suffering for them. Thus in a real sense he is their deputy. He is not an isolated individual, but he combines in himself the selves of a number of human beings. Any attempt to live as though he were alone is a denial of the actual fact of his responsibility. He cannot

194

evade the responsibility which is laid on him with his paternity. This reality shatters the fiction that the subject, the performer, of all ethical conduct is the isolated individual. Not the individual in isolation but the responsible man is the subject, the agent, with whom ethical reflexion must concern itself. This principle is not affected by the extent of the responsibility assumed, whether it be for a single human being, for a community or for whole groups of communities. No man can altogether escape responsibility, and this means that no man can avoid deputyship. Even the solitary lives as a deputy, and indeed quite especially so, for his life is lived in deputyship for man as man, for mankind as a whole. And, in fact, the concept of responsibility for oneself possesses a meaning only in so far as it refers to the responsibility which I bear with respect to myself as a man, that is to say, because I am a man. Responsibility for oneself is in truth responsibility with respect to the man, and that means responsibility with respect to mankind. The fact that Jesus lived without the special responsibility of a marriage, of a family or of a profession, does not by any means set Him outside the field of responsibility; on the contrary, it makes all the clearer His responsibility and His deputyship for all men. Here we come already to the underlying basis of everything that has been said so far. Jesus, life, our life, lived in deputyship for us as the incarnate Son of God, and that is why through Him all human life is in essence a life of deputyship. Jesus was not the individual, desiring to achieve a perfection of his own, but He lived only as the one who has taken up into Himself and who bears within Himself the selves of all men. All His living, His action and His dying was deputyship. In Him there is fulfilled what the living, the action and the suffering of men ought to be. In this real deputyship which constitutes His human existence He is the responsible person *par excellence*. Because He is life all life is determined by Him to be deputyship. Whether or not life resists, it is now always deputyship, for life or for death, just as the father is always a father, for good or for evil.

Deputyship, and therefore also responsibility, lies only

in the complete surrender of one's own life to the other man. Only the selfless man lives responsibly, and this means that only the selfless man *lives*. Wherever the divine 'yes' and 'no' become one in man, there there is responsible living. Selflessness in responsibility is so complete that here we may find the fulfilment of Goethe's saying about the man of action being always without conscience. The life .of deputyship is open to two abuses; one may set up one's own ego as an absolute, or one may set up the other man as an absolute. In the first case the relation of responsibility leads to forcible exploitation and tyranny; this springs from a failure to recognize that only the selfless man can act responsibly. In the second case what is made absolute is the welfare of the other man, the man towards whom I am responsible, and all other responsibilities are neglected. From this there arises arbitrary action which makes mock of the responsibility to God who in Jesus Christ is the God of all men. In both these cases there is a denial of the origin, the essence and the goal of responsible life in Jesus Christ, and responsibility itself is set up as a self-made abstract idol.

Responsibility, as life and action in deputyship, is essentially a relation of man to man. Christ became man, and He thereby bore responsibility and deputyship for men. There is also a responsibility for things, conditions and values, but only in conjunction with the strict observance of the original, essential and purposive determination of all things, conditions, and values through Christ (John 1.3), the incarnate God. Through Christ the world of things and of values is once more directed towards mankind as it was in the Creation. It is only within these limits that there is a legitimate sense in speaking, as is often done, about responsibility for a thing or for a cause. Beyond these limits it is dangerous, for it serves to reverse the whole order of life, making things the masters of men. There is a devotion to the cause of truth, goodness, justice and beauty which would be profaned if one were to ask what is the moral of it, and which indeed itself makes it abundantly clear that the highest values must be subservient to man. But there is also a deification of all these values which has no connexion at all with responsibility; it springs from a demoniacal possession which destroys the man in sacrificing him to the idol. 'Responsibility for a thing' does not mean its utilization for man and consequently the abuse of its essential nature, but it means the essential directing of it towards man. Thus that narrow pragmatism is entirely excluded which, in Schiller's words, 'makes a milch-cow of the goddess' when that which has value in itself is in a direct and short-sighted manner subordinated to human utility. The world of things attains to its full liberty and depth only when it is grasped in its original, essential and purposive relevance to the world of persons; for, as St Paul expresses it, the earnest expectation of the creature waits for the manifestation of the glory of the children of God; and indeed the creature itself shall be delivered from the bondage of corruption (which also consists in its own false self-deification) into the glorious liberty of the children of God (Rom. 8.19–21).

Correspondence with Reality

The responsible man is dependent on the man who is concretely his neighbour in his concrete possibility. His conduct is not established in advance, once and for all, that is to say, as a matter of principle, but it arises with the given situation. He has no principle at his disposal which possesses absolute validity and which he has to put into effect fanatically, overcoming all the resistance which is offered to it by reality, but he sees in the given situation what is necessary and what is 'right' for him to grasp and to do. For the responsible man the given situation is not simply the material on which he is to impress his idea or his programme by force, but this situation is itself drawn in into the action and shares in giving form to the deed. It is not an 'absolute good' that is to be realized; but on the contrary it is part of the self-direction of the responsible agent that he prefers what is relatively better to what is relatively worse and that he perceives that the 'absolute good' may sometimes be the very worst. The responsible man does not have to impose upon reality a law which is alien to it, but his action is in the true sense 'in accordance with reality'.

This concept of correspondence to reality certainly needs to be defined more exactly. It would be a complete and a dangerous misunderstanding if it were to be taken in the sense of that 'servile conviction in the face of the fact' that Nietzsche speaks of, a conviction which yields to every powerful pressure, which on principle justifies success, and which on every occasion chooses what is opportune as 'corresponding to reality'. 'Correspondence with reality' in this sense would be the contrary of responsibility; it would be irresponsibility. But the true meaning of correspondence with reality lies neither in this servility towards the factual nor yet in a principle of opposition to the factual, a principle of revolt against the factual in the name of some higher reality. Both extremes alike are very far removed from the essence of the matter. In action which is genuinely in accordance with reality there is an indissoluble link between the acknowledgement and the contradiction of the factual. The reason for this is that reality is first and last not lifeless; but it is the real man, the incarnate God. It is from the real man, whose name is Jesus Christ, that all factual reality derives its ultimate foundation and its ultimate annulment, its justification and its ultimate contradiction, its ultimate affirmation and its ultimate negation. To attempt to understand reality without the real man[1] is to live in an abstraction to which the responsible man must never fall victim; it is to fail to make contact with reality in life; it is to vacillate endlessly between the extremes of servility and revolt in relation to the factual. God became man; He accepted man in the body and thereby reconciled the world of man with God. The affirmation of man and of his reality took place upon the foundation of the acceptance, and not the acceptance upon the foundation of the affirmation. It was not because man

---

[1] In the first picture of his Dance of Death, which represents the Creation, Hans Holbein personifies the sun, the moon and the wind. In this way he gives expression in a naive form to the fact that reality consists ultimately in the personal. In this respect there is an element of truth in primitive animism.

and his reality were worthy of the divine affirmation that God accepted them and that God became man, but it was because man and his reality were worthy of divine being that God accepted man and affirmed him by Himself becoming man in the body and thereby taking upon Himself and suffering the curse of the divine 'no' to the human character. It is from this action of God, from the real man, from Jesus Christ, that reality now receives its 'yes' and its 'no', its right and its limitations. Affirmation and contradiction are now conjoined in the concrete action of him who has recognized the real man. Neither the affirmation nor the contradiction now comes from a world which is alien to reality, from a systematic opportunism or idealism; but they come from the reality of the reconciliation of the world with God which has taken place in Jesus Christ. In Jesus Christ, the real man, the whole of reality is taken up and comprised together; in Him it has its origin, its essence and its goal. For that reason it is only in Him, and with Him as the point of departure, that there can be an action which is in accordance with reality. The origin of action which accords with reality is not the pseudo-Lutheran Christ who exists solely for the purpose of sanctioning the facts as they are, nor the Christ of radical enthusiasm whose function is to bless every revolution, but it is the incarnate God Jesus who has accepted man and who has loved, condemned and reconciled man and with him the world.

Our conclusion from this must be that action which is in accordance with Christ is action which is in accordance with reality. This proposition is not an ideal demand, but it is an assertion which springs from the knowledge of reality itself. Jesus Christ does not confront reality as one who is alien to it, but it is He who alone has borne and experienced the essence of the real in His own body, who has spoken from the standpoint of reality as no man on earth can do, who alone has fallen victim to no ideology, but who is the truly real one, who has borne within Himself and fulfilled the essence of history, and in whom the law of the life of history is embodied. He is the real one, the origin, essence and goal of all that is real, and for that reason He is Himself the Lord and the Law of the real. Consequently the word of Jesus Christ is the interpretation of His existence, and it is therefore the interpretation of that reality in which history attains to its fulfilment. The words of Jesus are the divine commandment for responsible action in history in so far as this history is the reality of history as it is fulfilled in Christ, the responsibility for man as it is fulfilled in Christ alone. They are not intended to serve the ends of an abstract ethic; for an abstract ethic they are entirely incomprehensible and they lead to conflicts which can never be resolved, but they take effect in the reality of history, for it is from there that they originate. Any attempt to detach them from this origin distorts them into a feeble ideology and robs them of the power, which they possess in their attachment to their origin, of witnessing to reality.

Action which is in accordance with Christ is in accordance with reality because it allows the world to be the world; it reckons with the world as the world; and yet it never forgets that in Jesus Christ the world is loved, condemned and reconciled by God. This does not mean that a 'secular principle' and a 'Christian principle' are set up in opposition to one another. On the contrary, any such attempt to achieve some sort of commensurability between Christ and the world at least in the form of a general principle, any such attempt to provide a theoretical basis for Christian action in the world, leads, in the form of secularism or the theory of the autonomy of the various domains of life, or else in the form of enthusiasm, to the ruin and destruction of the world which in Christ is reconciled with God; it leads to those eternal conflicts which constitute the underlying material of all tragedy and which precisely in this destroy the totally untragic unity of Christian life and action. When a secular and a Christian principle are opposed, the ultimate reality is taken to be the law, or more exactly a multiplicity of irreconcilably contradictory laws. It is the essence of Greek tragedy that a man's downfall is brought about by the conflict of incompatible laws. Creon and Antigone, Jason and Medea,

Agamemnon and Clytemnestra, all are subject to the claim of these eternal laws which cannot be reconciled in one and the same life; obedience is rendered to the one law at the price of guilt in respect of the other law. The meaning of all genuine tragedies is not that one man is right and the other wrong, but that both incur guilt towards life itself; the structure of their life is an incurring of guilt in respect of the laws of the gods. This is the most profound experience of classical antiquity. Especially since the Renaissance it has exercised a decisive influence over western thought; in the early periods of the Church and in the Middle Ages there were no tragedies, but in modern times it has only very rarely been perceived that this tragic experience has been overcome by the message of Christ. Even the modern Protestant ethic invokes the pathos of tragedy in its representation of the irreconcilable conflict of the Christian in the world, and claims that in this it is expressing an ultimate reality. All this unconsciously lies entirely under the spell of the heritage of antiquity; it is not Luther, but it is Aeschylus, Sophocles and Euripides who have invested human life with this tragic aspect. The seriousness of Luther is quite different from the seriousness of the classical tragedians. For the Bible and for Luther what ultimately requires to be considered in earnest is not the disunion of the gods in the form of their laws, but it is the unity of God and the reconciliation of the world with God in Jesus Christ; it is not the inescapability of guilt, but it is the simplicity of the life which follows from the reconciliation; it is not fate, but the gospel as the ultimate reality of life; it is not the cruel triumph of the gods over falling man, but it is the election of man to be man as the child of God in the world which is reconciled through grace.

To contrast a secular and a Christian principle as the ultimate reality is to fall back from Christian reality into the reality of antiquity, but it is equally wrong to regard the Christian and the secular as in principle forming a unity. The reconciliation which is accomplished in Christ between God and the world consists simply and solely in the person of Jesus Christ; it consists in Him as the one who acts in the responsibility of deputyship, as the God who for love of man has become man. From Him alone there proceeds human action which is not worn away and wasted in conflicts of principle but which springs from the accomplishment of the reconciliation of the world with God, an action which soberly and simply performs what is in accordance with reality, an action of responsibility in deputyship. It is now no longer established in advance what is 'Christian' and what is 'secular'; both of these are recognized, with their special qualities and with their unity, only in the concrete responsibility of action which springs from the reconciliation that has been effected in Jesus Christ.

We have just said that for action which corresponds with reality the world remains the world, but in the light of our whole discussion so far it is clear that this cannot now mean that the world is in principle isolated or that it is declared to be autonomous. If the world remains the world, that must be because all reality is founded upon Jesus Christ Himself. The world remains the world because it is the world which is loved, condemned and reconciled in Christ. No man has the mission to overleap the world and to make it into the kingdom of God. Nor, on the other hand, does this give support to that pious indolence which abandons the wicked world to its fate and seeks only to rescue its own virtue. Man is appointed to the concrete and therefore limited responsibility which knows the world as being created, loved, condemned and reconciled by God and which acts within the world in accordance with this knowledge. The 'world' is thus the sphere of concrete responsibility which is given to us in and through Jesus Christ. It is not some general concept from which it is possible to derive a self-contained system. A man's attitude to the world does not correspond with reality if he sees in the world a good or an evil which is good or evil in itself, or if he sees in it a principle which is compounded of both good and evil and if he acts in accordance with this view; his attitude accords with reality only if he lives and acts in limited responsibility and thereby allows the world ever anew to disclose its essential character to him.

Action which is in accordance with reality is limited by our creatureliness. We do not ourselves create the conditions of our action, but we find ourselves placed in these conditions from the outset. Our action is limited by definite boundaries in the forward but never in the backward direction, and these boundaries cannot be overstepped. Our responsibility is not infinite; it is limited, even though within these limits it embraces the whole of reality. It is concerned not only with the good will but also with the good outcome of the action, not only with the motive but also with the object; it seeks to attain knowledge of the given totality of the real in its origin, its essence and its goal; it discerns it as subject to the divine 'yes' and 'no'. Since we are not concerned with the realization of an unrestricted principle, it is necessary in the given situation to observe, to weigh up, to assess and to decide, always within the limitations of human knowledge in general. One must risk looking into the immediate future; one must devote earnest thought to the consequences of one's action; and one must endeavour to examine one's own motives and one's own heart. One's task is not to turn the world upside-down, but to do what is necessary at the given place and with a due consideration of reality. At the same time one must ask what are the actual possibilities; it is not always feasible to take the final step at once. Responsible action must not try to be blind. And all this must be so because in Christ God became *man*, because He said 'yes' to mankind, and because it is only we ourselves, as men and in human restriction of judgement and of knowledge in relation to God and to our neighbour, who possess the right and the obligation to live and to act. But because it was *God* who became man, it follows that responsible action, in the consciousness of the human character of its decision, can never itself anticipate the judgement as to whether it is in conformity with its origin, its essence and its goal, but this judgement must be left entirely to God. All ideological action carries its own justification within itself from the outset in its guiding principle, but responsible action does not lay claim to knowledge of its own ultimate righteousness. When the deed is performed with a responsible weighing up of all the personal and objective circumstances and in the awareness that God has become *man* and that it is *God* who has become man, then this deed is delivered up solely to God at the moment of its performance. Ultimate ignorance of one's own good and evil, and with it a complete reliance upon grace, is an essential property of responsible historical action. The man who acts ideologically sees himself justified in his idea; the responsible man commits his action into the hands of God and lives by God's grace and favour.

A further consequence of this limitedness of responsible life and action is that it takes into account the responsibility of the other man who confronts it. Responsibility differs from violence and exploitation precisely in the fact that it recognizes the other man as a responsible agent and indeed that it enables him to become conscious of his responsibility. The responsibility of the father or of the statesman is limited by the responsibility of the child and of the citizen, and indeed the responsibility of the father and of the statesman consists precisely in rendering conscious and in strengthening the responsibility of those who are committed to their care. There can, therefore, never be an absolute responsibility, a responsibility which is not essentially limited by the responsibility of the other man.

We have now seen that the limit of responsible action lies in the fact that the deed ends in the grace and judgement of God and is bounded by the responsibility of our neighbours, and at the same time it becomes evident that it is precisely this limit which makes the action a responsible one. God and our neighbour, as they confront us in Jesus Christ, are not only the limit, but, as we have already perceived, they are also the origin of responsible action. Irresponsible action may be defined precisely by saying that it disregards this limit, God and our neighbour. Responsible action derives its unity, and ultimately also its certainty, from the fact that it is limited in this way by God and by our neighbour. It is precisely because it is not its own master, because it is not unlimited and arrogant but creaturely and humble, that it

THE WORLD OF THINGS

can be sustained by an ultimate joy and confidence and that it can know that it is secure in its origin, its essence and its goal, in Christ.

The World of Things—Pertinence—Statecraft

On the basis of our knowledge that responsibility is always a relation between persons which has its foundation in the responsibility of Jesus Christ for men, on the basis of our knowledge that the origin, essence and goal of all reality is the real, that is to say, God in Jesus Christ, we are now enabled and obliged to say something also about the relation of the responsible man to the domain of things. We will call this relation pertinence. That has two implications.

The first is that that attitude to things is pertinent which keeps steadily in view their original, essential and purposive relation to God and to men. This relation does not corrupt them in their character as things, but it purifies this character; it does not extinguish the ardour of devotion to a cause, but it refines and intensifies it. The greater the purity of the service to a cause or to a thing, and the more completely this service is free from personal subsidiary aims, the more thoroughly the thing itself will recover its original relation to God and to man, and the more completely it will set man free from himself. The thing for the sake of which the ultimate personal sacrifice is made must serve man precisely in this. If, for example, an attempt is made to render a science useful to men in an illegitimately direct manner for demagogic, pedagogic or moralistic purposes, then it is not only the man but also the science which is ruined. If, on the other hand, in this science man exclusively and unreservedly serves the cause of truth, then in the selfless surrender of all his own wishes he finds himself, and the thing for the sake of which he has rendered this selfless service must in the end serve him. Thus it is essential to the pertinence of the action, to the correspondence of the action with the thing, that one should never overlook this relation of the thing or the cause to the person. It is true that we know this relation only in a thoroughly imperfect form. Either the thing makes itself independent of the person or the person makes himself independent of the thing, or else the two stand side by side completely unrelated. What is needful is the restoration of the original relation on the basis of the responsibility which has its foundation in Jesus Christ.

The second implication is that from its origin there is inherent in every thing its own law of being, no matter whether this thing is a natural object or a product of the human mind, and no matter whether it is a material or an ideal entity. We take the word 'thing' in this sense as meaning any datum in which there is inherent an essential law of this kind, no matter whether or to what extent it is a neutral or rather a personal entity. This definition will include the axioms of mathematics and of logic as well as the state or the family, a factory or a commercial company; in every case it is necessary to discover the particular inherent law by virtue of which this entity exists. The more intense the connexion between the thing and the existence of man, the more difficult it becomes to define the law of its being. The laws of logical thought are more easily defined than, for example, the law of the state; and again it is easier to detect the law of a joint-stock company than the law of an organic growth, of the family or of a people. The correspondence of responsible action with reality also involves the detection and pursuit of these laws. The law appears in the first place as a formal technique which requires to be mastered; but the more closely the particular thing with which we are concerned is connected with human existence, the clearer it will become that the law of its being does not consist entirely in a formal technique, but rather that this law renders all technical treatment questionable. The problem of a technique of statecraft is the best example of this, while a technique of radio manufacture is relatively unproblematic. There can be no doubt that statecraft, political science, also has its technical side; there is a technique of administration and a technique of diplomacy; in its widest sense this technical side of statecraft includes all positive legislation, all positive treaties and agreements, and even all those rules and conventions of internal and international political coexistence which are not legally defined but which are sanctioned by history. Finally, it even includes all the generally accepted moral principles of the life of the state. No statesman can disregard any one of these laws and conventions with impunity. Arrogant disdain for them or violation of them denotes a failure to appreciate reality which sooner or later has to be paid for. Pertinent action will conform with these laws and conventions; its observance of them will not be merely hypocritical, but it will regard them as an essential element in all order; it will acknowledge and turn to advantage the wisdom of these conventions which has been achieved through the experience of many generations.[1] Precisely at this point pertinent action will be incontrovertibly compelled to recognize that the essential law of the state comprises something more than these rules and conventions of statecraft. Indeed, precisely because the state is indissolubly bound up with human existence, its essential law extends ultimately far beyond the range of anything that can be expressed in terms of rules. And it is precisely at this point that the full depth of responsible action is achieved.

In the course of historical life there comes a point where the exact observance of the formal law of a state, of a commercial undertaking, of a family, or for that matter of a scientific discovery, suddenly finds itself in violent conflict with the ineluctable necessities of the lives of men; at this point responsible and pertinent action leaves behind it the domain of principle and convention, the domain of the normal and regular, and is confronted by the extraordinary situation of ultimate necessities, a situation which no law can control. It was for this situation that Machiavelli in his political theory coined the term *necessità*. In the field of

[1] Pertinent action is not by any means necessarily dependent on specialist training, as was all too long supposed in Germany. In England pertinent action on a large scale is entrusted not to the specialist but to the amateur. Sociologically speaking, pertinent action will be most effectively ensured by a sound balance of specialism and dilettantism. *Translator's note: sachgemäss* ('pertinent') may bear various meanings within the range 'expedient–appropriate–realistic'.

politics this means that the technique of statecraft has now been supplanted by the necessity of state. There can be no doubt that such necessities exist; to deny their existence is to abandon the attempt to act in accordance with reality. But it is equally certain that these necessities are a primary fact of life itself and cannot, therefore, be governed by any law or themselves constitute a law. They appeal directly to the free responsibility of the agent, a responsibility which is bound by no law. They create a situation which is extraordinary; they are by nature peripheral and abnormal events. They no longer leave a multiplicity of courses open to human reason but they confront it with the question of the *ultima ratio*. In the political field this *ultima ratio* is war, but it can also be deception and the breaking of treaties for the sake of one's own vital needs. In the economic field it is the destruction of human livelihoods in the interest of the necessities of business. The *ultima ratio* lies beyond the laws of reason, it is irrational action. The true order is completely reversed if the *ultima ratio* itself is converted into a rational law, if the peripheral case is treated as the normal, and if *necessità* is made a technique. Baldwin was right when he said that there was only one greater evil than violence and that this was violence as a principle, as a law and a standard. He did not mean by this the extraordinary and abnormal necessity of the use of violence as the *ultima ratio*; if he had meant that he would have been a mere enthusiast and not a statesman; above all he did not wish to see the extraordinary and peripheral case confused with the normal case, with the law. He wished to preserve the relative order which is secured through the pertinent observance of law and convention, when to abandon this order for the sake of a peripheral event would mean chaos.

The extraordinary necessity appeals to the freedom of the men who are responsible. There is now no law behind which the responsible man can seek cover, and there is, therefore, also no law which can compel the responsible man to take any particular decision in the face of such necessities. In this situation there can only be a complete renunciation of every law, together with the knowledge that here one must make one's decision as a free venture, together also with the open admission that here the law is being infringed and violated and that necessity obeys no commandment. Precisely in this breaking of the law the validity of the law is acknowledged, and in this renunciation of all law, and in this alone, one's own decision and deed are entrusted unreservedly to the divine governance of history.

There can be no theoretical answer to the question whether in historical action the ultimate goal is the eternal law or free responsibility in the face of all law but before God. Great nations are opposed in this in an insurmountable and ultimate antinomy. The greatness of British statesmen, and I am thinking here, for example, of Gladstone, is that they acknowledge the law as the ultimate authority; and the greatness of German statesmen—I am thinking now of Bismarck—is that they come before God in free responsibility. In this neither can claim to be superior to the other. The ultimate question remains open and must be kept open, for in either case man becomes guilty, and in either case he can live only by the grace of God and by forgiveness. Each of these men, the one who is bound by the law and the one who acts in free responsibility, must hear and bow before the accusation of the other. Neither can be the judge of the other. It is always for God to judge.

The Acceptance of Guilt

From what has just been said it emerges that the structure of responsible action includes both readiness to accept guilt and freedom.

When we once more turn our attention to the origin of all responsibility it becomes clear to us what we are to understand by acceptance of guilt. Jesus is not concerned with the proclamation and realization of new ethical ideals; He is not concerned with Himself being good (Matt. 19.17); He is concerned solely with love for the real man, and for that reason He is able to enter into the fellowship of the guilt of men and to take the burden of their guilt upon Himself. Jesus does not desire to be regarded as the only perfect one at the expense of men; He does not desire to look down on mankind as the only guiltless one while mankind goes to its ruin under the weight of its guilt; He does not wish that some idea of a new man should triumph amid the wreckage of a humanity whose guilt has destroyed it. He does not wish to acquit Himself of the guilt under which men die. A love which left man alone in his guilt would not be love for the real man. As one who acts responsibly in the historical existence of men Jesus becomes guilty. It must be emphasized that it is solely His love which makes Him incur guilt. From His selfless love, from His freedom from sin, Jesus enters into the guilt of men and takes this guilt upon Himself. Freedom from sin and the question of guilt are inseparable in Him. It is as the one who is without sin that Jesus takes upon Himself the guilt of His brothers, and it is under the burden of this guilt that He shows Himself to be without sin. In this Jesus Christ, who is guilty without sin, lies the origin of every action of responsible deputyship. If it is responsible action, if it is action which is concerned solely and entirely with the other man, if it arises from selfless love for the real man who is our brother, then, precisely because this is so, it cannot wish to shun the fellowship of human guilt. Jesus took upon Himself the guilt of all men, and for that reason every man who acts responsibly becomes guilty. If any man tries to escape guilt in responsibility he detaches himself from the ultimate reality of human existence, and what is more he cuts himself off from the redeeming mystery of Christ's bearing guilt without sin and he has no share in the divine justification which lies upon this event. He sets his own personal innocence above his responsibility for men, and he is blind to the more irredeemable guilt which he incurs precisely in this; he is blind also to the fact that real innocence shows itself precisely in a man's entering into the fellowship of guilt for the sake of other men. Through Jesus Christ it becomes an essential part of responsible action that the man who is without sin loves selflessly and for that reason incurs guilt.

Conscience

There is a reply to all this which undeniably commands respect. It comes from the high authority of conscience; for conscience is unwilling to sacrifice its integrity to any other value, and it therefore refuses to incur guilt for the sake of another man. Responsibility for our neighbour is cut short by the inviolable call of conscience. A responsibility which would oblige a man to act against his conscience would carry within it its own condemnation. In what respects is this true and in what respects is it false?

It is true that it can never be advisable to act against one's own conscience. All Christian ethics is agreed in this. But what does that mean? Conscience comes from a depth which lies beyond a man's own will and his own reason and it makes itself heard as the call of human existence to unity with itself. Conscience comes as an indictment of the loss of this unity and as a warning against the loss of one's self. Primarily it is directed not towards a particular kind of doing but towards a particular mode of being. It protests against a doing which imperils the unity of this being with itself.

So long as conscience can be formally defined in these terms it is extremely inadvisable to act against its authority; disregard for the call of conscience will necessarily entail the destruction of one's own being, not even a purposeful surrender of it; it will bring about the decline and collapse of a human existence. Action against one's own conscience runs parallel with suicidal action against one's own life, and it is not by chance that the two often go together. Responsible action which did violence to conscience in this formal sense would indeed be reprehensible.

But that is not by any means the end of the question. The call of conscience arises from the imperilling of a man's unity with himself, and it is therefore now necessary to ask what constitutes this unity. The first constituent is the man's own ego in its claim to be 'like God', *sicut deus*, in the knowledge of good and evil. The call of conscience in natural man is the attempt on the part of the ego to justify itself in its knowledge of good and evil before God, before men and before itself, and to secure its own continuance in this self-justification. Finding no firm support in its own contingent individuality the ego traces its own derivation back to a universal law of good and seeks to achieve unity with itself in conformity with this law. Thus the call of conscience has its origin and its goal in the autonomy of a man's own ego. A man's purpose in obeying this call is on each occasion anew that he should himself once more realize this autonomy which has its origin beyond his own will and knowledge 'in Adam'. Thus in his conscience he continues to be bound by a law of his own finding, a law which may assume different concrete forms but which he can transgress only at the price of losing his own self.

We can now understand that the great change takes place at the moment when the unity of human existence ceases to consist in its autonomy and is found, through the miracle of faith, beyond the man's own ego and its law, in Jesus Christ. The form of this change in the point of unity has an exact analogy in the secular sphere. When the national socialist says 'My conscience is Adolf Hitler' that, too, is an attempt to find a foundation for the unity of his own ego somewhere beyond himself. The consequence of this is the surrender of one's autonomy for the sake of an unconditional heteronomy, and this in turn is possible only if the other man, the man to whom I look for the unity of my life, fulfils the function of a redeemer for me. This, then, provides an extremely direct and significant parallel to the Christian truth, and at the same time an extremely direct and significant contrast with it.

When Christ, true God and true man, has become the point of unity of my existence, conscience will indeed still formally be the call of my actual being to unity with myself, but this unity cannot now be realized by means of a return to the autonomy which I derive from the law; it must be realized in fellowship with Jesus Christ. Natural conscience, no matter how strict and rigorous it may be, is now seen to be the most ungodly self-justification, and it is overcome by the conscience which is set free in Jesus Christ and which summons me to unity with myself in Jesus Christ. Jesus

Christ has become my conscience. This means that I can now find unity with myself only in the surrender of my ego to God and to men. The origin and the goal of my conscience is not a law but it is the living God and the living man as he confronts me in Jesus Christ. For the sake of God and of men Jesus became a breaker of the law. He broke the law of the Sabbath in order to keep it holy in love for God and for men. He forsook His parents in order to dwell in the house of His Father and thereby to purify His obedience towards His parents. He sat at table with sinners and outcasts; and for the love of men He came to be forsaken by God in His last hour. As the one who loved without sin, He became guilty; He wished to share in the fellowship of human guilt; He rejected the devil's accusation which was intended to divert Him from this course. Thus it is Jesus Christ who sets conscience free for the service of God and of our neighbour; He sets conscience free even and especially when man enters into the fellowship of human guilt. The conscience which has been set free from the law will not be afraid to enter into the guilt of another man for the other man's sake, and indeed precisely in doing this it will show itself in its purity. The conscience which has been set free is not timid like the conscience which is bound by the law, but it stands wide open for our neighbour and for his concrete distress. And so conscience joins with the responsibility which has its foundation in Christ in bearing guilt for the sake of our neighbour. Human action is poisoned in a way which differs from essential original sin, yet as responsible action, in contrast to any self-righteously high-principled action, it nevertheless indirectly has a part in the action of Jesus Christ. For responsible action, therefore, there is a kind of relative freedom from sin, and this shows itself precisely in the responsible acceptance of the guilt of others.

From the principle of truthfulness Kant draws the grotesque conclusion that I must even return an honest 'yes' to the enquiry of the murderer who breaks into my house and asks whether my friend whom he is pursuing has taken refuge there; in such a case self-righteousness of conscience has become outrageous presumption and blocks the path of responsible action. Responsibility is the total and realistic response of man to the claim of God and of our neighbour; but this example shows in its true light how the response of a conscience which is bound by principles is only a partial one. If I refuse to incur guilt against the principle of truthfulness for the sake of my friend, if I refuse to tell a robust lie for the sake of my friend (for it is only the self-righteously law-abiding conscience which will pretend that, in fact, no lie is involved), if, in other words, I refuse to bear guilt for charity's sake, then my action is in contradiction to my responsibility which has its foundation in reality. Here again it is precisely in the responsible acceptance of guilt that a conscience which is bound solely to Christ will best prove its innocence.

It is astonishing how close Goethe came to these ideas with a purely profane knowledge of reality. In the dialogue in which Pylades tries to persuade Iphigenia to overcome the inner law and to act responsibly we read:

PYLADES   An over-strict demand is secret pride.

IPHIGENIA   The spotless heart alone is satisfied.[1]

PYLADES   Here in the temple you no doubt were so;
 And yet life teaches us to be less strict
 With others and ourselves; you too will learn.
 This human kind is intricately wrought
 With knots and ties so manifold that none
 Within himself or with the rest can keep
 Himself quiet disentangled and quite pure.
 We are not competent to judge ourselves;
 Man's first and foremost duty is to go
 Forward and think about his future course:
 For he can seldom know what he has done,
 And what he now is doing even less . . .
 One sees that you have rarely suffered loss;
 For if that were not so you would not now
 Refuse this one false word to escape this evil.

[1] (More exactly: . . . has enjoyment of itself.) The introduction of the characteristic concept of 'enjoyment' is also to be noted here.

IPHIGENIA   Would my heart like a man's could be resolved
And then be deaf to any other voice!

However greatly responsibility and the conscience which is set free in Christ may desire to be united, they nevertheless continue to confront one another in a relation of irreducible tension. Conscience imposes two kinds of limit upon that bearing of guilt which from time to time becomes necessary in responsible action.

In the first place, the conscience which is set free in Christ is still essentially the summons to unity with myself. The acceptance of a responsibility must not destroy this unity. The surrender of the ego in selfless service must never be confused with the destruction and annihilation of this ego; for then indeed this ego would no longer be capable of assuming responsibility. The extent of the guilt which may be accepted in the pursuit of responsible action is on each occasion concretely limited by the requirement of the man's unity with himself, that is to say, by his carrying power. There are responsibilities which I cannot carry without breaking down under their weight; it may be a declaration of war, the violation of a political treaty, a revolution or merely the discharge of a single employee who thereby loses the means of supporting his family; or it may be simply a piece of advice in connexion with some personal decisions in life. Certainly the strength to bear responsible decisions can and should grow; certainly any failure to fulfil a responsibility is in itself already a responsible decision; and yet in the concrete instance the summons of conscience to unity with oneself in Jesus Christ remains irresistible, and it is this which explains the infinite multiplicity of responsible decisions.

Secondly, even when it is set free in Jesus Christ conscience still confronts responsible action with the law, through obedience to which man is preserved in that unity with himself which has its foundation in Jesus Christ. Disregard for this law can give rise only to irresponsibility. This is the law of love for God and for our neighbour as it is explained in the decalogue, in the sermon on the mount and in the apostolic paranesis. It has been correctly observed that in the contents of its law natural conscience is in strikingly close agreement with that of the conscience which has been set free in Christ. This is due to the fact that it is upon conscience that the continuance of life itself depends; conscience, therefore, contains fundamental features of the law of life, even though these features may be distorted in detail and perverted in principle. The liberated conscience is still what it was as the natural conscience, namely the warner against transgression of the law of life. But the law is no longer the last thing; there is still Jesus Christ; for that reason, in the contest between conscience and concrete responsibility, the free decision must be given for Christ. This does not mean an everlasting conflict, but the winning of ultimate unity; for indeed the foundation, the essence and the goal of concrete responsibility is the same Jesus Christ who is the Lord of conscience. Thus responsibility is bound by conscience, but conscience is set free by responsibility. It is now clear that it is the same thing if we say that the responsible man becomes guilty without sin or if we say that only the man with a free conscience can bear responsibility.

When a man takes guilt upon himself in responsibility, and no responsible man can avoid this, he imputes this guilt to himself and to no one else; he answers for it; he accepts responsibility for it. He does not do this in the insolent presumptuousness of his own power, but he does it in the knowledge that this liberty is forced upon him and that in this liberty he is dependent on grace. Before other men the man of free responsibility is justified by necessity; before himself he is acquitted by his conscience; but before God he hopes only for mercy.

Freedom

We must therefore conclude our analysis of the structure of responsible action by speaking of freedom.

Responsibility and freedom are corresponding concepts. Factually, though not chronologically, responsibility presupposes freedom and freedom can consist only in responsibility. Responsibility is the freedom of men which is given only in the obligation to God and to our neighbour.

The responsible man acts in the freedom of his own self, without the support of men, circumstances or principles, but with a due consideration for the given human and general conditions and for the relevant questions of principle. The proof of his freedom is the fact that nothing can answer for him, nothing can exonerate him, except his own deed and his own self. It is he himself who must observe, judge, weigh up, decide and act. It is man himself who must examine the motives, the prospects, the value and the purpose of his action. But neither the purity of the motivation, nor the opportune circumstances, nor the value, nor the significant purpose of an intended undertaking can become the governing law of his action, a law to which he can withdraw, to which he can appeal as an authority, and by which he can be exculpated and acquitted.[1] For in that case he would indeed no longer be truly free. The action of the responsible man is performed in the obligation which alone gives freedom and which gives entire freedom, the obligation to God and to our neighbour as they confront us in Jesus Christ. At the same time it is performed wholly within the domain of relativity, wholly in the twilight which the historical situation spreads over good and evil; it is performed in the midst of the innumerable perspectives in which every given phenomenon appears. It has not to decide simply between right and wrong and between good and evil, but between right and right and between wrong and wrong. As Aeschylus said, 'right strives with right'. Precisely in this respect responsible action is a free venture; it is not justified by any law; it is performed without any claim to a valid self-justification, and therefore also without any claim to an ultimate valid knowledge of good and evil. Good, as what is responsible, is performed in ignorance of good and in the surrender to God of the deed

[1] This makes it unnecessary to raise the fallacious question of determinism and indeterminism, in which the essence of mental decision is incorrectly substituted for the law of causality.

which has become necessary and which is nevertheless, or
for that very reason, free; for it is God who sees the heart,
who weighs up the deed, and who directs the course of
history.

With this there is disclosed to us a deep secret of history in
general. The man who acts in the freedom of his own most
personal responsibility is precisely the man who sees his
action finally committed to the guidance of God. The free
deed knows itself in the end as the deed of God; the decision
knows itself as guidance; the free venture knows itself as
divine necessity. It is in the free abandonment of knowledge
of his own good that a man performs the good of God. It is
only from this last point of view that one can speak of good
in historical action. We shall have to take up these considerations again later at the point at which we have left off.

Before that we still have to give some space to a crucial
question which makes an essential contribution to the
clarification of our problem. What is the relationship between
free responsibility and obedience? It must seem at first sight
as though everything we have said about free responsibility is
applicable in practice only when a man finds himself in what
we call a 'responsible position' in life, in other words when he
has to take independent decisions on the very largest scale.
What connexion can there be between responsibility and the
monotonous daily work of the labourer, the factory worker,
the clerk, the private soldier, the apprentice or the schoolboy?
It is a different matter already with the owner-farmer, the
industrial contractor, the politician or statesman, the general,
the master craftsman, the teacher and the judge. But in their
lives, too, how much there is of technique and duty and how
little of really free decision! And so it seems that everything
that we have said about responsibility can in the end apply
only to a very small group of men, and even to these only in
a few moments of their lives; and consequently it seems as
though for the great majority of men one must speak not of
responsibility but of obedience and duty. This implies one
ethic for the great and the strong, for the rulers, and another
for the small and the weak, the subordinates; on the one hand

responsibility and on the other obedience, on the one hand freedom and on the other subservience. And indeed there can be no doubt that in our modern social order, and especially in the German one, the life of the individual is so exactly defined and regulated, and is at the same time assured of such complete security, that it is granted to only very few men to breathe the free air of the wide open spaces of great decisions and to experience the hazard of responsible action which is entirely their own. In consequence of the compulsory regulation of life in accordance with a definite course of training and vocational activity, our lives have come to be relatively free from ethical dangers; the individual who from his childhood on has had to take his assigned place in accordance with this principle is ethically emasculated; he has been robbed of the creative moral power, freedom. In this we see a deepseated fault in the essential development of our modern social order, a fault which can be countered only with a clear exposition of the fundamental concept of responsibility. As things stand, the large-scale experiential material for the problem of responsibility must be sought for among the great political leaders, industrialists and generals; for indeed those few others who venture to act on their own free responsibility in the midst of the pressure of everyday life are crushed by the machinery of the social order, by the general routine.

Yet it would be an error if we were to continue to look at the problem from this point of view. There is, in fact, no single life which cannot experience the situation of responsibility; every life can experience this situation in its most characteristic form, that is to say, in the encounter with other people. Even when free responsibility is more or less excluded from a man's vocational and public life, he nevertheless always stands in a responsible relation to other men; these relations extend from his family to his workmates. The fulfilment of genuine responsibility at this point affords the only sound possibility of extending the sphere of responsibility once more into vocational and public life. Where man meets man—and this includes the encounters of professional life—there arises genuine responsibility, and these responsible relationships cannot be supplanted by any general regulation or routine. That holds true, then, not only for the relation between married people, or for parents and children, but also for the master and the apprentice, the teacher and his pupil, the judge and the accused.

But we can go one step further than this. Responsibility does not only stand side by side with relationships of obedience; it has its place also within these relationships. The apprentice has a duty of obedience towards his master, but at the same time he has also a free responsibility for his work, for his achievement and, therefore, also for his master. It is the same with the schoolboy and the student, and indeed also with the employee in any kind of industrial undertaking and with the soldier in war. Obedience and responsibility are interlinked in such a way that one cannot say that responsibility begins only where obedience leaves off, but rather that obedience is rendered in responsibility. There will always be a relation of obedience and dependence; all that matters is that these should not, as they already largely do today, leave no room for responsibilities. To know himself to be responsible is more difficult for the man who is socially dependent than for the man who is socially free, but a relationship of dependence does not in any case in itself exclude free responsibility. The master and the servant, while preserving the relationship of obedience, can and should answer for each other in free responsibility.

The ultimate reason for this lies in that relation of men to God which is realized in Jesus Christ. Jesus stands before God as the one who is both obedient and free. As the obedient one He does His Father's will in blind compliance with the law which is commanded Him, and as the free one He acquiesces in God's will out of His own most personal knowledge, with open eyes and a joyous heart; He recreates this will, as it were, out of Himself. Obedience without freedom is slavery; freedom without obedience is arbitrary self-will. Obedience restrains freedom; and freedom ennobles obedience. Obedience binds the creature to the Creator, and freedom enables the creature to stand before the Creator as one who is made in His image. Obedience shows man that he must allow himself to be told what is good and what God requires of him (Micah 6.8); and liberty enables him to do good himself. Obedience knows what is good and does it, and freedom dares to act, and abandons to God the judgement of good and evil. Obedience follows blindly and freedom has open eyes. Obedience acts without questioning and freedom asks what is the purpose. Obedience has its hands tied and freedom is creative. In obedience man adheres to the decalogue and in freedom man creates new decalogues (Luther).

In responsibility both obedience and freedom are realized. Responsibility implies tension between obedience and freedom. There would be no more responsibility if either were made independent of the other. Responsible action is subject to obligation, and yet it is creative. To make obedience independent of freedom leads only to the Kantian ethic of duty, and to make freedom independent of obedience leads only to the ethic of irresponsible genius. Both the man of duty and the genius carry their justification within themselves. The man of responsibility stands between obligation and freedom; he must dare to act under obligation and in freedom; yet he finds his justification neither in his obligation nor in his freedom but solely in Him who has put him in this (humanly impossible) situation and who requires this deed of him. The responsible man delivers up himself and his deed to God.

We have tried to define the structure of responsible life in terms of deputyship, correspondence with reality, acceptance of guilt, and freedom. Now the demand for a more concrete formulation brings us to the question whether it is possible to advance a more exact definition of the place, the *locus*, at which responsible life is realized. Does responsibility set me in an unlimited field of activity? Or does it confine me strictly within the limits which are implied in my daily concrete tasks? What must I know myself to be responsible for? And what does not lie within the scope of my responsibility? Is there any purpose in regarding myself as responsible for everything that takes place in the world? Or can I stand by and watch these great events as an unconcerned spectator so long as my own tiny domain is in order? Am I to wear myself out in impotent zeal against all the wrong and all the misery that is in the world? Or am I entitled, in self-satisfied security, to let the wicked world run its course, so long as I cannot myself do anything to change it and so long as I have done my own work? What is the place and what are the limits of my responsibility?

THE PLACE OF RESPONSIBILITY
Vocation

In having recourse to this concept which has come to be of almost unique significance for the history of ethics, namely, the concept of the calling, we must from the outset bear clearly in mind the following four points. First of all we are not thinking here of the secularized concept of the calling which Max Weber defines as a 'limited field of accomplishments'. Secondly, we are not thinking of that pseudo-Lutheran view for which the concept of vocation simply provides the justification and sanctification of secular institutions. Thirdly, even Luther's own conception of vocation cannot unreservedly be identified with the New Testament conception, just as in his translation of Rom. 3.28 he very boldly ascribes to the New Testament concept (I Cor. 7.20) a fulness of meaning which is indeed essentially justified but which goes beyond the normal linguistic usage. We shall therefore base ourselves on the biblical text as we find it. Fourthly, even though the terms 'vocation' and 'responsibility' in our current language are not identical with the New Testament concepts, they nevertheless correspond so remarkably happily that there is especially good reason for employing them.

In the encounter with Jesus Christ man hears the call of God and in it the calling to life in the fellowship of Jesus Christ. Divine grace comes upon man and lays claim to him. It is not man who seeks out grace in its own place—God dwelleth in the light which no man can approach unto (I Tim. 6.16), but it is grace which seeks and finds man in *his* place—the Word was made flesh (John 1.14)—and which precisely in this place lays claim to him. This is a place which in every instance and in every respect is laden with sin and guilt, no matter whether it be a royal throne, the parlour of a respectable citizen or a miserable hovel. It is a place which is of this world. This visitation of man by grace occurred in the incarnation of Jesus Christ, and it occurs in the word of Jesus Christ which is brought by the Holy Ghost. The call comes to man as a Gentile or as a Jew, free man or slave, man or woman, married or single. At the precise place where he is he is to hear the call and to allow it to lay claim to him. This does not mean that servitude or marriage or celibacy in itself is thereby justified; but the man who has been called can in any of these places belong to God. It is only through the call which I have heard in Christ, the call of the grace which lays claim to me, that, as a slave or as a free man, married or celibate, I can live justified before God. From the standpoint of Christ this life is now my calling; from my own standpoint it is my responsibility.

This will have excluded two disastrous misunderstandings, the secular Protestant one and the monastic one. It is not in the loyal discharge of the earthly obligations of his calling as a citizen, a worker and a father that a man fulfils the responsibility which is imposed on him, but it is in hearing the call of Jesus Christ. This call does indeed summon him to earthly duties, but that is never the whole of the call, for it lies always beyond these duties, before them and behind them. The calling, in the New Testament sense, is never a sanctioning of worldly institutions as such; its 'yes' to them always includes at the same time an extremely emphatic 'no', an extremely sharp protest against the world. Luther's return from the monastery to the world, to the 'calling', is, in the true New Testament sense, the fiercest attack and assault to be launched against the world since primitive Christianity. Now a man takes up his position against the world *in* the world; the calling is the place at which the call of Christ is answered, the place at which a man lives responsibly. Thus the task which is appointed for me in my calling is a limited one, but at the same time the responsibility to the call of Jesus Christ breaks through all limits.

The misunderstanding on the part of medieval monasticism does not lie in its recognition of the fact that the call of Jesus Christ involves man in a struggle against the world but in its attempt to find a place which is not the world and at which this call can, therefore, be answered more fitly. In this vain endeavour to escape from the world no serious consideration is given either to the 'no' of God, which is addressed to the whole world, including the monastery, or to God's 'yes', in which He reconciles the world with Himself. Consequently, even in its 'no' to the world, God's call is taken less seriously in the monastic undertaking than in the secular calling as Luther (though not indeed pseudo-Lutheranism) understood it. It is entirely in line with Luther if we say that in a certain concrete instance the answer to the call of Jesus Christ may even consist in leaving a particular earthly calling in which one can no longer live responsibly. This thought is unacceptable only to pseudo-Lutheranism, with its belief in the sanctity of vocational duties and of earthly institutions as such, and with its belief that the world is everywhere good. Monasticism is right in so far as it is a protest against the misrepresentation of the New Testament idea of vocation. Luther, in his return to the world, was concerned solely for the total responsibility to the call of Christ. In this respect the monastic solution is doubly wrong. It restricts the compass of ultimately responsible life to the walls of the monastery, and it can only interpret as worthless compromise the life in which a man endeavours to unite in concrete responsibility to the call of Jesus Christ the 'yes' and the 'no' to life in the world which are implicit in that call. In answer to this failure to appreciate the responsibility of men, Luther invested this responsibility with a significance which is limited and yet at the same time has its foundations in the limitless. While doing this he rewarded the fulfilment of the earthly calling in responsibility to the call of Jesus Christ with the free and joyful conscience which springs from fellowship with Jesus Christ. The good and free conscience, therefore, does not come from the fulfilment of earthly vocational duty as such, for here conscience continues to be wounded by the unresolved conflict between a plurality of duties, so that the best that can be hoped for is the compromise of a divided conscience. It is only when the concrete vocation is fulfilled in responsibility towards the call of Jesus Christ, it is only upon the foundation of the knowledge of the incarnation of Jesus Christ, that conscience can be free in concrete action. The call of Christ alone, when it is responsibly obeyed in the calling, prevails over the compromise and over the conscience which this compromise has rendered insecure.

It follows from this that on the one side the centre of my responsibility is determined by the call of Jesus Christ which is addressed to me.

Our enquiry as to the place and the limit of responsibility has led us to the concept of the calling. This answer is properly applicable only when the calling is understood simultaneously in all its dimensions. The calling is the call of Jesus Christ to belong wholly to Him; it is the laying claim to me by Christ at the place at which this call has found me; it embraces work with things and relations with persons; it demands a 'limited field of accomplishments', yet never as a value in itself, but in responsibility towards Jesus Christ. Through this relation to Christ the 'limited field of accomplishments' is freed from its isolation. Its boundary is broken through not only from above, that is to say by Christ, but also in an outward direction. If, for example, I am a physician, then in the concrete instance I serve not only my patients but also medical science and with it science and the knowledge of truth in general. Although in practice I perform this service at my concrete position, for example at the bedside of a patient, yet I am continuously aware of my responsibility for the whole, and it is only in this that I fulfil my calling. Furthermore, it may happen that I, as a physician, am obliged to recognize and fulfil my concrete responsibility no longer by the sick-bed but, for example, in taking public action against some measure which constitutes a threat to medical science or to human life or to science as such. Vocation is responsibility

225

and responsibility is a total response of the whole man
to the whole of reality; for this very reason there can be no
petty and pedantic restricting of one's interests to one's
professional duties in the narrowest sense. Any such restriction
would be irresponsibility. The essential character of free
responsibility makes it impossible to establish laws defining
when and to what extent such a departure from the 'limited
field of accomplishments' forms part of a man's calling and
of his responsibility towards men. Such a departure can be
undertaken only after a serious weighing up of the vocational
duty which is directly given, of the dangers of interference in
the responsibility of others, and finally of the totality of the
question which is involved; when this is done I shall be
guided in the one direction or the other by a free responsibility towards the call of Jesus Christ. Responsibility in one's
calling obeys only the call of Christ. There is a wrong and a
right restriction and there is a wrong and a right extension
of responsibility; there is an enthusiastic breaking-down of
all limits, and there is a legalistic setting-up of limits. It is
difficult, or even impossible, to judge from outside whether in
a particular concrete instance an action is responsible or
whether it is enthusiastic or legalistic; there are, however,
criteria for self-examination, though even these cannot afford
complete certainty about one's own ego. The following are
among such criteria. Neither the limitation nor the extension
of my responsibility must be based on a principle; the only
possible basis for them is the concrete call of Jesus. If I know
myself to be by character inclined towards reforming zeal,
towards knowing better and towards fanaticism and unrestraint, then I shall be in danger of extending my responsibility in an arbitrary fashion and confusing my natural
impulses with the call of Jesus. If I know myself to be prudent,
cautious, diffident and law-abiding, then I shall have to
guard against representing the restriction of my responsibility to a narrow field as the call of Jesus Christ. And,
finally, it is never in thinking of myself, but it is always in
thinking of the call of Christ, that I shall be set free for
genuine responsibility.

Nietzsche, without knowing it, was speaking in the spirit of the New Testament when he attacked the legalistic and philistine misinterpretation of the commandment which bids us love our neighbour. He wrote: 'You are assiduous in your attentions to your neighbour and you find beautiful words to describe your assiduity. But I tell you that your love for your neighbour is a worthless love for yourselves. You go to your neighbour to seek refuge from yourselves and then you try to make a virtue of it; but I see through your "unselfishness" ... Do I advise you to love your neighbour? I advise you rather to shun your neighbour and to love whoever is furthest from you!' Beyond the neighbour who is committed to us by the call of Jesus there stands also for Jesus the one who is furthest from us, namely, Jesus Christ Himself, God Himself. If beyond his neighbour a man does not know this one who is furthest from him, and if he does not know this one who is furthest from him as this neighbour, then he does not serve his neighbour but himself; he takes refuge from the free open space of responsibility in the comforting confinement of the fulfilment of duty. This means that the commandment of love for our neighbour also does not imply a law which restricts our responsibility solely to our neighbour in terms of space, to the man whom I encounter socially, professionally or in my family. My neighbour may well be one who is extremely remote from me, and one who is extremely remote from me may well be my neighbour. By a terrible miscarriage of justice in the United States in 1831 nine young negroes, whose guilt could not be proved, were sentenced to death for the rape of a white girl of doubtful reputation. There arose a storm of indignation which found expression in open letters from some of the most authoritative public figures in Europe. A Christian who was perturbed by this affair asked a prominent cleric in Germany whether he, too, ought not to raise his voice in the matter, and on the grounds of the 'Lutheran' idea of vocation, that is to say, on the grounds of the limitation of his responsibility, the clergyman refused. In the event the protests which came in from all parts of the world led to a revision of the judgement.

Here perhaps it is from the point of view of the call of
Jesus Christ that we may understand the saying of Nietzsche:
'My brothers, I do not counsel you to love your neighbour;
I counsel you to love him who is furthest from you'. We do
not say this in order to pass judgement in the particular case
to which we have just referred. We say it in order to keep
open the boundary.

No one can fail to hear the Bible's admonitions to do what
is waiting to be done (Eccl. 9.10), to be exact in small
matters (Luke 16.10 and 19.17), to discharge one's domestic
obligations before undertaking greater duties (I Tim. 3.5),
and to refrain from interfering in the functions of others
(I Pet. 4.15). Yet all these admonitions are contingent on
the call of Christ, and they do not, therefore, imply any
law which sets limits to the free responsibility towards this
call. In the course of the struggle of the churches in Germany
it happened often enough that a minister refused to intervene
publicly and responsibly in cases of distress and persecution
of various kinds precisely because his own flock were not yet
themselves affected; he did not do this from cowardice or
from lack of enterprise but solely because he considered
such an intervention to be an unlawful overstepping of the
calling which had been given to him, namely, his vocation to
assist his flock in their distress and in their temptations. If
subsequently his own flock came to be involved, then there
often ensued an act of thoroughly authoritative and free
responsibility. This again is not said in order to anticipate
judgement but in order to preserve the openness of the
commandment of brotherly love in the face of any false
limitation and in order to safeguard the concept of vocation
in the liberty with which the gospel invests it.

But is not all responsible action in one's calling confined
within inviolable limits by the law of God as it is revealed in
the ten commandments as well as by the divine mandates of
marriage, labour and government? Would not any overstepping of these limits constitute an infringement of the
manifest will of God? Here there arises once again in its most
acute form the problem of law and liberty. This problem now

threatens to implant a contradiction in the will of God itself. Certainly there can be no responsible action which does not devote extremely serious consideration to the limit which is given through God's law, and yet it is precisely responsible action which will not separate this law from its Giver. It is only as the Redeemer in Jesus Christ that responsible action will be able to recognize the God who holds the world in order by His law; it will recognize Jesus Christ as the ultimate reality towards which it is responsible, and it is precisely by Him that it will be set free from the law for the responsible deed. For the sake of God and of our neighbour, and that means for the sake of Christ, there is a freedom from the keeping holy of the Sabbath, from the honouring of our parents, and indeed from the whole of the divine law, a freedom which breaks this law, but only in order to give effect to it anew. The suspension of the law can only serve the true fulfilment of it. In war, for example, there is killing, lying and expropriation solely in order that the authority of life, truth and property may be restored. A breach of the law must be recognized in all its gravity. 'Blessed art thou if thou knowest what thou doest; but if thou knowest it not, then art thou accursed and a transgressor of the law' (Luke 6.4 in Codex D). Whether an action arises from responsibility or from cynicism is shown only by whether or not the objective guilt of the violation of the law is recognized and acknowledged, and by whether or not, precisely in this violation, the law is hallowed. It is in this way that the will of God is hallowed in the deed which arises from freedom. But since this is a deed which arises from freedom, man is not torn asunder in deadly conflict, but in certainty and in unity with himself he can dare to hallow the law truly even by breaking it.[1]

---

[1] *Editor's note.* A further section was planned for inclusion here under the title *Love and Responsibility.* A preparatory note gives the following outline under the heading 'Responsibility': '1. The Word in its Comprehensive Sense. 2. The Structure of Responsible Life. (*a*) Liberty, Deputyship. (*b*) Realism. (*c*) Acceptance of Guilt. (*d*) Liberty, Venture, Delivering up of the Deed, the Question of Purpose or Significance. 3. The Sphere of Responsibility. (*a*) The Commandments. (*b*) The Divine Mandates. (*c*) The Given Calling. (*d*) Free,

Spontaneous, Accepted Responsibility (the Overcoming of these Spaces in Depth and in Breadth—What am I responsible for?). 4. Contradiction and Unity in Responsibility. (*a*) Love and Responsibility. (*b*) Politics and the Sermon on the Mount. (*c*) Christ the Vital Law of History. (*d*) The Cosmic Form of Love.'

VII

THE 'ETHICAL' AND THE 'CHRISTIAN' AS A THEME

The Warrant for Ethical Discourse

A CHRISTIAN ethic will have to begin by asking whether and to what extent it is possible at all to treat the 'ethical' and the 'Christian' as a theme, for that is not by any means so self-evident as one might assume from the confidence with which this repeatedly has been and is being done. We cannot, in fact, even set foot in the field of Christian ethics until we have first of all recognized how extremely questionable a course we are pursuing if we take the 'ethical' and the 'Christian' as a theme for our consideration or discussion or even as a subject for scientific exposition.

One particular treatment of the ethical as a theme is excluded from the outset so far as a Christian ethic is concerned. More perhaps than in a good many instructional manuals of Christian ethics, we may, within certain limits, detect a profound understanding of the essence of the 'ethical' in the saying 'morality is always self-evident', which F. T. Vischer puts into the mouth of his 'Another' as a gently ironical protest against any attempt to allow the ethical to become an independent topic of discussion. This protest is directed not merely against the over-loud and over-obtrusive spoken and written word, but also and especially against the inner process to which this word corresponds. 'The higher level goes without saying! It is the basis, the preconditions, that must be taken care of!' says 'Another'. The great decision, the great situation, what Vischer calls 'the upper storey', is self-evident, simple and clear without the need for many words. What is difficult and problematic, what requires the very closest attention, is the 'lower storey' of 'disharmonies and frustrations', irregularities and accidents.

'I cannot calculate them or organize them;' complains 'Another', 'they run round in circles and in all directions; it is quite impossible for me to tie them down ... after all there can be no plan for dealing with what is without a plan, and no system for dealing with what is entirely devoid of system.' In other words it is the sphere of everyday happenings which raises the really essential difficulties and which one must have experienced in order to perceive that the enunciation of general moral principles is completely inadequate and unfitted for coming to grips with it. For 'Another' there is no problem in the question of whether I shall help someone who is in distress or whether I shall intervene to prevent a man from tormenting an animal. It 'goes without saying'. But it is quite a different matter when we have to deal with the small everyday troubles such as the 'common cold' and the 'perversity of inanimate objects', that is to say, with all the thousand and one ways in which great and high-principled undertakings may be 'frustrated' by trivial and insignificant untoward outward happenings.

The 'ethical' as a theme is tied to a definite time and a definite place. That is so because man is a living and mortal creature in a finite and destructible world and because he is not essentially or exclusively a student of ethics. It is one of the great naivetés, or, more exactly, one of the great follies, of the moralists that they deliberately overlook this fact and start out from the fiction that at every moment of his life man has to make a final and infinite choice, the fiction that every moment of life involves a conscious decision between good and evil. They seem to imagine that every human action has had a clearly-lettered notice attached to it by some divine police authority, a notice which reads either 'permitted' or 'forbidden'. They assume that a man must continually be doing something decisive, fulfilling some higher purpose and discharging some ultimate duty. This represents a failure to understand that in historical human existence everything has its time (Eccl. 3), eating, drinking and sleeping as well as deliberate resolve and action, rest as well as work, purposelessness as well as the fulfilment of purpose, inclination as well as duty, play as well as earnest endeavour, joy as well as renunciation. Their presumptuous misjudgement of this creaturely existence leads either to the most mendacious hypocrisy or else to madness. It turns the moralist into a dangerous tormentor, tyrant and clown, a figure of tragi-comedy.

Certainly there is a necessary time and place in human existence for the so-called 'ethical phenomenon', that is to say, the experience of obligation, the conscious and deliberate decision between something which is, on principle, good and something which is, on principle, evil, the ordering of life in accordance with a supreme standard, moral conflict and moral resolve. One may, therefore, suppose that within these limits it can and indeed should be made a theme for discussion. But precisely this proper delimiting of the place and of the time is of crucial importance if one is to prevent a pathological overburdening of life by the ethical, if one is to prevent that abnormal fanaticization and total moralization of life which has as its consequence that those processes of concrete life which are not properly subject to general principles are exposed to constant criticism, fault-finding, admonition, correction and general interference. The 'ethical phenomenon', in the sense which we have just described, is fundamentally misunderstood if the unconditional character of the experience of obligation is taken to imply an exclusive and all-embracing claim. To understand it in this way is to injure and to destroy the creaturely wholeness of life. To confine the ethical phenomenon to its proper place and time is not to invalidate it; it is, on the contrary, to render it fully operative. Big guns are not the right weapons for shooting sparrows.

In respect of its contents as well as of its character as an experience the ethical phenomenon is a peripheral event. 'Shall' and 'should', both as contents and as experience, are appropriate to a situation in which something is not, either because it cannot be or else because it is not desired. My living in the fellowship of a family, of a marriage and of the organization in which I work and own property is primarily an obligation in which I acquiesce freely and one in which the 'ethical phenomenon', the objective and subjective aspects of 'shall' and 'should', does not come to light but remains dormant. 'Shall' and 'should' make themselves heard only at the point where this fellowship is disrupted or the organization is endangered, and as soon as order is restored they have nothing more to say. It is true that they fall silent only in their acute form, as a concrete demand and accusation, but they persist as an awareness of one's own limitations, as the awareness, which arises from the actual concrete disruption of a community, that every community is in the true sense always involved in a process of disintegration. In other words, they continue to occupy a place in human life as self-limitation, as resignation or 'humility' in the profane sense of the word. This is the profane analogy to the doctrine of original sin. But both in its permanent and in its acute form, and as regards both its contents and its character as an experience, the obligation of 'shall' and 'should' applies only to a peripheral situation, and this obligation is inwardly disrupted if from being a peripheral concept it is converted into a pedagogical method. 'Shall' or 'should' is always an 'ultimate' word. If it is made a theme for discussion, this character of qualitative 'ultimateness' must always be safeguarded, and in certain circumstances the better way to safeguard this qualitatively 'ultimate' concept may be to refrain from treating it as a theme at all, 'because it goes without saying'. If this obligation, the obligation which goes without saying, is made a topic for discussion, then it all too easily loses its quality as an ultimate and becomes a penultimate, a method.

There are, of course, undoubtedly occasions and situations in which the moral course is not self-evident, either because it is not, in fact, followed or because it has become questionable from the point of view of its contents. It is at such times that the ethical becomes a theme. For one thing, it brings with it a refreshing simplification of the problems of life; it reduces them to broad general principles and it compels men to make clear decisions and to adopt unequivocal attitudes. In such circumstances the discussion will be more than usually dominated by convictions, by judgements of value, by opinions and flat assertions, and by outbursts of natural indignation and unreserved admiration; everything will be reduced to universal principles, that is to say, simplified; interest in principle will largely take the place of interest in the real processes of life with all their various levels of meaning. Sociologically speaking, this will mean the elimination of that upper stratum whose attitude is predominantly intellectual, relativistic and individualistic, and of the approach to the theme which this stratum dictates. The theme of the public discussion will now have become universally intelligible, so that everybody can take part in the debate. Respectability of outlook will now constitute a sufficient bond to form a community of enemies of intellectual and material corruption. These occasions, when the ethical becomes a theme for discussion, purify and restore the human community and are necessary for it, and yet, precisely because of the essential character of this theme, they must always be considered only as exceptional occurrences. If they are prolonged beyond their necessary duration they become in many respects disastrous; the ethical ceases to be understood as an 'ultimate' word, and its place is taken by a trite and jejune moralization and a pedantic regimentation of the whole of life; all the problems of life are reduced to a bleak and monotonous uniformity; all cultural functions are reduced to a primitive triviality and there is an enforced mental and social levelling-down. What suffers the decisive loss here is not merely the abundant fulness of life but the very essence of the ethical itself. Times in which the ethical has become, and has had to become, a theme for discussion must be followed by times when the moral course goes without saying, times when a man's activity lies not merely on the periphery but in the centre and in the fulness of everyday life. That is true of the life of the individual no less than of the human community. From the sociological point of view, one may say that the stubborn effort to prolong the discussion of the ethical theme beyond its proper time springs from an unsatisfied desire for an extension of influence on the part of those who possess effective opinions but who are themselves ineffectual in life. They have failed to seize the opportunity which history has offered them of demonstrating their effectiveness not only by their opinions but also by their performance in life during times when society is being reshaped under the impact of the ethical theme. Now that 'the moral course once again goes without saying' and is no longer a topic of discussion, they see their chances in life diminishing, cling insistently to the ethical theme, and thereby finally exclude themselves from the vital process. What we have said here about the human community is exactly paralleled in the life of the individual. That convulsive clinging to the ethical theme, which takes the form of a moralization of life, arises from fear of the fulness of everyday life and from an awareness of incapacity for life; it is a flight into a position which lies outside real life, a position from which one can only view life at a distance with an eye which is at the same time arrogant and envious. It ought by now to be sufficiently clear that in such a case it is not only life that has been forfeited, but also the essence of the ethical itself, precisely because it has been treated as a theme when it ought not to have been so treated.

What then, in view of all this, is an 'ethic' which by definition makes a theme of the ethical? And what is an ethicist? We can begin more easily by saying what, in any case, an ethic and an ethicist cannot be. An ethic cannot be a book in which there is set out how everything in the world actually ought to be but unfortunately is not, and an ethicist cannot be a man who always knows better than others what is to be done and how it is to be done. An ethic cannot be a work of reference for moral action which is guaranteed to be unexceptionable, and the ethicist cannot be the competent critic and judge of every human activity. An ethic cannot be a retort in which ethical or Christian human beings are produced, and the ethicist cannot be the embodiment or ideal type of a life which is, on principle, moral.

Ethics and ethicists do not intervene continuously in life. They draw attention to the disturbance and interruption of life by the 'shall' and the 'should' which impinge on all life from its periphery. Ethics and ethicists do not wish to represent goodness as such, that is to say, as an end in itself, but, precisely by speaking strictly from the standpoint of the 'ethical', from the standpoint of the peripheral event of 'shall' and 'should', they wish to help people to learn to share in life, to share in life within the limits of the obligation of 'shall' and 'should', and not hold themselves aloof from the processes of life as spectators, critics and judges; to share in life not out of the motive of 'shall' and 'should', but from the full abundance of vital motives, from the natural and the organic, and from free acceptance and will, not in humourless hostility towards every vital force and towards every weakness and disorder. They would help them to learn to join in life not in mistrustful surveillance and appraisal of everything that is and everything that ought to be, and not in the timidly over-scrupulous subordination of the natural to the deontological, of the free to the necessary, of the concrete to the universal and of the purposeless to purpose—for in that case, as W. Hermann says, the limits of the 'ethical' are in the end so grotesquely stretched that the last paragraph of a Christian ethic must have as its subject 'morally permitted behaviour'; but to share in life within the bounds of 'shall' and 'should' (not, however, from the motives of 'shall' and 'should') in the abundant fulness of the concrete tasks and processes of life with all their infinite multiplicity of different motives.

We will for the moment disregard a large number of problems which we have already touched upon and confine ourselves to what is here our guiding question, namely, the question of the fixed place and the fixed time of the ethical. In addition to what we have already said on this subject, a few further definitions may now be given.

Timeless and placeless ethical discourse lacks the concrete warrant which all authentic ethical discourse requires. It is an adolescent, presumptuous and illegitimate declamation of ethical principles, and however intense may be the subjective earnestness with which it is propounded, it is contrary to the essential character of ethical discourse in a way which is clearly felt, even though it may be difficult to define. In such cases it is often impossible to find fault with the process of abstraction and generalization or with the theories advanced, and yet they do not possess the specific gravity of ethical propositions. The words are correct but they have no weight. In the end it must be felt that they are not helpful but chaotic. For some obscure but, in the end, undeniable reason it is in the nature of things simply not possible, not in accordance with any true state of affairs, if a youth recites ethical generalities to a circle of experienced and grown men. The young man will over and over again be faced with that situation which he finds so annoying, so astonishing and incomprehensible, the situation in which his words are lost in the empty air while the words of an old man, even if their contents are exactly the same, are heard and carry weight. It will be a sign of maturity or of immaturity whether one perceives or fails to perceive from this experience that what confronts us here is not the stubborn and narrow-minded self-complacency of old age or its fear of allowing youth to assert itself, but it is a question of the safeguarding or the violation of an essential ethical law. Ethical discourse requires a warrant such as the adolescent cannot simply confer upon himself, however pure and earnest may be his ethical conviction. In ethical discourse what matters is not only that the contents of the assertion should be correct, but also that there should be a concrete warrant, an authorization for this assertion. It is not only what is said that matters, but also the man who says it.

In what does this warrant or authorization consist? Who receives it and who confers it? This warrant, without which there can be no ethical discourse, means first of all that ethical discourse is subjected to a concrete limitation. Ethical discourse cannot be conducted in a vacuum, in the abstract, but only in a concrete context. Ethical discourse, therefore, is not a system of propositions which are correct in themselves, a system which is available for anyone to apply at any time and in any place, but it is inseparably linked with particular persons, times and places. This limitation does not mean that the ethical loses any of its significance, but it is precisely from this that it derives its warrant, its weight; whereas whenever it is not restricted in this way, whenever it is available for general application, it is enfeebled to the point of impotence.

No one can confer upon himself the warrant for ethical discourse; it is imparted to a man, it is assigned to him, not primarily on the basis of subjective accomplishments and merits, but on the basis of an objective position in the world. Thus the authorization for ethical discourse is conferred upon the old man and not upon the young one, upon the father and not the child, the master and not the servant, the teacher and not the pupil, the judge and not the accused, the ruler and not the subject, the preacher and not the parishioner. What finds expression here is that disparity which is so extremely offensive to modern sensibilities but which is inherent and essential in the ethical, namely, the disparity between the superior and the inferior. Without this objective subordination of the lower to the higher, and without that courage to accept superiority which modern man has so completely lost, ethical discourse is dissipated in generalities, it lacks an object and its essential character is destroyed.

The ethical, therefore, is not a principle which levels out, invalidates and disrupts the whole order of human precedence and subordination, but already in itself it implies a definite structure of human society; it implies certain definite sociological relations which involve authority. It is only within these relationships that it makes its appearance and acquires the concrete warrant or authorization which is essential to it. These assertions are in direct contradiction to the interpretation of the ethical as a universally valid rational principle which implies the invalidation of all concrete factors, all limitations of time and place and all relations of subordination and authority, and which proclaims the equality of all men by virtue of their innate universal human reason. One must be quite clear about the fact—and the history of the past hundred and fifty years has demonstrated it clearly enough—that the actual goal of this

new conception of the ethical, which was to establish a
universal union of mankind in the place of a fossilized form
of society characterized by the antagonism of privileged and
unprivileged members, has not only not been achieved but
has turned out to be exactly the opposite of what was
intended. The ethical, in this sense of the formal, the universally valid and the rational, contained no element of
concretion, and it therefore inevitably ended in the total
atomization of human society and of the life of the individual,
in unlimited subjectivism and individualism. When the
ethical is conceived without reference to any local or temporal
relation, without reference to the question of its warrant or
authority, without reference to the concrete, then life falls
apart into an infinite number of unconnected atoms of time,
and human society resolves itself into individual atoms of
reason. It makes no practical difference whether one interprets the ethical as a purely formal universally valid principle
or whether one refers it to the 'existential' decision which the
individual takes completely anew at every separate 'moment'.
The underlying factor is always that the ethical is destroyed
by its being detached from its concrete relations. That is so
simply because the ethical is not essentially a formal rational
principle but a concrete relation between the giver and the
receiver of commands; formal reason is not a socially constructive principle but a principle of atomization, and society
consists solely in the concrete and infinitely manifold relationships of responsibility of men one for another.

On the other hand, one must not simply jettison the
contribution of the Enlightenment towards the understanding
of the ethical. In its polemical context the Enlightenment
must still be allowed to have been right to oppose a system
under which society was divided into privileged and unprivileged sections. The ethical is in actual fact connected with
the universally and humanly rational; and in actual fact
the inherent tendency of the ethical, in its subordination
of the inferior to the superior, does not in any way imply a
sanctioning of privileges. The Enlightenment was certainly
entirely right to point out that the ethical is not concerned

with an abstract order of society, or with representatives of particular strata of society, or with 'upper' and 'lower' as such, but with men. On that basis it was right also in giving such extremely emphatic support to the equal dignity of men before the ethical. It was wrong only when it went beyond these polemical arguments and once more made man himself an abstraction, employing this abstraction as a weapon against all human order in the name of human equality and human dignity. It was wrong when it made a formal abstract principle of human reason, for the essence of human reason is that it freely perceives and accepts reality, which in the present context means that it freely perceives and accepts ethical propositions, and this abstract principle dissolves and disrupts all these contents of reason. Notwithstanding all this, it is still important to keep the Enlightenment in mind as a corrective to any attempt to misuse the ethical as a sanction for privilege.

Nevertheless, fear of the misuse of the ethical must not lead us simply to discount or conceal its inherent tendency to subordinate the lower to the higher. We can no longer escape the fact that the ethical calls for clear relationships in terms of superiority and inferiority. Nor can superiority and inferiority simply be interchanged to accord with the fluctuations in the value of subjective accomplishment and character. Superiority does not consist in the subjective value of the superior man, but it derives its legitimation from a concrete objective commission. The master craftsman is still the master even for his talented journeyman, and the father is still the father even for his worthy and meritorious son. Quite independently of the subjective side of the matter, it is still the master and the father who possess the warrant for ethical discourse. The warrant goes with the office and not with the person.

This means at the same time that for ethical discourse a certain duration and stability are presupposed in the relationships of authority. Genuine ethical discourse is not exhausted in a single proclamation, but requires repetition and continuity; it requires time. Precisely in this lies the burden, but also the dignity and the authenticity, of ethical discourse. Single pronunciamentos are nothing. The warrant for ethical discourse shows itself in constancy under trial, in persistence and reiteration. But to enquire into the basis for the warrant for ethical discourse is already to go beyond the bounds of the ethical.

All this, however, is possible only on the basis of inner acquiescence and resolute perseverance in superiority and inferiority. The two are possible only in conjunction with one another. There can be acquiescence and perseverance in inferiority only if there is acquiescence and perseverance in superiority, and *vice versa*. If no one dares to be superior, if no one 'thinks he needs' to be inferior, or if superiority seeks its foundation only in the inferior, if, that is to say, the father derives his authority from his children's confidence in him and the government derives its authority from its popularity, and if, therefore, inferiority is always regarded as a mere preliminary to superiority, in other words, as a catalyst of all superiority, then there can be no authentic ethical discourse but there is already the beginning of ethical chaos. Consequently the requirement of an inner acquiescence and perseverance in superiority and inferiority already introduces the crucial question of the basis for the warrant for ethical discourse, and with this question the ethical takes a decisive step beyond its own boundaries.

What has been said so far can, in our view rightly, be regarded as a general phenomenology of the ethical, but we now find ourselves confronted with a final decisive question which lies beyond the sphere of the ethical-phenomenological. What is the basis for the concrete warrant for ethical discourse? Two answers at first present themselves. The warrant for ethical discourse may positivistically, without any further attempt at explanation, be found in reality as it is given. Or else one may construct a system of orders and values within which the father, the master and the government all have this warrant assigned to them. It is evident that the positivistic argument forms a very shaky foundation, for it possesses no criteria beyond the reality which is at any particular time given and which may always change. Furthermore, the positivistic argument cannot succeed in defining the boundaries between the various different authorities which claim for themselves the warrant for ethical discourse, for example the government, the father, the teacher and the Church; it is now actual power that comes to be regarded as the sole criterion for the warrant. Thus positivism fails to provide a basis for the ethical. It might at first sight appear that more reliance can be placed upon the attempt to construct a rigid system of authorities and subordinations such as has repeatedly been undertaken by Christian philosophers; in the nineteenth century especially by the conservative romanticists, notably J. Stahl, and in the twentieth century by the Catholic, Max Scheler. The difference in principle between this and positivism is obvious; there are now other criteria, beyond the positive data, for the classification of the authorities and of their warrants. These criteria are of a religious, or more exactly a Christian, nature. The concrete authorities are divine appointments, direct manifestations of the divine will which demands submission to them. By this means there is no doubt achieved a certain independence from the shaky foundation of the positive empirical given reality of a particular time. On the other hand, empirical positivism is now replaced by a metaphysical and religious positivism, and here again this is in itself enough to frustrate any attempt to establish any but arbitrary boundaries between the various authorities and warrants. Either the idea of the state or the idea of fatherhood or the idea of the Church will become the dominant principle. The conflict which ensues from the direct divine appointment of these various competing authorities is decided by a more or less arbitrary ruling in favour of the claim of one of these authorities to be absolute. Systematic construction and metaphysical deduction alike lead to inertness in real life. Consequently the question of the basis of the concrete warrant for ethical discourse still remains open. And the question, therefore, also remains open why the ethical must be understood not as a timeless principle but as being locally and temporally restricted. Finally, there remains open the further question, to what extent and within what limits the 'ethical' can become a theme.

The Commandment of God

This brings us to the only possible object of a 'Christian ethic', an object which lies beyond the 'ethical', namely, the 'commandment of God'.

In what we have been saying about the 'ethical' we have, perhaps unconsciously, encountered the living rock, an outcrop of the commandment of God itself.

The commandment of God is something different from what we have so far referred to as the ethical. It embraces the whole of life. It is not only unconditional; it is also total. It does not only forbid and command; it also permits. It does not only bind; it also sets free; and it does this by binding. Yet the 'ethical', in a sense which still has to be explained, is part of it. God's commandment is the only warrant for ethical discourse.

The commandment of God is the total and concrete claim laid to man by the merciful and holy God in Jesus Christ. We cannot here develop a general theory or doctrine of the commandment of God; but we will indicate the points which are most significant in the present context.

Unlike the ethical, the commandment of God is not a summary of all ethical propositions in the most general terms. It is not the universally valid and timeless in contrast to the historical and temporal. It is not principle, as distinct from the application of principle. It is not the abstract as opposed to the concrete, or the indefinite as opposed to the definite. If it were anything of the kind it would have ceased to be *God's* commandment, for on each occasion it would then have been left to us to deduce the definite from the indefinite, the application from the principle and the temporal from the timeless. This would mean that precisely at the crucial juncture the decisive factor would no longer be the commandment, but our understanding, our interpretation and our application. The commandment of God would once again be replaced by our own choice.

God's commandment is the speech of God to man. Both in its contents and in its form it is concrete speech to the concrete man. God's commandment leaves man no room for application or interpretation. It leaves room only for obedience or disobedience. God's commandment cannot be found and known in detachment from time and place; it can only be heard in a local and temporal context. If God's commandment is not clear, definite and concrete to the last detail, then it is not God's commandment.

Either God does not speak at all or else He speaks to us as definitely as He spoke to Abraham and Jacob and Moses and as definitely as in Jesus Christ He spoke to the disciples and through His apostles to the Gentiles. Does this mean that at every moment of our lives we may be informed of the commandment of God by some special direct divine inspiration, or that at every moment, in an unmistakable and unequivocal manner, God causes what Karl Heim calls the 'accent of eternity' to rest on a particular action which He wills? No, it does not mean that, for the concreteness of the divine commandment consists in its historicity; it confronts us in a historical form. Does this mean, then, that we are utterly lacking in certainty in the face of the extremely varying claims of the historical powers, and that, so far as the commandment of God is concerned, we are groping in the darkness? No, the reason why it does not mean this is that God makes His commandment heard in a definite historical form. We cannot now escape the question where and in what historical form God makes His commandment known. For the sake of simplicity and clarity, and even at the risk of a direct misunderstanding, we will begin by answering this question in the form of a thesis. God's commandment, which is manifested in Jesus Christ, comes to us in the Church, in the family, in labour and in government.

It is a necessary premise which must never be lost sight of, even though for the time being it may not be fully intelligible, that the commandment of God is and always remains the commandment of God which is made manifest in Jesus Christ. There is no other commandment of God than that which is revealed by Him and which is manifested according to His will in Jesus Christ.

This means that the commandment of God does not spring from the created world. It comes down from above. It does not arise from the factual claim on men of earthly powers and laws, from the claim of the instinct of self-preservation or from the claim of hunger, sex or political force. It stands beyond all these as a demand, a precept and a judgement. The commandment of God establishes on earth an inviolable superiority and inferiority which are independent of the factual relations of power and weakness. In establishing this superiority it confers that warrant for ethical discourse of which we have already spoken, or, more comprehensively, it confers the warrant to proclaim the divine commandment.

Because the commandment of God is the commandment which is revealed in Jesus Christ, no single authority, among those which are authorized to proclaim the commandment, can claim to be absolute. The authorization to speak is conferred from above on the Church, the family, labour and government, only so long as they do not encroach upon each other's domains and only so long as they give effect to God's commandment in conjunction and collaboration with one another and each in its own way. No single one of these authorities can exclusively identify itself with the commandment of God. The supremacy of the commandment of God is shown precisely by the fact that it juxtaposes and coordinates these authorities in a relation of mutual opposition and complementarity and that it is only in this multiplicity of concrete correlations and limitations that the commandment of God takes effect as the commandment which is manifest in Jesus Christ.

God's commandment, revealed in Jesus Christ, is always concrete speech *to* somebody. It is never abstract speech *about* something or *about* somebody. It is always an address, a claim, and it is so comprehensive and at the same time so definite that it leaves no freedom for interpretation or application, but only the freedom to obey or to disobey.

God's commandment, revealed in Jesus Christ, embraces the whole of life. It does not only, like the ethical, keep watch on the untransgressible frontier of life, but it is at the same time the centre and the fulness of life. It is not only obligation but also permission. It does not only forbid, but it also sets free for life; it sets free for unreflected doing. It does not only interrupt the process of life when this process goes astray, but it guides and conducts this process even though there is not always need for consciousness of this fact. God's commandment becomes the daily divine guidance of our lives. We may make this clear by an example, the relationship of a child to his parents. The commandment of God is not only a threat, a correction and a warning for the child who rebels against his parents, but it comes upon the child, accompanies him and guides him, in all the countless situations in which in his daily life he honours and loves his parents. The commandment of God does not exist only in the solemn form of, for example, the Fifth Commandment; it exists also in the form of everyday words, exhortations and appeals for some particular concrete conduct and action within the community of the family. This does not imply a cleavage in God's commandment; on the contrary, it implies its all-embracing unity; it means that it is perfectly concrete and that through the commandment life does not fall apart into countless new beginnings, but it is given a clear direction, an inner continuity and a firm security. The commandment of God becomes the element in which one lives without always being conscious of it, and, thus it implies freedom of movement and of action, freedom from the fear of decision, freedom from fear to act, it implies certainty, quietude, confidence, balance and peace. I honour my parents, I am faithful in marriage, I respect the lives and property of others, not because at the frontiers of my life there is a threatening 'thou shalt not', but because I accept as holy institutions of God these realities, parents, marriage, life and property, which confront me in the midst and in the fulness of life. It is only when the

247

commandment no longer merely threatens me as a transgressor of the limits, it is only when it convinces and subdues me with its real contents, that it sets me free from the anxiety and the uncertainty of decision. If I love my wife, if I accept marriage as an institution of God, then there comes an inner freedom and certainty of life and action in marriage; I no longer watch with suspicion every step that I take; I no longer call in question every deed that I perform. The divine prohibition of adultery is then no longer the centre around which all my thought and action in marriage revolves. (As though the meaning and purpose of marriage consisted of nothing except the avoidance of adultery!) But it is the honouring and the free acceptance of marriage, the leaving behind of the prohibition of adultery, which is now the precondition for the fulfilment of the divine commission of marriage. The divine commandment has here become the permission to live in marriage in freedom and certainty.

The commandment of God is the permission to live as man before God.

The commandment of God is permission. It differs from all human laws in that it commands freedom. It is by overcoming this contradiction that it shows itself to be God's commandment; the impossible becomes possible, and that which lies beyond the range of what can be commanded, liberty, is the true object of this commandment. That is the high price of God's commandment; it is no cheaper than that. Permission and liberty do not mean that God now after all allows man a domain in which he can act according to his own choice, free from the commandment of God, but this permission and this liberty arise solely from the commandment of God itself. They are possible only through and in the commandment of God; they are never detached from God; it is still always *God's* permission, and it is only as such that it gives freedom from the torment of anxiety in the face of each particular decision and deed; it is only as such that it gives the certainty of personal accomplishment and of guidance by the divine command. Kant and Fichte are right to reject the concept of the 'permitted' in ethics, so long as the 'permitted' is taken to mean that which in relation to the commandments of God is neutral, independent and indifferent, but they are wrong when they thereby eliminate the concept of the permission of God, the permission which derives from the commandment of God, and when they replace this concept with an exclusive concept of duty which will necessarily always prove to be too narrow to comprise and to sustain the whole of human life.

The commandment of God permits man to live as man before God, as man, and not merely as a taker of ethical decisions or as a student of ethics. What this involves can best be stated by quoting the verses which Matthias Claudius wrote under the title *Man*.

> Conceived and nursed by woman wondrously,
> He comes, sees, hears, is easily deceived.
> He hankers, craves, and sheds the tear that's due,
> Scorns and reveres, knows joy, knows danger too,
> Believes and doubts, errs, teaches, builds, destroys,
> Torments himself with telling truth from falsehood.
> He sleeps and watches, grows and eats and drinks.
> His hair is one year brown, another grey.
> And, if he lives so long, when four-score years
> Are done he lays himself beside his fathers
> And never comes again.

This poem well expresses the temporal character of human life, its fulness and its frailty. This is the life with which we are concerned when we speak of the commandment of God, and it is precisely of this life that the 'ethical' knows nothing. The 'ethical' can only wish to keep interrupting this life, confronting it at every moment with nothing but the conflict of its duties. The 'ethical' can always only make this life appear questionable to itself. It can only resolve it into countless separate decisions. The flow of life, from the conception to the grave, is incomprehensible to the ethical; it is 'pre-ethical'. The 'ethical' is repelled and horrified by the obscurity of the motives for action, by the way in which every deed is compounded of conscious and unconscious elements, natural and supernatural elements, inclination and duty, egotism and altruism, volition and compulsion, activity and passivity, so that all active doing is at the same time passive undergoing and *vice versa*. In all circumstances the 'ethical' demands clarity, directness, purity and consciousness in human motives and deeds. It cuts any knotty growth in life. The commandment of God permits man to be man before God. It allows the flood of life to flow freely. It lets man eat, drink, sleep, work, rest and play. It does not interrupt him. It does not continually ask him whether he ought to be sleeping, eating, working or playing, or whether he has some more urgent duties. It does not make man a critic and judge of himself and of his deed, but it allows him to live and to act with certainty and with confidence in the guidance of the divine commandment. The self-tormenting and hopeless question regarding the purity of one's motives, the suspicious observation of oneself, the glaring and fatiguing light of incessant consciousness, all these have nothing to do with the commandment of God, who grants liberty to live and to act. The permission to live, which is granted in the commandment of God, takes account of the fact that the roots of human life and action lie in darkness and that activity and passivity, the conscious and the unconscious, are inextricably interwoven. Light comes into this life only through taking advantage of this divine permission; it comes only from above.

Before the commandment of God man does not permanently stand like Hercules at the crossroads. He is not everlastingly striving for the right decision. He is not always wearing himself out in a conflict of duties. He is not continually failing and beginning again. Nor does the commandment of God itself make its appearance only in these great, agitated and intensely conscious moments of crisis in life. On the contrary, before the commandment of God man may at last really move forward along the road and no longer stand endlessly at the crossroads. He can now have the right decision really behind him, and not always before him. Entirely without inner conflict he can do one thing and leave undone another thing which, according to theoretical ethics, is perhaps equally urgent. He can already have made a beginning and he can allow himself to be guided, escorted and protected on his way by prayers as though by a good angel. And God's commandment itself can give life unity of direction and personal guidance only in the form of seemingly small and insignificant everyday words, sayings, hints and help.

The purpose of the commandment lies not in the avoidance of transgression, and not in the torment of ethical conflict and decision, but in freely accepted, self-evident life in the Church, in marriage, in the family, in work and in the state. The 'ethical' defines only the boundary, the formal and the negative, and is therefore possible as a theme only on the periphery, formally and negatively. The commandment of God, on the other hand, is concerned with the positive contents and with man's freedom to accept these positive contents. From this it follows that God's commandment can be treated as the theme of a Christian ethic only by dint of keeping these positive contents and this liberty of man simultaneously in view. The commandment, as the theme of a Christian ethic, is satisfied neither by a system of casuistry, a decision which anticipates concrete cases at the expense of man's freedom, nor by a formal doctrine of freedom which discounts the positive contents. In the last analysis the 'ethical' was concerned with staking out and defining a space in which man could share in the whole fulness of life, but the commandment is concerned with this 'sharing in life' itself in its concrete contents and in that liberty of man which these contents render possible in such a 'sharing in life'. Thus it becomes clear that the commandment of God also comprises the 'ethical'. The crucial point here is that we do not say the opposite, namely, that the ethical also comprises the commandment. For in this latter case the commandment would be the secondary factor and no more than a special case, a concrete 'application' of the ethical, whereas in reality it is the commandment which is the original factor, with its concrete contents and with that liberty of man which it makes possible; from its own resources the commandment fixes the boundaries and creates the space within which it can be heard and fulfilled. The boundary arises from the centre and the fulness of life with the commandment of God; it is not the other way round. If we now conclude by substituting for the philosophical concept of the 'ethical' the biblical concept of the 'law', the result must be that the commandment and the law are inseparably linked together but that a distinction must be drawn between them. The law is comprised within the commandment; it arises from it; and it must be understood by reference to it.

Quite automatically, therefore, our next considerations must fall into two parts, the concrete commandment of God[1] and the law.

THE CONCRETE COMMANDMENT AND THE DIVINE MANDATES

In its unity which embraces the whole of human life and in its undivided claim to man and to the world through the reconciling love of God, God's commandment, revealed in Jesus Christ, confronts us concretely in four different forms which it alone unites: the Church, marriage and the family, culture and government.

The commandment of God is not to be found anywhere and everywhere. It is not to be found in theoretical speculation or in private inspiration, nor yet in historical forces or sublime ideals. It is to be found only where it presents itself. The

1 *Editor's note.* The following summary was sketched out under the heading *'Fallacious* Questions'. 1. How does the will of God become concrete? Answer: the will of God is always concrete, or else it is not the will of *God*. In other words, the will of God is not a principle from which one has to draw inferences and which has to be applied to 'reality'. A 'will of God' which can be recognized without immediately leading to action is a general principle, but it is not the will of God. 2. How does the good will of the Christian become concrete? The good will is from the outset a concrete deed; otherwise it is not Christian will. Man is from the outset engaged in concrete action. 3. What is the will of God for this or that particular case? This is the casuistic misinterpretation of the concrete. The concrete is not achieved in this way, for it is once again already anticipated by a principle. 4. The formalistic misinterpretation. 5. The philosophical attempt to reach a solution in the theory of values.

commandment of God can be spoken only where God Himself gives the warrant for it, and only in so far as God gives the warrant for it can the commandment of God legitimately be performed. The commandment of God is not to be found where there are historical forces, powerful ideals and convincing perceptions. It is to be found where there are the divine mandates which are founded upon the revelation of Christ. Such mandates are the Church, marriage and the family, culture and government.[1]

[1] *Editor's note.* A letter from prison dated 23rd January 1944 contains the following passage concerning the place of friendship in this scheme. 'Friendship is not easy to classify sociologically. Probably one should regard it as a subdivision of the concept of culture, while brotherhood belongs to the concept of the Church and comradeship comes under the concept of labour and the concept of the political. Marriage, labour, the state and the Church each have their concrete divine mandate. But what is the situation as regards culture? I do not believe that one can simply subordinate it to the concept of labour, though in many ways one is tempted to do so. Its place is not in the domain of obedience but in the free expanse of liberty which encompasses the three domains of the divine mandates. A man who has no knowledge of this free expanse of liberty may be a good father, a good citizen and a good worker; and no doubt he may also be a Christian; but I rather doubt whether he is a complete human being; and to this extent I doubt also whether he can be a Christian in the full meaning of the term. Our "Protestant (not Lutheran) Prussian world" is so completely governed by the four mandates that these entirely overshadow the free expanse of liberty. It almost seems today, and is perhaps in fact the case, that the concept of the Church can alone make it possible once again to understand the free expanse of liberty, the field which includes art, culture, friendship and play. Perhaps, then, what Kierkegaard calls the "aesthetic existence", far from being excluded from the domain of the Church, should be given a new foundation within the Church. I really think so; and this would provide yet another point of contact with the Middle Ages! Who, for example, in our time can still with an easy mind cultivate music or friendship, play games and enjoy himself? Certainly not the "ethical" man, but only the Christian. It is precisely because friendship belongs to the domain of this liberty (the liberty of the "Christian man") that one must confidently defend oneself against all the frowns of "ethical" existences, certainly without appealing to the *necessitas* of a divine commandment, but appealing nevertheless to the *necessitas* of liberty. I believe that within the domain of this liberty friendship is the rarest and most precious treasure. It is rare indeed, for where is it now to be found in this world of ours which is predominantly governed by the first three mandates? Friendship is not to be compared with the values of the mandates. In relation to them it is *sui generis*, yet it is as much in place among them as the cornflower in the wheatfield.' (*Cf.* the poem *The Friend*.)

The Concept of the Mandate

By the term 'mandate' we understand the concrete divine commission which has its foundation in the revelation of Christ and which is evidenced by Scripture; it is the legitimation and warrant for the execution of a definite divine commandment, the conferment of divine authority on an earthly agent. The term 'mandate' must also be taken to imply the claiming, the seizure and the formation of a definite earthly domain by the divine commandment. The bearer of the mandate acts as a deputy in the place of Him who assigns him his commission. In its proper sense the term 'institution' or 'order' might also be applied here, but this would involve the danger of directing attention rather towards the actual state of the institution than towards its foundation, which lies solely in the divine warrant, legitimation and authorization. The consequence of this can all too easily be the assumption of a divine sanction for all existing orders and institutions in general and a romantic conservatism which is entirely at variance with the Christian doctrine of the four divine mandates. If the concept of the 'institution' could be purged of these misinterpretations it would no doubt be capable of expressing very effectively what is here intended. The concept of the 'estate' also suggests itself in this connexion; it did good service from the time of the Reformation onwards, but in the course of history it has acquired so many new connotations that it is now quite impossible to employ it in its pure original sense. These words now suggest human prerogatives and privileges and no longer convey their original meaning of dignity in humility. Finally, the term 'office' is now so completely secularized, and has come to be so closely associated with institutional bureaucratic thinking, that it cannot possibly render the sublime quality of the divine decree. For lack of a better word, therefore, we will for the time being retain the term 'mandate', but it is still our purpose, by dint of clarifying the concept itself, to help to renew and to restore the old notion of the institution, the estate and the office.

The divine mandates are dependent solely on the *one* commandment of God as it is revealed in Jesus Christ. They are introduced into the world from above as orders or 'institutions' of the reality of Christ, that is to say, of the reality of the love of God for the world and for men which is revealed in Jesus Christ. This means that they are not in any sense products of history; they are not earthly powers, but divine commissions. It is only from above, with God as the point of departure, that it is possible to say and to understand what is meant by the Church, by marriage and the family, by culture and by government. The bearers of the mandate do not receive their commission from below; their task is not to expound and execute desires of the human will, but in a strict and unalterable sense they hold their commission from God, they are deputies and representatives of God. This remains true whatever may be the historical origins of a church, a family or a government. In this way, by virtue of the divine warrant, there is established in the sphere of the mandate an unalterable relation of superiority and inferiority.

This means that the commandment of God wishes to find man always in an earthly relation of authority, in a clearly defined order of superiority and inferiority. But at this point it is immediately necessary to define this superiority and inferiority more closely. First of all, it is not identical with an earthly relation of superior and inferior power. The stronger can certainly not without further ado claim for himself the authority of the divine mandate *vis-à-vis* the weaker. On the contrary, it is characteristic of the divine mandate that it corrects and regulates the earthly relations of superior and inferior power in its own way. Secondly, it must be emphasized that the divine mandate establishes not only superiority but also inferiority. Superiority and inferiority pertain to one another in an indissoluble relation of mutual limitation which we shall later have to define more closely. Thirdly, superiority and inferiority here represent a relation not of concepts or of things but of persons; it is a relation between those persons who, whether they be superior or inferior, submit to the commission of God and to it alone. The master, too, has a

Master, and this fact alone establishes his right to be master and authorizes and legitimates his relation to the servant. Master and servant owe to one another the honour which arises from any particular act of participation in the mandate of God. There may be abuse of superiority to the detriment of the inferior, but at the same time there may also be abuse of inferiority. Quite apart from personal aberrations, abuse of both superiority and inferiority is inevitable whenever it is no longer recognized that both have their foundation in the mandate of God. In such a case superiority is thought of as a fortuitous favour of fortune; it is seized upon and exploited without compunction, and, in return, inferiority is thought of as an unjust disadvantage, which necessarily gives rise to indignation and rebellion. The whole relation of superiority and inferiority is reversed when the inferior becomes conscious of the forces which are inherent within itself. This is the critical moment at which the inferior suddenly breaks free; it perceives itself to be armed with the dark forces of destruction, denial, doubt and rebellion, and, with these chaotic powers at its disposal, it feels itself to be superior to all established order and to all superiority. There is now no longer any genuine superiority or inferiority; the superior derives its authority and legitimation solely from below, and this superiority, which is superior only on the basis of the inferior, is regarded by the inferior only as the personified claim of the inferior to become superior. Thus in such a case the inferior becomes a permanent and inevitable menace to the superior; in the face of this threat the man who is superior can maintain his 'superior' position only by tormenting and provoking the inferior still more actively while at the same time combating the rebellious forces of the inferior with terror and violence. At this stage, when the relation between superior and inferior is reversed or confused, there arises between them the most intense hostility, mistrust, deceit and envy. And in this atmosphere, too, purely personal abuse of superiority and inferiority flourishes as never before. In the horror which is aroused by the violence of this rebellion the fact that there was ever the possibility of a genuine institutional order established from above can only appear as a miracle, and so, in reality, it is. The genuine order of superior and inferior draws its life from belief in the commission from 'above', belief in the 'Lord of lords'. This belief alone can exorcize the demonic forces which emerge from below. The collapse of this belief means the total collapse and destruction of the whole structure and order which is established in the world from above. Some will say it was a hoax and a fraud, and others will say it was a miracle, but both sides alike must surely be astonished by the power of belief.

It is only in conjunction, in combination and in opposition with one another that the divine mandates of the Church, of marriage and the family, of culture and of government declare the commandment of God as it is revealed in Jesus Christ. No single one of these mandates is sufficient in itself or can claim to replace all the others. The mandates are *conjoined*; otherwise they are not mandates of God. In their conjunction they are not isolated or separated from one another, but they are directed towards one another. They are 'for' one another; otherwise they are not God's mandates. Moreover, within this relation of conjunction and mutual support, each one is limited by the other; even within the relation of mutual support this limitation is necessarily experienced as a relation of mutual opposition. Wherever this mutual opposition no longer exists there is no longer a mandate of God.

Superiority, therefore, is subject to three limitations which each take effect in a different way; it is limited first by God, who confers the commission, second by the other mandates, and third by the relation of inferiority. Yet these limitations also constitute a protection for superiority. This protection affords encouragement for the observance of the divine mandates, just as the limitation gives warning against the abuse of superiority.

Protection and limitation are two sides of the same thing. God protects by limiting, and He encourages by warning.

We will now begin by saying something of the commandment of God in each of the four mandates in turn, and we will then go on to discuss the relation of these mandates 'with', 'for' and 'against' one another.

The Commandment of God in the Church

The commandment of God confronts us in the Church in two different ways, in preaching and in confession or ecclesiastical discipline; in other words, it confronts us publicly and privately, addressed on the one hand to the assembled hearers of the preaching and on the other to the individual man. These two forms of the divine commandment necessarily belong together. If confession or church discipline is lost, then the commandment of God in preaching will be understood as no more than a proclamation of general moral principles which in themselves are devoid of any concrete claim. If public preaching is entirely relegated to the background and attention is concentrated on the confessional, then there is indeed no lack of concrete application, but there nevertheless arises a dangerous legalistic casuistry which destroys liberty of faith and which inevitably results in a constant covert interference in the domains of the other divine mandates, family, culture and government, and so brings about the destruction of the free cooperation of the mandates in order to establish the absolute authority of the mandate of the Church. There can be no doubt that these two possibilities indicate the shortcomings of the Protestant and Catholic Churches respectively. The Protestant Church ceased to possess a concrete ethic when the minister no longer found himself constantly confronted by the problems and responsibilities of the confessional. With a fallacious appeal to Christian liberty, he evaded his responsibility of concrete proclamation of the divine commandment. It is, therefore, only by rediscovering the divine office of confession that the Protestant Church can find its way back to a concrete ethic such as it possessed at the time of the Reformation. The Catholic cleric throughout his course of study is prepared for his office as a father confessor by discussing innumerable 'cases' in which he will have to make decisions. There can be no doubt that this procedure involves very serious danger of reducing the divine commandment to a mere code of laws and pedagogic method. This danger can be overcome only by a rediscovery of the Christian office of preaching.

The two forms of the divine commandment in the Church have this in common, that they are both the proclamation of divine revelation. The mandate which is given to the Church is the mandate of proclamation. God desires a place at which His word is repeatedly spoken, expounded, interpreted and disseminated until the end of the world. The word which came from heaven in Jesus Christ desires to return again in the form of human speech. The mandate of the Church is the word of God. God Himself desires to be present in this word. God Himself desires to speak His word in the Church.

What the Church proclaims is the word of the revelation of God in Jesus Christ. This word does not proceed from any man's own heart or understanding or character; it comes down to man from heaven, from the will and the mercy of God; it is a word commanded and instituted by Jesus Christ, and from this it follows that the word, by the manner of its coming, establishes a clearly differentiated relation of superiority and inferiority. Above there is the office of proclamation, and below there is the listening congregation. In the place of God and of Jesus Christ there stands before the congregation the bearer of the office of preaching with his proclamation. The preacher is not the spokesman of the congregation, but, if the expression may be allowed, he is the spokesman of God before the congregation. He is authorized to teach, to admonish and to comfort, to forgive sin, but also to retain sin. And at the same time he is the shepherd, the pastor of the flock. This office is instituted directly by Jesus Christ Himself; it does not derive its legitimation from the will of the congregation but from the will of Jesus Christ. It is established *in* the congregation and not *by* the congregation, and at the same time it is *with* the congregation. When this office is exercised in the congregation to its full extent, life is infused into all the other offices of the congregation, which can after all only be subservient to the office of the divine word; for wherever the word of God rules alone, there will be found faith and service. The congregation which is being awakened by the proclamation of the word of God will demonstrate the genuineness of its faith by honouring the office of preaching in its unique glory and by serving it with all its powers; it will not rely on its own faith or on the universal priesthood of all believers in order to depreciate the office of preaching, to place obstacles in its way, or even to try to make it subordinate to itself. The superior status of the office of preaching is preserved from abuse, and against danger from without, precisely by a genuine subordination of the congregation, that is to say, by faith, prayer and service, but not by a suppression or disruption of the divine order or by a perverse desire for superiority on the part of the congregation.

The office of proclamation, the testimony to Jesus Christ, is inseparably bound up with Holy Scripture. At this point we must venture to advance the proposition that Scripture is essentially the property of the office of preaching and that it is the preaching which properly belongs to the congregation. Scripture requires to be interpreted and preached. By its nature it is not a book of edification for the congregation. What rightly belongs to the congregation is the text of the sermon together with the interpretation of this text, and on this basis there is a 'searching of the Scriptures, whether these things be so' (Acts 17.11), that is to say, whether they are really as the preaching has proclaimed them to be; in certain unusual circumstances, therefore, there arises the necessity for contradicting the preaching on the basis of Holy Scripture.[1] But even here it is presupposed that Holy Scripture belongs essentially to the office of teaching. If individual Christians, or groups of Christians, seize hold of the Bible, appealing to the equal right of all Christians, to the right of the faithful to speak for themselves and to the self-evident truth of the scriptural word, it is by no means a sign of special reverence

[1] In normal circumstances the examination of the preaching is the business not of the congregation but of the ecclesiastical visiting commission. It creates an unhealthy situation if the congregation is always obliged to listen to the preaching in a critical frame of mind.

or special spiritual understanding for the essential character of the divine revelation. In this lies the source of a great deal of presumption, disorder, rebellion and spiritual confusion. Respect for the holy character of the Scripture demands recognition of the fact that it is only by grace that a man is called upon to interpret and proclaim it and that it is also by grace that a man is permitted even to be a hearer of the interpretation and proclamation. The book of homilies and the prayer-book are the principal books for the congregation; the Holy Scripture is the book for the preacher; there can be little doubt that this formulation correctly represents the divinely ordained relationship between the congregation and the office. It must at the same time be borne clearly in mind that these ideas do not spring from a clergyman's desire to schoolmaster the laity; they follow from the revelation of God Himself.[1]

On the basis of Holy Scripture, the office of preaching proclaims Christ as the Lord and Saviour of the world. There can be no legitimate proclamation by the Church which is not a proclamation of Christ. The Church does not proclaim two different messages, a message of universal reason and natural law for unbelievers, and a Christian message for believers. Only a pharisaical self-conceit can impel the Church to withhold the proclamation of Christ from one man and not from another. The Church's word derives its sole right and its sole authority from the commission of Christ, and consequently any word which she may utter without reference to this authority will be devoid of all significance. In her encounter with the government, for example, the Church must not simply cease to be the Church; the mandate of the government is certainly not to confess Christ; the government is concerned rather with quite concrete abuses which its divine mandate requires it to remedy. It is only when the Church fulfils what is essentially her own mandate that she

[1] It goes without saying that there can be no question here of a prohibition of Bible reading, corresponding, for example to the Hindoo exclusion of the fourth caste from the study of the Vedas. We are concerned here with the recognition of the place which is essentially appropriate to the Scripture.

can legitimately call for the fulfilment of the mandate of the government. Nor does the Church have two different commandments at her disposal, one for the world and another for the Christian congregation; her commandment, which she proclaims to all mankind, is the one commandment of God which is revealed in Jesus Christ.

The Church proclaims this commandment by testifying to Jesus Christ as the Lord and Saviour of his people and of the whole world, and so by summoning all men to fellowship with Him.

Jesus Christ, the eternal Son with the Father for all eternity: this means that no created thing can be conceived and essentially understood without reference to Christ, the Mediator of creation. All things were created by Him and for Him, and have their existence only in Him (Col. 1.15ff.). It is vain to seek to know God's will for created things without reference to Christ. Jesus Christ, the incarnate God: this means that God has taken upon himself bodily all human being; it means that henceforward divine being cannot be found otherwise than in human form; it means that in Jesus Christ man is made free to be really man before God. The 'Christian' element is not now something which lies beyond the human element; it requires to be in the midst of the human element. The 'Christian' element is not an end in itself, but it consists in man's being entitled and obliged to live as man before God. In the incarnation God makes Himself known as Him who wishes to exist not for Himself but 'for us'. Consequently, in view of the incarnation of God, to live as man before God can mean only to exist not for oneself but for God and for other men.

Jesus Christ, the crucified Reconciler: this means in the first place that the whole world has become godless by its rejection of Jesus Christ and that no effort of its own can rid it of this curse. The reality of the world has been marked once and for all by the cross of Christ, but the cross of Christ is the cross of the reconciliation of the world with God, and for this reason the godless world bears at the same time the mark of reconciliation as the free ordinance of God. The cross of atonement is the setting free for life before God in the midst of the godless world; it is the setting free for life in genuine worldliness. The proclamation of the cross of the atonement is a setting free because it leaves behind it the vain attempts to deify the world and because it has overcome the disunions, tensions and conflicts between the 'Christian' element and the 'secular' element and calls for simple life and action in the belief that the reconciliation of the world with God has been accomplished. A life in genuine wordliness is possible only through the proclamation of Christ crucified; true worldly living is not possible or real in contradiction to the proclamation or side by side with it, that is to say, in any kind of autonomy of the secular sphere; it is possible and real only 'in, with and under' the proclamation of Christ. Without or against the proclamation of the cross of Christ there can be no recognition of the godlessness and godforsakenness of the world, but the worldly element will rather seek always to satisfy its insatiable longing for its own deification. If, however, the worldly element establishes its own law side by side with the proclamation of Christ, then it falls victim entirely to itself and must in the end set itself in the place of God. In both these cases the worldly element ceases to be worldly; if it is left to its own devices the worldly element will not and cannot be merely worldly. It strives desperately and convulsively to achieve the deification of the worldly, with the consequence that precisely this emphatically and exclusively worldly life falls victim to a spurious and incomplete worldliness. The freedom and the courage are lacking for genuine and complete worldliness, that is to say, for allowing the world to be what it really is before God, namely, a world which in its godlessness is reconciled with God. We shall have something to say later on about the definition of the contents of 'genuine worldliness'. What is decisive at the present juncture is that a genuine worldliness is possible solely and exclusively on the basis of the proclamation of the cross of Jesus Christ.

Jesus Christ, the risen and ascended Lord: this means that Jesus Christ has overcome sin and death and that He is the living

Lord to whom all power is given in heaven and on earth. All the powers of the world are made subject to Him and must serve Him, each in its own way. The lordship of Jesus Christ is not the rule of a foreign power; it is the lordship of the Creator, Reconciler and Redeemer, the lordship of Him through whom and for whom all created beings exist, of Him in whom indeed all created beings alone find their origin, their goal and their essence. Jesus Christ imposes no alien law upon creation; but at the same time He does not tolerate any 'autonomy' of creation in detachment from His commandments. The commandment of Jesus Christ, the living Lord, sets creation free for the fulfilment of the law which is its own, that is to say, the law which is inherent in it by virtue of its having its origin, its goal and its essence in Jesus Christ. The commandment of Jesus does not provide the basis for any kind of domination of the Church over the government, of the government over the family, or of culture over government or Church, or for any other relation of overlordship which may be thought of in this connexion. The commandment of Jesus Christ does indeed rule over Church, family, culture and government; but it does so while at the same time setting each of these mandates free for the fulfilment of its own allotted functions. Jesus Christ's claim to lordship, which is proclaimed by the Church, means at the same time the emancipation of family, culture and government for the realization of their own essential character which has its foundation in Christ.[1] The liberation which results from the proclamation of the lordship of Christ alone renders possible that relation of the divine mandates 'with', 'for' and 'against' one another, of which we shall later have to speak in detail.

We have just said that the dominion of the commandment of Christ over all creation is not to be equated with the dominion of the Church. This raises a crucial problem in connexion with the Church's mandate, a problem which we can now no longer avoid.

[1] The antinomy of heteronomy and autonomy is here resolved in a higher unity which we may call Christonomy.

The mandate of the Church is to proclaim the revelation of God in Jesus Christ. But the mystery of this name lies in the fact that it does not only designate an individual man but embraces at the same time the whole of human nature. We can testify to Jesus Christ and proclaim Him always only as Him in whom God took manhood upon Himself in the body. In Jesus Christ is the new humanity, the congregation of God. In Jesus Christ the word of God and the congregation of God are indissolubly linked together. Through Jesus Christ the word of God and the congregation of God are inseparably united. Consequently, wherever Jesus Christ is proclaimed in accordance with the divine mandate, there, too, there is always the congregation. In the first instance this means only that men are there who accept the word concerning Christ, and who believe it and acquiesce in it, unlike others who do not accept it but reject it. It means, then, that men are there who allow that to happen to themselves which properly, as an act of God, should happen to all men; it means that men are there who stand as deputies for the other men, for the whole world. Certainly these are men who at the same time lead their worldly lives in the family, culture and government; they do so as men whom the word of Christ has set free for life in the world, but now they also form a community, a body which is distinct and separate from worldly institutions, for they are assembled together around the word of God and they are men who are chosen and live in this word. It is with this particular 'community' that we must now concern ourselves, and we must first turn our attention to the necessary distinction between this and the divine mandate of proclamation. The word of God, proclaimed by virtue of a divine mandate, dominates and rules the entire world; the 'community' which comes into being around this word does not dominate the world, but it stands entirely in the service of the fulfilment of the divine mandate. The law of this 'community' cannot and must not ever become the law of the worldly order, for by doing so it would be establishing an alien rule; conversely the law of a worldly order cannot and must not ever become the law of this community. Thus the peculiarity of the divine mandate of the Church lies in the fact that the proclamation of the lordship of Christ over the whole world must always be distinguished from the 'law' of the Church as a community, while on the other hand the Church as a community is not to be separated from the office of proclamation.

The Church as a self-contained community serves to fulfil the divine mandate of proclamation. She does this in two ways: first by the adaptation of the whole organization of this community for the effective proclamation of Christ to the whole world, which means that the congregation itself is merely an instrument, merely a means to an end; secondly, by virtue of the fact that, precisely through the congregation's acting on behalf of the world in this way, the purpose is achieved and the divine mandate of proclamation has begun to be fulfilled. This means that, precisely through its willingness to be merely the instrument and the means to the end, the congregation has become the goal and centre of all God's dealing with the world. The concept of deputyship characterizes this twofold relationship most clearly. The Christian congregation stands at the point at which the whole world ought to be standing; to this extent it serves as deputy for the world and exists for the sake of the world. On the other hand, the world achieves its own fulfilment at the point at which the congregation stands. The earth is the 'new creation', the 'new creature', the goal of the ways of God on earth. The congregation stands in this twofold relation of deputyship entirely in the fellowship and disciplehood of its Lord, who was Christ precisely in this, that He existed not for His own sake but wholly for the sake of the world.

The Church as a self-contained community is subject to a twofold divine ordinance and rule. She must be adapted to the purpose of the world, and precisely in this she must be adapted to her own purpose as the place at which Jesus Christ is present. The peculiar character of the Church as a self-contained community lies in the fact that in the very limitation of her spiritual and material domain she gives expression to the unlimited scope of the message of Christ, and that it is precisely this unlimited scope of the message of Christ which in its turn is a summons into the limited domain of the congregation.

The danger of Catholicism lies in the fact that it regards the Church essentially as an end in itself, and so tends to neglect the divine mandate of the proclamation of the word. The danger of the Reformation, on the other hand, lies in the fact that it devotes its whole attention to the mandate of the proclamation of the word and, consequently, almost entirely neglects the proper domain and function of the Church as an end in herself, and this consists precisely in her existence for the sake of the world. One need only call to mind the liturgical poverty and uncertainty of our present-day Protestant services, the feebleness of our ecclesiastical organization and law, the almost complete absence of any genuine ecclesiastical discipline, and the inability of most Protestants even to understand the significance of such disciplinary practices as spiritual exercises, asceticism, meditation and contemplation. One need only consider the general uncertainty about the special functions of the clergy, or the startlingly confused or presumptuous attitude of countless Protestant Christians towards those Christians who refuse to take oaths, those Christians who refuse to perform military service, etc., and one cannot help perceiving at once where the Protestant Church is at fault. Exclusive interest in the divine mandate of proclamation, and, together with this, interest in the Church's mission in the world, has resulted in failure to perceive the inner connexion between this mission and the Church's internal functions. This failure has necessarily detracted from the power, the abundance and the fulness of the proclamation itself, because the proclamation finds no fertile soil. In terms of parable, the commission of proclamation has been implanted in the congregation like the corn-seed in the field; if the soil has not been prepared the seed withers away and loses its own inherent fruitfulness.[1]

[1] This chapter was not completed. The plan for its further development has already been made clear.

PART TWO

I

THE DOCTRINE OF THE
PRIMUS USUS LEGIS
ACCORDING TO THE
LUTHERAN SYMBOLIC WRITINGS

1. *The Concept and its Usefulness*

WE find the term *usus legis* in the Latin heading of F.C.[1] VI: *de tertio usu legis* (in the German version: *Vom dritten Brauch des Gesetzes*). It occurs again in the Latin text of S.D. VI, 1, but in the German text *usus* is here replaced by the term *Nutzen* (advantage or profit). Ep. VI states that the law is given to men 'for three reasons' (corresponding to the Schmalkalden Article 'Of the Law'). From this it follows that no explicit answer is given to the question of the subject of the *usus*, *i.e.* whether the subject is God or the preacher, but that it is implicit that the subject is God. This view is also supported by Ep. VI, 7: 'Thus both for the penitent and for the impenitent, both for men who are born again and for men who are not born again, the law is and remains one and the same law, namely, the unalterable will of God, and the difference, so far as obedience is concerned, lies solely in the men themselves; for one who has not been born again performs the law as it is required of him, but he does it under compulsion and against his will (as do also those who are born again according to the flesh). The believer, however, without compulsion and willingly, if he has been born again, does what no threat of the law could ever force from him.' This means that the concept of the *usus legis* must not be taken to refer primarily to various different ways of preaching, *i.e.* different ways in which the preacher may use the

1 For the full names of the Lutheran symbolic writings discussed in this book, see p. 342.

law. On the contrary, it is primarily concerned with the various different effects of one and the same law. As for the subject or motivator of these effects, they must be regarded both as the free working of God upon man and as belief and unbelief on the part of man, so that the subject of the use must be not the preacher but God, and, in the proper sense, also the hearer of the preaching, man. However, this question is not explicitly clarified by the symbolic writings, and consequently there arise dangerous obscurities when it is expounded. The question of the active subject is of crucial importance for the whole problem of the preaching of the law, and it ought therefore to have been answered. For if the preacher were the subject of the three *usus* there would be a preaching of the law for the world which would be fundamentally distinct from the preaching of the law for the congregation, but if God is the subject there is only one preaching of the law, and this has a different effect with believers and with unbelievers. The preacher as subject of the *usus* would recognize an isolated preaching of works, but God as subject of the *usus* exercises a varying effect on man by the preaching of the one law. The concept of the *usus* fails to clarify this preliminary question, and its applicability is therefore questionable (*vide infra* §12).

2. *The Theological Justification for the Doctrine*

The law of God is 'a divine doctrine in which the just and unalterable will of God is revealed as to how man is to be framed in his nature, his thoughts, his words and his works, so that it may be pleasing and acceptable to God; and transgressors are threatened with the wrath of God, with punishment in time and in eternity' (S.D. V, 17) (*duplex usus* here?). This *primus usus legis* concerns the establishment of a *disciplina externa et honestas* (S.D. VI, 1). The *secundus usus* concerns the knowledge of sins. The *tertius usus* serves as a rule of conduct for converts and as a punishment for the flesh, which is still alive even in them. Even though the symbolic writings do not explicitly exclude it, it is in the nature of the case not possible to substantiate the view that the distinction between

272

the three *usus* relates to a chronological succession in the proclamation or to two fundamentally distinct classes of men, believers and unbelievers, in that order. The *externa disciplina* still applies also to the believers; and so do the threat and punishment of the law, so far as the believer is still flesh ('for the old Adam, the obstinate and contentious ass, is still also a part of them which cannot be subdued and made obedient to Christ solely with the teaching of the law or by admonition, by driving and by threatening, but which often also requires the cudgel of punishments and torments' (S.D. VI, 24)). The believer also still has need of the knowledge of sin through the law. Furthermore, already the *primus usus* comprises the whole contents of the law, namely, the entire decalogue. It also contains the threat and the promise which are addressed to the transgressor and the performer of the law respectively. It is uncertain whether or not the *usus paedagogicus* acquires an independent significance as a fourth *usus* between the *primus* and *secundus usus*; the Schmalkalden Articles recognize only two *usus*. These facts make it clear that the distinctions between the *usus* must not be understood chronologically; they do not refer to fundamentally different classes of men; they must be understood in relation to their substance. The *primus usus* defines the contents of the law with reference to the accomplishment of certain particular external works; the *secundus usus* defines the relation between the law and the person, leading the person to recognize that he is in opposition to the law and is condemned for it; the *tertius usus* defines the law as God's merciful help in the performance of the works which are commanded. The *primus usus* is the law as the preaching of works; the *secundus* is the law as the preaching of the knowledge of sin; the *tertius* is the law as the preaching of the fulfilment of the law. The proclamation of the law always comprises all three elements; if it is otherwise, then the unity of the law of God is disrupted and it becomes necessary to ask not only whether it is expedient to employ the concept of *usus* (§1) but also whether the doctrine of *usus* is justified theologically (*vide infra* §12).

3. *Interest in the Concept*

The *primus usus* is not treated with systematic coherence in the symbolic writings. It is not an object of interest as an independent topic. It is mentioned in connexion with various topics to which it is relevant. It receives a positive emphasis in the polemic against the monastic doctrine of perfection, against the ecclesiastical claim to secular authority, and against the enthusiasts, as well as in the doctrine of secular government; it receives a negative emphasis in the doctrine of justification and in the related critique of justification by works, as well as in the doctrine of free will. Finally, it appears with no particular emphasis, as a neutral formula, in the discussion of the *tertius usus legis*. The *primus usus* is of interest to the symbolic writings only so far as it stands in relation to the gospel.

4. *Definition*

By means of the *primus usus* 'outward discipline and seemliness are preserved against wild and disobedient people' (Ep. VI, 1). We will now consider the contents, the purpose, the means of execution, the proclaimer and the hearer of the *primus usus*.

5. *Contents*

The contents of the *primus usus* are the entire decalogue with reference to the works which it requires and together with the threat and the promise which it comprises. 'Here we maintain that the law is given by God, firstly in order to curb sin with threats and fear of punishment and with the promise and offer of grace and beneficence' (Schmalkalden Article 'Of the Law'—A.S.: C. II). With respect to its contents the whole of the law is comprised within the *primus usus* (A.C. IV, 8). Nowhere in the symbolic writings do we find the idea that the second table of the decalogue may be preached without the first. On the contrary, this dichotomy is everywhere sharply criticized. Already the first table includes a reference to the fact that the second table, too, cannot be fulfilled by works alone; and this means that the *primus usus* is superseded (A.C. IV, 8, 35). However, the law is not to be found only in the decalogue; it runs through the entire New Testament. 'What can be a more solemn and terrible telling forth and preaching of the wrath of God against sin, than the passion and death of Christ, His Son? But so far as all this preaches the wrath of God and makes man afraid, it is not the preaching of the gospel and of Christ, but Moses and the law for the unrepentant' (S.D. V, 12).

From what has just been said it follows that the *primus usus* also includes the preaching of the cross of Christ as preaching of the law. This conclusion is necessary, even though it is not expressed and presumably not intended in the symbolic writings; the S.D. (V, 10) even speaks of a preaching 'without Christ' and *sine mentione Christi*, which can presumably refer only to the *primus usus*. Yet the cross is always also preaching of the gospel, and from this point of view the preaching of the gospel is contained already in the decalogue; thus the *primus usus* can never be preached in abstract detachment from the gospel. Nevertheless, the essential purpose of the *primus usus* is to demand those works of the law which pertain to outward discipline and seemliness. By threats and by the enticement of the earthly benefits which God has promised for an honourable life men's fear and their longing for happiness are employed to compel them to perform the works of the law. This demonstrates that the *primus usus* is exclusively directed towards the achievement of works, that is to say, of particular conditions. From this standpoint the contents of the *primus usus* can now be designated as the 'natural law, innate in the heart, the law which coincides with the law of Moses or the ten commandments' (A.C. IV, 7). This formulation does not envisage the possibility of a *lex naturae* which deviates from the decalogue and gives rise to a conflict; the decalogue in any case always remains the sole criterion. It is, therefore, the will of God and not the will of man which takes effect in the *primus usus* or the *lex naturae*. 'God demands and requires such an outwardly seemly life, and for the sake of God's commandment one must do these same good works which are commanded in the ten commandments' (A.C. IV, 22). The organ through which the *lex naturae* takes effect is reason. Reason is opposed by the demonic forces ('evil lust and devils'), and these are more powerful than reason, so that despite its 'violent efforts' reason seldom achieves its purpose (A.C. XVIII, 71f.). This makes it clear that not every human impulse can pretend to be a natural law. The ultimate criterion is always the decalogue.

6. *Its Purpose*

The purpose of the *primus usus* is the establishment of the *iustitia civilis, rationis* or *carnis* (A.C. IV, 22–24; XVIII, 70). This consists in a seemly life in accordance with both tables of the decalogue (speaking of God, outward service of God and holy bearing, honouring of parents, not stealing (A.C. XVIII, 70)). It lies 'to some extent' within the power of free will and of reason, even though it will only seldom be realized (A.C. XVIII, 72). It wins praise from men and from God, 'for in this life and worldly being there is indeed nothing better than honesty and virtue ... and God rewards such virtue with bodily gifts' (A.C. IV, 24). This means that the whole of worldly life is subject to the decalogue so far as works are concerned. God desires *iustitia civilis* of all men, including Christians. This is the reply to the Enthusiasts, 'who teach that Christian perfection is to leave house and home, wife and child, bodily' (C.A. XVI, 4) and who thus seek to make of the gospel a new law for the world. The answer to this is that the gospel is not 'an outward and temporal being but an inward and eternal being and righteousness of hearts' and that it does not give 'new laws for civil life' (A.C. XVI, 55–57). This statement about the gospel, therefore, necessarily presupposes the proclamation of the decalogue for the establishment of *iustitia civilis*. Apart from this context it would itself be enthusiastic. Thus it is the opinion of the symbolical writings that the decalogue teaches the whole of the contents of the law and that the gospel adds nothing to it.

7. *Means of Execution*

As the means for the execution of the *primus usus*, *i.e.* for the establishment of *iustitia civilis*, 'God gives laws, institutes government, and provides learned and wise people to serve as rulers' (A.C. IV, 22). This means that civil government is placed under God's law and in His service. The law of the decalogue, which is preached by the Church, is executed by the government with force, and for this purpose the government is given the sword. The symbolic writings assume indeed that reason will dictate to governments the same law as the revealed law of the decalogue; thus they do not consider the possibility of a conflict of principle between the *lex naturae* and the decalogue. Yet this does not mean that government has a twofold basis and is founded both on a natural law and on a revealed law; it is only because these two laws have been declared to be identical (*vide supra* §5) that natural law, reason, can be represented as the basis for governmental action. Natural law can never lay claim to divine authority in opposition to the decalogue. Although, or rather because, the government has its origin in the law of God, as the Church proclaims it, and serves this law, it possesses a dignity of its own in relation to the Church, which proclaims the gospel; its dignity does not lie in a freedom from the law of God, from the decalogue, a freedom based upon a law of its own; it lies in the obedience with which it executes the law of God. By doing God's will in this way, by punishing the wicked and rewarding the good, the government glorifies its divine office and establishes its claim to obedience; in this the rulers may have a clear conscience (A.C. XVI, 64). The symbolic writings praise the Protestant doctrine for having restored to government its own proper dignity as distinct from human institutions. Thus the doctrine of *iustitia civilis* serves polemically the emancipation and honouring of worldly life under the decalogue, in opposition to the Roman doctrine of the perfection of the monastic life. But whenever a natural law sets itself up in opposition to the law of God in the decalogue, whenever the sword of government is no longer willing to serve the law of God (an eventuality which is not envisaged in this form by the symbolic writings), then this perverted nature and reason cannot lay claim to a divine right of their own, but they must be made subject to the law of God by the proclamation of the Church. For the symbolic writings the 'natural' is determined solely by the decalogue.

8. *The Proclaimer*

The proclaimer of the *primus usus* is primarily the Church and secondarily the government, the head of the family and the master. The Church proclaims the *primus usus* by preaching the whole law according to all three *usus*, that is to say indirectly; the government proclaims the *primus usus* directly. The Church proclaims the *primus usus* in the service of the gospel; and the government proclaims it as an end in itself. The place of the decalogue is both in the church and in the government building.

9. *The Hearer*

The hearers of the *primus usus* are the 'unbelievers, savages and un-Christians'. In other words the preaching is addressed to men, not to institutions as such; the institutions belong rather on the side of the proclaimers. For the symbolic writings there is no theological problem as to whether and what it is necessary to preach to the unbelievers. The practical problem, moreover, as to whether the unbelievers can be reached, is assumed to have been solved; some are reached by the Church and the others by the government. By unbelievers the symbolic writings certainly understand a particular class of men, but this idea is already partly negated by the fact that, according to the symbolic writings, the Christian, too, is still in the flesh and consequently has as much need of the *primus usus legis* as the unbeliever has (*cf.* the New Testament catalogues of vices). Conversely, the unbelievers, too, are subject to the call of the gospel, and because of the gospel they become subject to the Church's proclamation of the *primus usus*. There is no proclamation which is *only* for the unbelievers, but only a proclamation which is intended *also* for the unbelievers. There is no theological basis for a clear division of men into two classes. Such a division is not explicitly excluded by the symbolic books, and indeed it is occasionally suggested by them, but it is incompatible with their theological assertions.

10. *The Primus Usus and the Gospel*

(*a*) The *primus usus* conflicts with the gospel because it demands a righteousness of works and so makes man presumptuous (Schmalkalden Article 'Of the Law'—A.S. C. II, S.D. V, 10). For the gospel, therefore, *iustitia civilis* is sin and hypocrisy (A.C. II, 34; IV, 35). 'Whatever does not proceed from faith is sin. The person must first be pleasing to God if this person's works are to please Him' (S.D. IV, 8).

(*b*) The *primus usus* is relative to the gospel. 1. Through the *primus usus* there comes into being the worldly order which, according to God's will, preserves the world from disorder and arbitrariness. 2. Within this order man receives from God all the goodly gifts of earthly life and is able to do good works in faith in the gospel. In the symbolic writings this idea that secular institutions exist for the sake of life in faith in the gospel predominates over the idea that these institutions serve as a prerequisite for salvation through the gospel. 3. The government, which protects these institutions, provides for the maintenance of the Christian proclamation ('the Lord God demands this of *all* kings and princes . . .'[A.C. XXI, 44]) and is itself, as an institution of God, 'preserved and protected by God against the devil' (A.C. VIII, 50.4). Within the *iustitia civilis* observance of the first commandment means attendance at church, hearing the sermon, hearing the gospel, and a certain amount of reflection; one is not to 'wait for God to impart his gift from heaven directly' (S.D. II, 53, 46, 24). Attendance at the preaching, the 'means' whereby this gift is imparted, constitutes at the same time the closest link and the sharpest distinction between the *primus usus* and the gospel. Certainly, within the *primus usus*, this obedience is still always outward divine worship and sin, yet at this point it becomes positively the 'prerequisite' for faith in the gospel, even though it is at the same time in direct opposition to it. 5. The *primus usus* is both superseded and preserved by the gospel. In faith in Jesus Christ it is both broken down and fulfilled.

(*c*) The *primus usus* cannot be separated from the proclamation of the gospel. It applies both to unbelievers and to believers (Ep. VI, 6; S.D. VI, 9); it is not a method of proclamation but an integral part of the 'one unalterable will of God', and it cannot, therefore, be detached from the other two *usus*. There can be no Christian preaching of works without the preaching of the acknowledgement of sin and of the fulfilment of the law. And the law cannot be preached without the gospel. It is true that, according to the symbolic writings, some sayings of Scripture proclaim the law and others the gospel ('in some places it holds up the law to us and in some places it offers us grace . . .' [A.C. IV, 5]); yet at the same time the symbolic writings recognize that the law and the gospel are everywhere linked together from the decalogue through the preaching of the cross, and they teach that the preaching of both has always 'been side by side' (S.D. V, 23). Thus ultimately it is not the preacher but God alone who distinguishes between the law and the gospel. If the *primus usus* is preached in isolation it becomes a moral sermon and ceases to be the living word of God. It is clericalism and pharisaism if to a certain class of men one preaches only works, and is satisfied if these works are performed, and if one withholds from them the totality of the proclamation. The moral preacher can only produce hypocrites. The exposition of the decalogue in the *Great Catechism* affords the best practical rule for the preaching of the *primus usus*.

(*d*) The *primus usus* has its origin and goal in the gospel. The gospel is to be preached to all men; Jesus Christ became man and died for the sins of all men; He won salvation for His enemies; for these reasons the Christian proclamation summons all men to the faith. It, therefore, has no independent interest in the establishment of particular secular institutions. It summons men to the secular order because it summons them to the faith. In Christ God loved man and the world, and it is for that reason that there is also to be order among men and in the world. Man belongs to God in grace, and that is why he is to obey Him in works. It is because there exists a congregation of God that there can and must exist also justice, peace and order. Faith remains the prerequisite and origin of all works. And it is only from this point of view that the gospel is also the goal of the *primus usus*. God desires the outward order not only because the gospel exists but also in order that it may exist. Understood in this way the *primus usus* bears a 'pedagogical' character with regard to Christ (A.C. IV, 22). Both sequences are, therefore, theologically justified and necessary: gospel and law as well as law and gospel. In the symbolic writings the second sequence predominates. But in both sequences the gospel is the 'actual' kingdom of God.

(*e*) The *primus usus* and the kingdom of Christ. The biblical doctrine of the dominion of Christ over all earthly dominions and powers is taken up by the symbolic writings solely in the Christological article, but not in any way in connexion with the *primus usus*. The symbolic writings relate the concept of the kingdom of Christ entirely to the Church.

11. *Some Deductions and Questions*

(*a*) The proclamation of the *primus usus* is coextensive with the proclamation of the gospel. In other words, it is, according to God's will, unlimited. But it encounters a concrete inward limit in the unbelief and the disobedience of men and an outward limit in the power of government to resist the proclamation and to deprive the proclaimers and hearers of all secular responsibility. So long as the Christian bears secular responsibility the *primus usus* forms part of his confession of Christ. The more completely the proclamation brings about the situation of Rev. 13, and the more completely the Christians cease to share in the responsibility for the world's wrongdoing and themselves become the sufferers of wrong, so much the more will the responsibility which is laid upon them through the *primus usus* prove itself in obedient acceptance of suffering and in strict congregational discipline. But even the congregation in the catacombs will never be deprived of the universality of its mission. In preaching the law and the gospel it openly professes this mission and so keeps in view its responsibility for the world. The congregation can never be content to cultivate its own internal life; for to do so would be to deny its Master. Even when it can maintain the *iustitia civilis* only among its own members, because its word is not received by the world, it still does this in the service of the world and of its own universal mission. It will learn that the world is in disorder and that the kingdom of Christ is not of this world, but precisely in this it will be reminded of its mission towards the world. If it did otherwise, it would become a mere religious association. There is in principle no limit to the mission of the congregation; how it is to fulfil this mission will always have to be decided by the congregation itself in accordance with the signs of the times. The complete fulfilment of its mission will always be gravely endangered if the congregation supposes itself too directly to be placed in the situation of Rev. 13. The apocalyptic proclamation may well be a flight from the *primus usus*. The congregation will not try to compensate for the weakness of the word of God by religious fanaticism; nor will it confuse its own weakness with the weakness of the word.

(*b*) The symbolic writings maintain silence with regard to the question of the form of the proclamation of the *primus usus*, whether it is to be proclaimed only by preaching and instruction, that is to say, only by way of address to the congregation, or whether it is to be proclaimed in direct public or private address to persons in positions of governmental authority, whether it must on every single occasion contain an explicit reference to the gospel, whether it is to consist in a direct naming of concrete sins or in a general proclamation of the law, and whether it is to appear as a protest, a warning or a request. This means that the proclaimer who asks himself these questions is free to decide for himself, so long as he is conscious in faith of the aim which he is pursuing and of the situation in which he finds himself (as preacher, a head of a family, or as a ruler). The Reformation period, in fact, provides examples of all these possibilities.

(c) The *primus usus* is far removed from the moral preaching which sees its proper task in the adopting of certain attitudes towards current events and which consequently ascribes an independent significance to secular institutions and regards the gospel only as a means to an end. It is far removed also from the preaching which is, in principle, 'purely religious' and which separates the gospel from the worldly existence of man. Both of these ways of preaching are thematically determined and are, therefore, arbitrary curtailments and denials of the word of the living God which sets the believer in a situation of worldly responsibility. This false antithesis of moralizing and religious themes must be replaced by the true distinction and connexion between the law and the gospel. A relatively sure mark of these spurious themes is the polemical apologetic which is predominant in preaching of this kind; in such cases even the greatest religious or 'prophetic' emphasis cannot conceal the fact that the ultimate criterion for the proclamation is here the world and man and not the word of God. The preaching of false themes deprives the hearer of both the claim and the comfort of Jesus Christ.

(d) The *primus usus* marks the interest of the Christian proclamation in the contents of the law. It excludes a purely formal interpretation of the law. It is not concerned with the situation of the responsible man in the conflict of duties, but with the realization of particular conditions; it is not concerned with the place of the Christian in secular institutions, but with the form of the secular order in accordance with the will of God; it is not concerned with the christianization of worldly institutions or with their incorporation in the Church, but with their genuine worldliness, their 'naturalness' in obedience to God's word.

(e) In the field of *iustitia civilis* collaboration is possible and necessary between Christians and non-Christians in the clarification of certain questions of fact and in the furthering of certain concrete tasks. Because of their essentially different motivations the results which ensue from this cooperation do not bear the character of a proclamation of the word of God but rather that of a responsible counsel or demand on the basis of human knowledge. This distinction must be maintained. Cooperation may be desired and promoted by either the secular or the spiritual authority. The further question, whether or not cooperation between Christians of different denominations can lead to a proclamation by the Churches in common, depends solely on their unanimity in the interpretation of the word of God in faith in Jesus Christ. Within the proclamation the concrete formulation will relate essentially to the punishment of concrete sins, but in the field of responsible counsel it will be enabled and obliged to assume the form of positive demands.

(*f*) Unlike the other *usus*, the *primus usus* receives no explicit biblical corroboration in the symbolic writings. Does this mean that it is unbiblical? 1. The Bible recognizes no proclamation of the *primus usus* in detachment from the gospel. 2. The Bible recognizes no difference of principle between preaching for unbelievers and preaching for believers. 3. The Bible teaches that the proclamation and activity of the congregation take place in responsibility for the world. This responsibility can never be disregarded, for God loved the world and desires that all men shall be helped. 4. The Bible's attitude to the secular institutions is stated mainly in the form of concrete instructions to the congregation (Rom. 13; duties of the householder; catalogues of vices; Philemon). Nevertheless, there is also direct preaching to secular authorities (Paul before Felix on the resurrection of the dead, on justice, chastity and the judgement which is to come, Acts 24.14ff.; before Festus, the reference to the law of the state against arbitrary action, Acts 25.9; before Agrippa, Acts 26.1; John before Herod, Matt. 14.4). In any case, however, it is a question of concrete obedience to Him to whom all power is given in heaven and upon earth.

284

12. *Critique of the Doctrine of Usus in the Lutheran Symbolic Writings*

(*a*) The concept of *usus* is open to misunderstanding with regard to its subject or agent.

(*b*) The relating of the *primus usus* to the unbelievers threatens to lead to a disruption of the unity of the law and of the totality of the proclamation.

(*c*) The distinction between the three *usus* is not absolutely clear. This results from the association with the doctrine of *usus* of a distinction between different classes of men and a failure to refrain entirely from regarding the *usus* as different methods of proclamation.

(*d*) The relation between the preaching of the *primus usus* and the natural law is not clarified. In its present form the doctrine of the *primus usus* may give rise to a fallacious theology of institutions.

(*e*) A revision of the doctrine of *usus* would have to avoid any distinction between classes of hearers and represent the one law in its threefold form as the preaching of works, as the preaching of the acknowledgement of sin, and as the preaching of the fulfilment of the law. Alternatively, or in addition, it would have to treat the validity and effect of the whole law of God (in its threefold form) as a question which is to be systematically separated from the foregoing one. It would have to deal with the validity of the law in its two aspects, in relation to unbelievers and to believers, and with its effect, in the four aspects of righteousness of works, the example of Christ, despair and the guidance of grace. The old Lutheran dogmatics hesitated between *duplex, triplex* and *quadruplex usus legis* because it mixed together all these questions regarding the law; the question of its form requires treatment under three headings, that of its validity under two and that of its effect under four. Any attempt to reduce one of these questions to terms of another necessarily leads to confusion. The term *usus* itself, however, involves the danger of this confusion.

II

'PERSONAL' AND 'REAL' ETHOS

1. *Personal or Real Ethos?*

DILSCHNEIDER put forward a formulation in his ethics which today receives very wide acceptance, especially in supposedly Lutheran circles. 'Protestant ethics is concerned with man's personality and with this personality alone. All the other things of this world remain untouched by this Protestant ethos. The things of the world do not enter ethically into the zone of the demands of ethical imperatives.'[1] This is intended to provide a basis for the view that Christian ethics is concerned with the Christian economist, the Christian statesman, etc., but not with economics, the state, etc. To make this clear: the distinction between a 'personal' and a 'real' ethos is not identical with the distinction between an 'individual' and a 'social' ethic; on the contrary, it is recognized that the Christian also possesses social obligations in the world. Nor does the rejection of the 'real ethos' imply the rejection of all concrete ethics in favour of a formal ethic; on the contrary, within the personal ethos completely concrete terms are employed. Thus, in order to refute Dilschneider's thesis it is not sufficient to refer either to the biblical commandments which relate to life in society or to the concrete character of the biblical ethic. On the contrary, to put it very briefly, the question here is whether within the field of Christian ethics any assertions may be made with regard to worldly institutions and conditions, *e.g.* the state, economics or science, *i.e.* whether Christian ethics has an interest in worldly institutions and conditions or whether these things of the world are, in fact, 'ethically neutral' and do not fall within 'the zone of the demands of ethical

[1] Otto Dilschneider, *Die evangelische Tat*, Bertelsmann, 1940, p. 87.

286

imperatives'. In other words, is it the Church's sole task to practise love and charity within the given worldly institutions, *i.e.* to inspire these institutions so far as possible with a new outlook, to mitigate hardships, to care for the victims of these institutions, and to establish a new order of her own within the congregation? Or is the Church charged with a mission towards the given worldly orders themselves, a mission of correction, improvement, etc., a mission to work towards a new worldly order? Has the Church merely to gather up those whom the wheel has crushed or has she to prevent the wheel from crushing them?

2. *The New Testament*

A. The liberal theologians, especially Troeltsch and Naumann, treated the original gospel as a 'purely religious' power which encompasses the individual man in his outlook but is at the same time indifferent and unconcerned with regard to worldly institutions and conditions. They have drawn attention on the one hand to its solicitude for the 'infinite value of the human soul' and on the other hand to its alleged indifference with regard, for example, to slavery or the political régime. In view of this deficiency of the New Testament gospel Naumann concluded that he could be a Christian in only five or ten per cent of his life, *i.e.* only in so far as he was not concerned with worldly institutions. In reply to this liberal theology the religious-socialist theologians based their argument on the socially revolutionary character of the sayings of Jesus about the poor and the rich, about justice and peace, and about the coming of the kingdom of God on earth. They saw in the gospel of Jesus the world-reforming power κατ' ἐξοχήν. 'God and the soul' and 'the kingdom of God on earth'—these were the opposing watchwords. We have already perceived that this is a false antithesis and that the question is wrongly formulated. For both views have failed to discern the central feature of the New Testament, the person of Jesus Christ as the salvation of the world. The ethical question is contingent on the question of

Christ, and it is only on the basis of the New Testament answer to the question of Christ that it is possible to answer the question of the relation of the gospel to secular institutions.

(a) All created things are through and for Christ and exist only in Christ (Col. 1.16). This means that there is nothing, neither persons nor things, which stands outside the relation to Christ. Indeed it is only in relation to Christ that created things have their being. This is true not only of man but also of the state, economy, science, nature, etc.

(b) In Christ 'all things' (Col. 1.17) (*i.e.* the world [II Cor. 5.19]) are reconciled with God; *all things* are 'summed up under one head'—ἀνακεφαλαίωσις (Eph. 1.10). Nothing is excepted. In Christ God loved 'the world' (John 3.16).

(c) The congregation of Jesus Christ is the place at which Christ is believed and obeyed as the salvation of the whole world. This means that from the outset the congregation, according to its essential character, bears responsibility for the world which God loved in Christ. If the congregation fails to fulfil this responsibility it ceases to be the congregation of Christ.

(d) Christ as the salvation of the world implies the dominion of Christ over men and things. The dominion of Christ does not here mean the same in the case of the individual person as it means, for example, in the case of the state or the economy, etc. It is only through the dominion of Christ that everything, man, the state, the economy, etc., attains to its proper essence. But all these things belong together and must not be arbitrarily torn apart.

(e) Because all created things exist for the sake and purpose of Christ they are all subject to Christ's commandment and claim. For the sake and purpose of Christ there is and ought to be worldly order in state, family and economy. For the sake of Christ the worldly order is subject to the commandment of God. It is to be noted that there is no question here of a 'Christian state' or a 'Christian economy', but only of the rightful state and the rightful economy as a secular institution for the sake of Christ. There exists, therefore, a

Christian responsibility for secular institutions, and within a Christian ethic there exist propositions which relate to this responsibility.

B. What concrete expression does the New Testament give to this responsibility of the congregation for the world?

(*a*) The crucial point is that an interest in the conditions of the world is found only within the context of the whole proclamation of Christ. The New Testament cannot conceive of a proclamation to the world without testimony to Christ, *i.e.* without the only solid basis for such a proclamation. Consequently the decisive responsibility of the congregation for the world is always the proclamation of Christ. But in the service of this proclamation of Christ St Paul appeals to the Roman law and testifies before the heathen authority to chastity and righteousness (Acts 16, 24.14ff., 25.10, 26.1).

(*b*) But why does the New Testament not fight against slavery? The most far-reaching conclusions have been drawn from this one single fact with a complete disregard for all the New Testament statements of principle. The usual explanation by reference to the expectation of the imminent return of Jesus is not conclusive. Either the fact of the dominion of Christ over all fields of life was to be taken seriously, in which case the expectation of the impending end could only call for an even quicker realization of this dominion in order to prepare the way for the coming of Christ (*cf.* Luke 12.45), or else it was not to be taken seriously at all. In that case it was not to be taken seriously even when the coming of the Lord was delayed. However, according to the New Testament, there can be no doubt of the seriousness of Christ's claim upon all created things; so that only the following simple explanations remain. St Paul did not regard the form of slavery which was practised in his time as an institution which conflicted with the commandment of God. This view can be supported by sources which refer to the relative mildness of the slavery of that period. Above all, St Paul was able to observe that the slave was clearly not prevented by his actual situation as a slave from living as a Christian. An order of the world which left room for the congregation of

Jesus Christ and for life in accordance with the commandments of God was not in itself unacceptable; it required to be
corrected from within. It may well have been much the same
with the political and economic situation; here it is necessary
to remember that the Roman Empire was precisely at this
time characterized by a certain stability and legal security.
It must also be borne in mind that it was only very much
later that the Apostle came in contact with the sometimes
far harsher form of slavery which was practised in the western
part of the Empire, and that he could have taken up a
position with regard to these questions only within the context
of his proclamation of Christ. It is, however, clear that he did
not do so even in Rome, as can be deduced from the subse-
quent attitude of the Church. Of greater importance than
any of these possible explanations is the fact that there are a
number of completely different ways in which the congregation may fulfil its responsibility towards the world. It will
fulfil it differently when it is in the situation of a mission and
when it is in a situation in which the Church is recognized
by the state, and differently again in times of persecution.
The mission community, as a minority, will have to con-
centrate at first entirely on the preaching of Christ as a
summons to the congregation, in order to open up a way for
itself towards sharing in some kind of responsible work in
the world. For the Church which is recognized by the state,
and for the Christians who bear secular office and responsibility, the confession of Christ must include testimony to the
commandment of God with regard to the state, economy,
etc. The more completely the Christians find themselves in
the situation of Rev. 13 and are not responsible for the wrong-
doings of the world but are themselves sufferers under wrong,
so much the more completely will their responsibility for the
world be tested solely in obedience under suffering and in
strict congregational discipline. But even the congregation in
the catacombs will never be deprived of the universality of its
task. The congregation will always have to decide for itself
how it is to perform this task in view of the character of the
times. The New Testament, too, refers to political and

economic forms which in themselves conflict with the commandment of God (Rev. 13). Soon after this period it was
questionable whether it was permissible to serve as a soldier
or official in the Roman Empire.

3. *The Symbolic Writings*

In the symbolic writings the interest of the Church of
Christ in secular institutions is defined in the doctrine of the
primus usus legis. It is to be noted here that the *primus usus* is
possible only within the unity of the whole law and of the
whole proclamation. It is only for Christ's sake that there
exists a *primus usus* and a *iustitia civilis*. Whenever the *primus
usus* threatens to detach itself from this unity it becomes an
abstract natural law without any foundation. The best
example to follow is Luther's *Great Catechism*, in which this
unity is preserved. In the *primus usus* the Church demonstrates that she does not leave the world to its own devices,
but that she summons it to submit to the dominion of Christ.
In other words, the *primus usus* is not concerned with the
situation of the Christian in the secular institution, but with
the secular institutions themselves in accordance with the
will of God. It is not concerned with the christianizing of
the secular institutions or with subordinating them to the
Church, that is to say, with abolishing their 'relative'
autonomy; it is concerned rather with their true worldliness
or 'naturalness' in obedience to God's word. It is, therefore,
precisely in their genuine worldliness that the secular
institutions are subject to the dominion of Christ. This, and
nothing else, constitutes their 'autonomy'. They are 'autonomous' not in relation to the law of Christ but in relation to
earthly heteronomies.

4. *Some Criticisms of Dilschneider's Thesis*

(*a*) The isolation of the person from the world of things is
idealistic and not Christian. Christ does not detach the
person from the world of things but from the world of sin;
there is a great difference. There are no things 'in themselves',
which are not related to the person. There is no realm of

things which, on principle, stand outside the realm of persons and therefore outside the range of the divine commandments. That is true not only of historical entities but also of the realm of nature, though even this distinction is questionable from the point of view of the Bible. Nature is subject to commandments which are revealed to us in the word, the commandments of fruitfulness, of growth, of praising God (Ps. 148) and of service towards man. Thus in the Bible there is no distinction drawn between the world of persons and a world of things which is not affected by God's commandments.

(b) The alleged immunity of the world of things from the commandment of God rests on a false interpretation of the doctrine of *adiaphora*. The fact that *adiaphora* exist does not at all mean that the world of things is neutralized; it means, on the contrary, that it is appointed by God to serve the liberty of men. Nothing is in principle an *adiaphoron*; the assertion that a thing is an *adiaphoron* is only a statement of belief and it does not imply at all that a certain quality is possessed by the 'thing in itself' independently of the person, but rather expresses a particular relationship of the person to the thing. A doctrine which states that things may in principle be *adiaphora* is antinomistic.

(c) How far does the world of things actually extend? Does it not extend into the midst of the congregation? To sever the world of things from the commandments of God is to proclaim its autonomy; this constitutes the abandonment of the dominion of Christ over one sphere of life, and that means antinomism.

(d) The untheological terms 'person' and 'thing' must be discarded in favour of the biblical distinction between the congregation and the secular institution.

5. *Systematic Considerations Concerning the Assertions Which Christian Ethics May Make With Regard to Secular Institutions*

(a) All the possible assertions with regard to secular institutions are founded upon Jesus Christ and must, therefore, be brought into relation with Him as the origin, essence and goal of all created things. It is the dominion of Christ which renders all these assertions possible and significant.

(*b*) In the proclamation of the dominion of Christ over secular institutions these institutions are not made subject to an alien rule, for 'he came unto his own' (John 1.11) and 'by him all things consist' (Col. 1.17). They are not made subject to a clerical, humanitarian, rational or Jewish law or to a form of moral natural law. Under the dominion of Christ they attain to their own true character and become subject to their own innate law, which is theirs according to the manner of their creation. Nor, on the other hand, are they made subject to the arbitrary rule of a so-called 'autonomy' which is fundamentally nothing but lawlessness, ἀνομία, and sin, but within the world which is created, loved and reconciled by God in Christ they receive the place which is characteristic, proper and right for them. Thus, under the dominion of Christ they receive their own law and their own liberty.

(*c*) The decalogue is the law of living, revealed by God, for all life which is subject to the dominion of Christ. It signifies liberation from alien rule and from arbitrary autonomy. It discloses itself to believers as the law of the Creator and the Reconciler. The decalogue is the framework within which a free obedience becomes possible in worldly life. It affords liberty for free life under the dominion of Christ.

(*d*) The dominion of Christ and the decalogue do not mean that the secular institutions are made subservient to a human ideal or 'natural law', nor yet to the Church (this being a contradiction of the medieval Thomist doctrine), but they mean their emancipation for true worldliness, for the state to *be* a state, etc. The primary implication for secular institutions of the dominion of Christ and of the decalogue is not, therefore, the conversion of the statesman or the economist, nor yet the elimination of the harshness and unmercifulness of the state for the sake of a falsely interpreted christianization of the state and its transformation into a part of the Church. It is precisely in the dispensation of strict

justice and in the administration of the office of the sword, in
maintaining the unmerciful character of the institutions of
the state, that is to say, their genuine worldliness, that the
dominion of Christ, *i.e.* the rule of mercy, is given its due.
The incarnation of God, that is to say, the incarnation of love,
would be misinterpreted if one were to fail to perceive that
the worldly institutions of strict justice, of punishment and
of the wrath of God are also a fulfilment of this incarnate
love and that the commandment of the sermon on the mount
is also observed in genuine action by the state. The purpose
and aim of the dominion of Christ is not to make the worldly
order godly or to subordinate it to the Church but to set it
free for true worldliness.

(*e*) The emancipation of the worldly order under the
dominion of Christ takes concrete form not through the conversion of Christian statesmen, etc., but through the concrete encounter of the secular institutions with the Church
of Jesus Christ, her proclamation and her life. By allowing
this Church of Jesus Christ to continue, by making room for
her and by enabling her proclamation of the dominion of
Christ to take effect, the secular institutions attain to their
own true worldliness and law which has its foundation in
Christ. Their attitude to the Church of Jesus Christ will
always be the measure of the true worldliness which is not
impeded by any ideological and alien law or by any arbitrary
autonomy. A false attitude to the Church will always have
as its consequence a failure to achieve genuine worldliness on
the part of the secular institutions, the state, etc., and *vice
versa*.

(*f*) With regard to the relationship of the secular institutions to one another and to the Church, the Lutheran
doctrine of the three estates, *oeconomicus, politicus* and *hierarchi-
cus*, has as its decisive characteristic and permanent significance that it is based on coordination rather than any kind
of priority and subordination, so that the worldly order is
safeguarded against the alien rule of the Church, and *vice
versa*. In my opinion this doctrine must be replaced by a
doctrine which is drawn from the Bible, the doctrine of the

four divine mandates, marriage and family, labour, government, and Church. These institutions are divine in that they possess a concrete divine commission and promise which has its foundation and evidence in the revelation. Amid the changes of all historical institutions these divine mandates continue until the end of the world. Their justification is not simply their historical existence; in this they differ from such institutions as the people, the race, the class, the masses, the society, the nation, the country, the Empire, etc. It is a positive divine mandate for the preservation of the world for the sake and purpose of Christ. It is perhaps not by chance that precisely these mandates seem to have their type in the celestial world. Marriage corresponds with Christ and the congregation; the family with God the Father and the Son, and with the brotherhood of men with Christ; labour corresponds with the creative service of God and Christ to the world, and of men to God; government corresponds with the dominion of Christ in eternity; the state corresponds with the πόλις of God.

(g) A word of the Church with regard to the secular institutions will consequently have to place these divine mandates, in whatever may be their concrete form at the time, under the dominion of Christ and under the decalogue. In doing this it will not be subjecting the secular institutions to an alien law, but it will be setting them free for concrete and genuine worldly service. It will speak of the divine mandates of the worldly order in such a way that the dominion of Christ is maintained *over* them and the divine mandate of the Christian Church is maintained *side by side* with them. It cannot deprive the secular institutions of their responsible decision and their service, but it can direct them to the only place at which they can decide and act responsibly.

(h) It may be remarked that the secular institutions are able to perform their service even without the encounter with the word of the Church of Jesus Christ (*cf.* Luther and the Turks). First of all, there is never more than a limited truth in this observation; genuine worldliness is achieved only through emancipation by Christ; without this there is the rule of alien laws, ideologies and idols. Secondly, the very limited correctness of this remark can only afford the Church a thankfully accepted confirmation of the truth which is revealed to her; it cannot lead her to suppose that this is in itself sufficient, but it must lead her to proclaim the dominion of Christ as the full truth in the midst of all partial truths. When the Church perceives that a worldly order is on some few occasions possible without the preaching being heard (but still never without the existence of Jesus Christ), this will not impel her to disregard Christ, but it will elicit from her the full proclamation of the grace of the dominion of Christ. The unknown God will now be preached as the God who is known because He is revealed.

III

STATE AND CHURCH

1. *The Concepts Involved*

THE concept of the state is foreign to the New Testament. It has its origin in pagan antiquity. Its place is taken in the New Testament by the concept of government ('power'). The term 'state' means an ordered community; government is the power which creates and maintains order. The term 'state' embraces both the rulers and the ruled; the term 'government' refers only to the rulers. The concept of the *polis*, which is a constituent of the concept of the state, is not necessarily connected with the concept of *exousia*. For the New Testament the *polis* is an eschatological concept; it is the future city of God, the new Jerusalem, the heavenly society under the rule of God. The term government does not essentially refer to the earthly *polis*; it may go beyond it; it is, for example, applicable even in the smallest form of community, in the relation of father and child or of master and servant. The term government does not, therefore, imply any particular form of society or any particular form of state. Government is divinely ordained authority to exercise worldly dominion by divine right. Government is deputyship for God on earth. It can be understood only from above. Government does not proceed from society, but it orders society from above. If it is exegetically correct to regard it as an angelic power, this would still serve only to define its position between God and the world. Only the concept of government, and not the concept of the state, can have a theological application. Nevertheless, in a concrete study the concept of the state naturally cannot be avoided.

In using the term 'church', and especially in clarifying its relation to the terms 'government' and 'state', we have to distinguish between the spiritual office or ministry and the congregation or the Christians. The spiritual office is the divinely ordained authority to exercise spiritual dominion by divine right. It does not proceed from the congregation, but from God. A clear distinction must be drawn between the secular and the spiritual authority, but the Christians are, nevertheless, at the same time citizens, and the citizens, whether they be believers or not, are at the same time subject to the claim of Jesus Christ. Consequently the relationship of the spiritual office to the government differs from that of the Christians. In order to avoid constant misunderstandings this difference should be kept clearly in view.

2. *The Basis of Government*

A. *In the Nature of Man*

The ancients, especially Aristotle, base the state on the character of man. The state is the supreme consummation of the rational character of men, and to serve it is the supreme purpose of human life. All ethics is political ethics. Virtues are political virtues. This theory of the state was taken over in principle by Catholic theology. The state is a product of human nature. Man's ability to live in society derives from the Creation, as does also the relation of ruler and ruled. The state fulfils the assigned purpose of the human character within the sphere of the natural and creaturely. The state is the 'highest development of the natural society' (Schilling, *Moraltheologie*, II, p. 609). This Aristotelian and Thomist doctrine is found in a somewhat modified form in Anglican theology. And indeed it has also penetrated into modern Lutheranism. With the Anglicans the connexion between natural theology and incarnational theology opens up the possibility of a peculiar natural-cum-Christian theory of the state. (Incidentally, the questionableness of this combination of natural and incarnational theology is now clearly perceived by the young Anglo-Catholics, who provide the corrective of a *theologia crucis*.) Modern Lutheranism acquired the notion of the natural state through Hegel and romanticism. In this case the state is the fulfilment not of the universally human and rational character of man, but of the creative will of God in the people. The state is essentially a nation-state. The people fulfils its divinely-willed destiny in such a state. The detailed contents are of no significance here. The Ancient Greek concept of the state persists in the forms of the rational state, the nation-state, the culture-state, the social state, and finally, as the decisive factor, the Christian state. The state is the executor of certain given contents, and indeed, when this theory is carried to its ultimate conclusion, the state becomes the actual subject or originator of these contents, *i.e.* of the people, the culture, the economy or the religion. It is 'the real god' (Hegel). All these theories alike regard the state as a community, so that it is only with difficulty and by indirect means that they admit of the idea of government. Fundamentally it is necessary in these cases to derive government, too, from the natural character of man. It consequently becomes difficult to understand it at the same time as the coercive power which directs itself against man, for it is precisely this coercive power which essentially distinguishes the government of the state from that voluntary priority and subordination which is to be found in every community. Whenever the basis of the state is sought in the created nature of man, the concept of government is broken up and is then reconstructed from below, even when this is not at all intended. Whenever the state becomes the executor of all the vital and cultural activities of man, it forfeits its own proper dignity, its specific authority as government.

B. *In Sin*

The Reformation, by taking up ideas of St. Augustine, broke away from the ancient Greek concept of the state. The Reformation does not represent the state as a community arising from the created nature of man, although traces of this idea, too, can be found in the writings of some of the Reformers; it places the origin of the state, as government, in the Fall. It was sin that made necessary the divine institution of government. The sword which God has given to government is to be used by it in order to protect men against the chaos which is caused by sin. Government is to punish the criminal and to safeguard life. Thus a reason is provided for the existence of government both as a coercive power and as the protector of an outward justice. The Reformation attached equal importance to both of these aspects, but its thinking subsequently developed along two divergent lines. Some thinkers subordinated the concept of justice to the concept of coercive force, and were thus led on to the concept of the state which is founded on power; others subordinated power to justice, and so attained to the concept of the state which is founded on law and order. The former believed that there was *exousia* only where there was power, the latter only where there was justice. In this way both parties failed to give its full meaning to the Reformation concept of *exousia*. Both parties perceived that the state is not a consummation of creaturely characteristics but an institution of God which is ordained from above. They did not understand the state 'from below', on the basis of the people, the culture, etc., but from above, that is to say, in the true sense, as government. In this way the original idea of the Reformation and of the Bible was faithfully followed out. Thus the state is not essentially a culture-state, etc. These are only possible, divinely permitted forms of political society, and there may well be an abundance of other such forms which have hitherto remained unknown to us. Unlike these forms of society, which are merely permitted by God, government is actually established and ordained by God Himself. People, culture, social organization, etc., are of the world. Government is order in the world, an order which bears the authority of God. Government is not itself of the world, but of God. On this basis the notion of the Christian state is also untenable; for the state possesses its character as government independently of the Christian character of the persons who govern. There is government also among the heathen.

C. *In Christ*

It becomes clear from these last remarks, and indeed from everything that we have said so far on this subject, that the basing of the state on sin or on the nature of man leads to a conception of the state as a self-contained entity, a conception which fails to take account of the relation of the state to Jesus Christ. Whether it be as an institution of creation or as an institution of preservation, the state exists here by itself, more or less independently of the revelation of God in Jesus Christ. This conclusion cannot be avoided even in the case of the second theory, which is in many ways superior to the first. But now the question arises, what basis can there be for a theologically tenable assertion (as distinct from a philosophy in general Christian terms) with regard to Paradise and the Fall—what basis can there be other than Jesus Christ? It is through Jesus Christ and for Jesus Christ that all things are created (John 1.3; I Cor. 8.6; Heb. 1.2), and in particular 'thrones, dominions, principalities and powers' (Col. 1.16). It is only in Jesus Christ that all these things 'consist' (Col. 1.17). And it is He who is 'the head of the church' (Col. 1.1). A theological proposition with regard to government, with regard, that is to say, to the government which is instituted by God and not to some general philosophical idea of government, is therefore in no circumstances possible without reference to Jesus Christ, and to Jesus Christ as the head of His Church; no such proposition is possible without reference to the Church of Jesus Christ. The true basis of government is therefore Jesus Christ Himself. The relation of Jesus Christ to government can be expressed under seven headings:

I. As the Mediator of Creation, 'through whom' government, too, is created, Jesus Christ is the sole and necessary medium between government and the Creator. There is no immediate relation between government and God. Christ is its Mediator.

II. Government, like all created things, 'consists only in Jesus Christ'; in other words, it is only in Him that it has its essence and being. If Jesus Christ did not exist, there would be no created things; all created things would be annihilated in the wrath of God.

III. Government, like all created things, is designed and

directed 'towards Jesus Christ'. Its goal is Jesus Christ Himself. Its purpose is to serve Him.

IV. Jesus Christ possesses all power in heaven and on earth (Matt. 28.18), and He is, therefore, also the Lord of government.

V. Through the atonement on the cross Jesus Christ has restored the relation between government and God (Col. 1.20 —τα πάντα).

VI. In addition to these relations to Jesus Christ which government shares with all created things, there is also a special relation in which government stands with respect to Jesus Christ.

(a) Jesus Christ was crucified with the permission of government.

(b) By acknowledging and openly declaring the innocence of Jesus (John 18.38; cf. also the part played by Lysias, Felix, Festus and Agrippa in the trial of St Paul), government gave evidence of its proper character.

(c) When government did not dare to exercise its governmental power in maintaining its own knowledge and judgement, it abandoned its office under pressure from the people. This does not constitute a condemnation of the office, but only of the faulty discharge of this office.

(d) Jesus submitted to government; but He reminded government that its power is not human arbitrary will, but a 'gift from above' (John 19.10).

(e) With this Jesus showed that government can only serve Him, precisely because it is a power which comes down from above, no matter whether it discharges its office well or badly. Both in acquitting Him of guilt and in delivering Him up to be crucified, government was obliged to show that it stands in the service of Jesus Christ. Thus it was precisely through the cross that Jesus won back His dominion over government (Col. 2.15), and, at the end of all things, 'all dominion and government and power' will be both abolished and preserved through Him.

VII. So long as the earth continues, Jesus will always be at the same time Lord of all government and Head of the Church, without government and Church ever becoming one and the same. But at the end there will be a holy city (*polis*) without temples, for God and the Lamb will Themselves be the Temple (Rev. 21), and the citizens of this city will be the faithful of the congregation of Jesus throughout all the world, and dominion in this city will be exercised by God and the Lamb. In the heavenly *polis* state and Church will be one.

Only the derivation of government from Jesus Christ can supersede the derivations in terms of natural law which are the ultimate consequences of the derivations from the nature and the sin of man. The derivation from the nature of man regards the actual conditions of peoples, etc., as providing the basis for the state in terms of natural law. This argument affords a justification for imperialism and for revolution (for both inward and outward revolution). The derivation from sin has to devise natural-law standards in order to restrict the concept of power by means of the concept of justice; these standards will imbue it with a more strongly conservative tendency. But both the concept and the contents of natural law are equivocal (depending on whether this natural law is derived from certain particular data or from certain particular standards); and it therefore fails to provide an adequate basis for the state. Natural law can furnish equally cogent arguments in favour of the state which is founded on force and the state which is founded on justice, for the nation-state and for imperialism, for democracy and for dictatorship. A solid basis is afforded only by the biblical derivation of government from Jesus Christ. Whether and to what extent a new natural law can be established on this foundation is a theological question which still remains open.

3. *The Divine Character of Government*

A. *In its Being*

Government is given to us not as an idea or a task to be fulfilled but as a reality and as something which 'is (αἰ δε οὖσαι Rom. 13.1c). It is in its being that it is a divine office. The persons who exercise government are God's 'ministers', servants and representatives (Rom. 13.4). The being of government is independent of the manner of its coming into being. No matter if man's path to governmental office repeatedly passes through guilt, no matter if almost every crown is stained with guilt (*cf.* Shakespeare's histories), the being of government lies beyond its earthly coming into being; for government is an institution of God, not in its coming into being but in its being. Like all existing things, government, too, stands in a certain sense beyond good and evil; that is to say, it possesses not only an office but also a historical existence. An ethical failure does not *eo ipso* deprive it of its divine dignity. This situation is clearly expressed in the saying 'my country, right or wrong'. This is that historical relationship of one actual entity to another which is found again in the relationship between father and child, between brother and brother, and between master and servant, and which is immediately obvious in these cases. There can be no ethical isolation of the son from his father, and indeed, on the basis of actual being, there is a necessity of sharing in the assuming and carrying of the guilt of a father or a brother. There is no glory in standing amid the ruins of one's native town in the consciousness that at least one has not oneself incurred any guilt. That is rather the self-glorification of the moral legalist in the face of history. The clearest expression of this dignity of government, one source of which is its historical existence, is its power, the sword which it wields. Even when the government incurs guilt and is open to ethical attack, its power is from God. It has its existence solely in Jesus Christ, and through the cross of Christ it is reconciled with God (*vide supra*).

B. *In its Task*

The being of government is linked with a divine commission. Its being is fulfilled only in the fulfilment of the commission. A total apostasy from its commission would jeopardize its being. But by God's providence this total apostasy is possible only as an eschatological event, and as such it leads amidst grievous torments to a total separation of the congregation from the government as the embodiment of Antichrist. The mission of government consists in serving the dominion of Christ on earth by the exercise of the worldly power of the sword and of justice. Government serves Christ by establishing and maintaining an outward justice by means of the sword which is given to it, and to it alone, in deputyship for God. And it has not only the negative task of punishing the wicked, but also the positive task of praising the good or 'them that do well' (I Pet. 2.14). It is therefore endowed, on the one hand, with a judicial authority, and on the other hand, with a right to educate for goodness, *i.e.* for outward justice or righteousness. The way in which it exercises this right of education is, of course, a question which can be considered only in the context of the relation of government to the other divine mandates. The much-discussed question of what constitutes this goodness or outward justice which government is charged with promoting is easily resolved if one keeps in view the derivation of government from Jesus Christ. This good cannot in any case be in conflict with Jesus Christ. Good consists in allowance being made in every action of government for the ultimate purpose, namely, the service of Jesus Christ. What is intended here is not a Christian action, but an action which does not exclude Christ. Government achieves such an action if it takes the contents of the second table as its criterion in its various particular historical situations and decisions. But whence does government derive its knowledge of these contents? Primarily from the preaching of the Church. But for pagan government the answer is that there is a providential congruity between the contents of the second table and the inherent law of historical life itself. Failure to observe the second table destroys the very life which government is charged with preserving. Thus, if it is properly understood, the task of protecting life will itself lead to observance of the second table. Does this mean that the state is after all based on natural law? No; for in fact it is a matter here only of the government which does not understand itself but which now is, nevertheless, providentially enabled to acquire the same knowledge, of crucial significance for its task, as is disclosed to the government which does understand itself in the true sense in Jesus Christ. One might, therefore, say that in this case natural law has its foundation in Jesus Christ.

Consequently, whether or not government is aware of its own true basis, its task consists in maintaining by the power of the sword an outward justice in which life is preserved and is thus held open for Christ.

Does the task of government also include observance of the first table, that is to say, the decision for the God and Father of Jesus Christ? We intend to consider this question in the section on government and Church, and at this point we will say only that the knowledge of Jesus Christ is part of the assignment of all men, including, therefore, those persons who exercise government. But the praise and the protection of the righteous (I Pet. 2.14) is an integral part of the mission of government, independently of the decision of faith of the persons who exercise government. Indeed it is only in protecting the righteous that government fulfils its true mission of serving Christ.

The mission of government to serve Christ is at the same time its inescapable destiny. Government serves Christ no matter whether it is conscious or unconscious of this mission or even whether it is true or untrue to it. If it is unwilling to fulfil this mission, then, through the suffering of the congregation, it renders service to the witness of the name of Christ. Such is the close and indissoluble relation of government to Christ. It cannot in either case evade its task of serving Christ. It serves Him by its very existence.

C. *In its Claim*

The claim of government, which is based on its power and its mission, is the claim of God and is binding upon conscience. Government demands obedience 'for conscience sake' (Rom. 13.5), which may also be interpreted as 'for the Lord's sake' (I Pet. 2.13). This obedience is combined with deference

(Rom. 13.7; I Pet. 2.17). In the exercise of the mission of government the demand for obedience is unconditional and qualitatively total; it extends both to conscience and to bodily life. Belief, conscience and bodily life are subject to an obligation of obedience with respect to the divine commission of government. A doubt can arise only when the contents and the extent of the commission of government become questionable. The Christian is neither obliged nor able to examine the rightfulness of the demand of government in each particular case. His duty of obedience is binding on him until government directly compels him to offend against the divine commandment, that is to say, until government openly denies its divine commission and thereby forfeits its claim. In cases of doubt obedience is required; for the Christian does not bear the responsibility of government. But if government violates or exceeds its commission at any point, for example by making itself master over the belief of the congregation, then at this point, indeed, obedience is to be refused, for conscience sake, for the Lord's sake. It is not, however, permissible to generalize from this offence and to conclude that this government now possesses no claim to obedience in some of its other demands, or even in all its demands. Disobedience can never be anything but a concrete decision in a single particular case. Generalizations lead to an apocalyptic diabolization of government. Even an anti-Christian government is still in a certain sense government. It would, therefore, not be permissible to refuse to pay taxes to a government which persecuted the Church. Conversely, the fact of obedience to government in its political functions, payment of taxes, acceptance of loyalty oaths and military service, is always a proof that this government is not yet understood in the sense of the apocalypse. An apocalyptic view of a particular concrete government would necessarily have total disobedience as its consequence; for in that case every single act of obedience obviously involves a denial of Christ (Rev. 13.7). In all political decisions the historical entanglement in the guilt of the past is too great to be assessed, and it is therefore generally impossible to pass judgement on the justice of a single particular decision. It is here that the venture of responsibility must be undertaken, but the responsibility for such a venture on the part of the government can be borne *in concreto* (*i.e.* apart from the general share in responsibility for political action which is borne by individuals) only by the government. Even in cases where the guilt of the government is extremely obvious, due consideration must still be given to the guilt which has given rise to this guilt. The refusal of obedience in the case of a particular historical and political decision of government must therefore, like this decision itself, be a venture undertaken on one's own responsibility. A historical decision cannot be entirely resolved into ethical terms; there remains a residuum, the venture of action. That is true both of the government and of its subjects.

4. *Government and the Divine Institutions in the World*

Government has the divine task of preserving the world, with its institutions which are given by God, for the purpose of Christ. For this purpose government alone bears the sword. Everyone is subject to an obligation of obedience towards government. But, both with its task and with its claim, government always presupposes the created world. Government maintains created things in their proper order, but it cannot itself engender life; it is not creative. However, it finds already in the world which it governs two institutions through which God the Creator exercises His creative power, and upon which it must therefore, in the nature of things, rely; these are marriage and labour. The Bible discloses both of these to us already in Paradise, and thereby shows that they are part of God's creation, which is through and for Jesus Christ. Even after the Fall, *i.e.* in the only form in which we know them, both are still divine institutions of discipline and grace, because God desires to show Himself even to the fallen world as the Creator, and because He causes the world to consist in Christ and makes it Christ's own. Marriage and labour are from the beginning subject to a definite divine mandate which must be executed in faith and obedience towards God. Marriage and labour, therefore, possess their own origin in God, an origin which is not established by government, but which requires to be acknowledged by government. Through marriage bodily life is propagated and men are brought into being for the glorification and service of Jesus Christ. But this implies also that marriage is there not only for begetting children but also for educating them in obedience to Jesus Christ. The parents are for the child the deputies of God, both as its begetters and as its educators. Through labour a world of values is created for the glorification and service of Jesus Christ. Here, too, as in the case of marriage, there is not a divine creation out of nothing, but on the basis of the first creation there is a creation of new things, in marriage of new life and in labour of new values. Labour embraces here the whole range of work which extends from agriculture by way of industry and commerce to science and art (*cf.* Gen. 4.17ff.). Thus, for the sake of Jesus Christ, a right of their own is conferred both upon marriage, together with the family, and upon labour, together with economic life, culture, science and art. This means that for these fields the significance of government is regulative and not constitutive. Marriage is performed not by government but in the presence of government. Industry and commerce, science and art, are not cultivated by government itself, but they are subject to its supervision, and within certain limits (which cannot be discussed in detail here) to its direction. But government never becomes the subject or originator of these fields of labour. If it asserts its authority beyond the limits of its assigned task it will in the long run forfeit its genuine authority over these fields.

Distinct from the order or institution of marriage and that of labour is the order or institution of the people. According to Scripture, its origin lies neither in Paradise nor in an explicit divine mandate. The people is, on the one hand (according to Gen. 10), a natural consequence of the spreading of the succeeding generations; on the other hand (Gen. 11), it is a divine institution which causes mankind to live in dissension and mutual incomprehension, and which thereby reminds men that their unity does not lie in their own achievement of complete power but solely in God, the Creator and Redeemer. Yet in Scripture there is no special commission of God for the people. Marriage and labour are divine offices, but the people is a historical reality, which in a special sense has reference to the divine reality of the one people of God, the Church. Scripture offers no indication with regard to the relation between people and government; it does not demand the nation-state; it recognizes the possibility that several peoples may be united under one government. It knows that the people grows from below, but that government is instituted from above.

5. *Government and Church*

Government is instituted for the sake of Christ; it serves Christ, and consequently it also serves the Church. Yet the dominion of Christ over all government does not by any means imply the dominion of the Church over government. But the same Lord, whom government serves, is the Head of the congregation, the Lord of the Church. The service of government to Christ consists in the exercise of its commission to secure an outward justice by the power of the sword. This service is thus an indirect service to the congregation, which only by this is enabled to 'lead a quiet and peaceable life' (I Tim. 2.2). Through its service towards Christ, government is intimately linked with the Church. If it fulfils its mission as it should, the congregation can live in peace, for government and congregation serve the same Master.

A. *Government's Claim on the Church*

The claim of government to obedience and deference extends also to the Church. With respect to the spiritual office, government can indeed only demand that this office shall not interfere in the secular office, but that it shall fulfil its own mission, which does, in fact, include the admonition to obey government. Government possesses no authority over this mission itself, as it is exercised in the pastoral office and in the office of Church management. So far as the spiritual office is an office which is exercised publicly, government has a claim to supervise it, to see that everything is done in an orderly manner, that is to say, in accordance with outward justice. It is only in this connexion that it has a claim to intervene in the question of appointments and organization within the office. The spiritual office itself is not subject to government. Yet government possesses a full claim to obedience with regard to the Christian members of the congregation. In this it does not appear as a second authority side by side with the authority of Christ, but its own authority is only a form of the authority of Christ. In his obedience to government the Christian is obedient to Christ. As a citizen the Christian does not cease to be a Christian, but he serves Christ in a different way. This in itself also provides an adequate definition of the contents of the authentic claim of government. It can never lead the Christian against Christ; on the contrary, it helps him to serve Christ in the world. The person who exercises government thus becomes for the Christian a servant of God.

B. *The Church's Claim on Government*

The Church has the task of summoning the whole world to submit to the dominion of Jesus Christ. She testifies before government to their common Master. She calls upon the persons who exercise government to believe in Christ for the sake of their own salvation. She knows that it is in obedience to Jesus Christ that the commission of government is properly executed. Her aim is not that government should pursue a Christian policy, enact Christian laws, etc., but that it should be true government in accordance with its own special task. Only the Church brings government to an understanding of itself. For the sake of their common Master the Church claims to be listened to by government; she claims protection for the public Christian proclamation against violence and blasphemy; she claims protection for the institution of the Church against arbitrary interference, and she claims protection for Christian life in obedience to

Jesus Christ. The Church can never abandon these claims; and she must make them heard publicly so long as government itself maintains its claim to acknowledge the Church. Of course, if government opposes the Church, explicitly or in fact, there may come a time when the Church no longer wastes her words, even though she still does not give up her claim; for the Church knows that, whether government performs its mission well or badly, it must always serve only its Master, and therefore also the Church. The government which denies protection to the Church thereby places the Church all the more patently under the protection of her Master. The government which blasphemes its Master testifies thereby all the more evidently to the power of this Master who is praised and glorified in the torments and martyrdoms of the congregation.

C. *The Ecclesiastical Responsibility of Government*

To the claim of the Church there corresponds the responsibility of government. Here it becomes necessary to answer the question of the attitude of government to the first commandment. Must goverment make a religious decision, or does its task lie in religious neutrality? Is government responsible for maintaining the true Christian service of God, and has it the right to prohibit other kinds of divine service? Certainly the persons who exercise government ought also to accept belief in Jesus Christ, but the office of government remains independent of the religious decision. Yet it pertains to the responsibility of the office of government that it should protect the righteous, and indeed praise them, in other words that it should support the practice of religion. A government which fails to recognize this undermines the root of true obedience and, therefore, also its own authority (*e.g.* France in 1905). At the same time the office of government as such remains religiously neutral and attends only to its own task. And it can, therefore, never become the originator in the foundation of a new religion; for if it does so it disrupts itself. It affords protection to every form of service of God which does not undermine the office of government. It takes care that the differences between the various forms of service of God do not give rise to a conflict which endangers the order of the country. But it achieves this purpose not by suppressing one form of service of God, but by a clear adherence to its own governmental commission. It will thereby become evident that the true Christian service of God does not endanger this commission, but, on the contrary, continually establishes it anew. If the persons who exercise government are Christian they must know that the Christian proclamation is delivered not by means of the sword but by means of the word. The idea of *cuius regio eius religio* was possible only in certain quite definite political circumstances: namely, the agreement of the princes to admit each other's exiles; as a general principle it is incompatible with the office of government. In the case of some special situation of ecclesiastical emergency it would be the responsibility of the Christians who exercise government to make their power available, if the Church requests it, in order to remove the source of the disorder. This does not mean, however, that in such circumstances government as such would take over the functions of ecclesiastical control. It is here exclusively a matter of restoring the rightful order within which the spiritual office can be rightfully discharged and both government and Church can perform their own several tasks. Government will fulfil its obligation under the first commandment by being government in the rightful manner and by discharging its governmental responsibility also with respect to the Church. But it does not possess the office of confessing and preaching faith in Jesus Christ.

D. *The Political Responsibility of the Church*

If political responsibility is understood exclusively in the sense of governmental responsibility, then it is clearly only upon government that this responsibility devolves. But if the term is taken to refer quite generally to life in the *polis*, then there are a number of senses in which it is necessary to speak of a political responsibility of the Church in answer to the claim of government upon the Church. Here again we distinguish between the responsibility of the spiritual office and the responsibility of the Christians. It is part of the Church's office of guardianship that she shall call sin by its name and that she shall warn men against sin; for 'righteousness exalteth a nation', both in time and in eternity, 'but sin is perdition for the people', both temporal and eternal perdition (Prov. 14.34). If the Church did not do this, she would be incurring part of the guilt for the blood of the wicked (Ezek. 3.17ff.). This warning against sin is delivered to the congregation openly. and publicly, and whoever will not hear it passes judgement upon himself. The intention of the preacher here is not to improve the world, but to summon it to belief in Jesus Christ and to bear witness to the reconciliation which has been accomplished through Him and to His dominion. The theme of the proclamation is not the wickedness of the world but the grace of Jesus Christ. It is part of the responsibility of the spiritual office that it shall devote earnest attention to the proclamation of the reign of Christ as King, and that it shall with all due deference address government directly in order to draw its attention to shortcomings and errors which must otherwise imperil its governmental office. If the word of the Church is, on principle, not received, then the only political responsibility which remains to her is in establishing and maintaining, at least among her own members, the order of outward justice which is no longer to be found in the *polis*, for by so doing she serves government in her own way.

Is there a political responsibility on the part of individual Christians? Certainly the individual Christian cannot be made responsible for the action of government, and he must not make himself responsible for it; but because of his faith and his charity he is responsible for his own calling and for the sphere of his own personal life, however large or however small it may be. If this responsibility is fulfilled in faith, it is effectual for the whole of the *polis*. According to Holy Scripture, there is no right to revolution; but there is a responsibility of every individual for preserving the purity of his office and mission in the *polis*. In this way, in the true sense, every individual serves government with his responsibility. No one, not even government itself, can deprive him of this responsibility or forbid him to discharge it, for it is an integral part of his life in sanctification, and it arises from obedience to the Lord of both Church and government.

E. *Conclusions*

Government and Church are connected in such various ways that their relationship cannot be regulated in accordance with any single general principle. Neither the separation of state and Church, nor the form of the state church can in itself constitute a solution of the problem. Nothing is more dangerous than to draw theoretical conclusions by generalizing from single particular experiences. The recommendation for a withdrawal of the Church from the world and from the relations which she still maintains with the state under the impact of an apocalyptic age is, in this general aspect, nothing but a somewhat melancholy interpretation of the times in terms of the philosophy of history. If it were really acted upon in earnest, it would necessarily lead to the most drastic consequences, which are described in Rev. 13. But, conversely, a philosophy of history may equally easily be the source for a scheme for a state church or a national church. No constitutional form can as such exactly represent the actual relative closeness and remoteness of government and Church. Government and Church are bound by the same Lord and are bound together. In their task government and Church are separate, but government and Church have the same field of action, man. No single one of these relationships must be isolated so as to provide the basis for a particular constitutional form (for example in the sequence state church, free church, national church); the true aim is to provide room within every given form for the relationship which is, in fact, instituted by God and to entrust the further development to the Lord of both government and Church.

6. *The Church and the Form of the State*

In both Protestant and Catholic political theory the question of the form of the state is always treated as a secondary problem. Certainly, so long as government fulfils its assigned mission, the form in which it does so is of no great importance for the Church. Still, there is justification for asking which form of the state offers the best guarantee for the fulfilment of the mission of government and should, therefore, be promoted by the Church. No form of the state is in itself an absolute guarantee for the proper discharge of the office of government. Only concrete obedience to the divine commission justifies a form of the state. It is, nevertheless, possible to formulate a few general propositions in order to discern those forms of the state which provide a relatively favourable basis for rightful governmental action and, therefore, also for a rightful relationship between church and state; precisely these relative differences may be of great practical consequence.

i. That form of the state will be relatively the best in which it becomes most evident that government is from above, from God, and in which the divine origin of government is most clearly apparent. A properly understood divine right of government, in its splendour and in its responsibility, is an essential constituent of the relatively best form of the state. (Unlike other western royalty, the kings of the Belgians called themselves kings 'by the grace of the people'.)

ii. That form of the state will be relatively the best which sees that its power is not endangered but is sustained and secured

(a) by the strict maintenance of an outward justice,
(b) by the right of the family and of labour, a right which has its foundation in God, and
(c) by the proclamation of the gospel of Jesus Christ.

iii. That form of the state will be relatively the best which does not express its attachment to its subjects by restricting the divine authority which has been conferred upon it, but which attaches itself to its subjects in mutual confidence by just action and truthful speech. It will be found here that what is best for government is also best for the relationship between government and church.

IV

ON THE POSSIBILITY
OF THE WORD OF THE CHURCH
TO THE WORLD

1. What lies behind that longing, which is awakening every-where among the Christians of the world, for the Church's word of solution to the world? There are essentially the following ideas: The social, economic, political and other problems of the world have become too much for us; all the available offers of ideological and practical solutions are inadequate. In this way the world of technical progress has reached its limits. The car is caught in the mud; the wheels are rotating at the highest possible speed, but they still cannot draw the car clear. In their extent and in their character the problems are so universally human that some quite fundamental remedy has become necessary. The Church has so far failed to master the social, economic, political, sexual and educational problems. By her own guilt she has given offence, so that men are prevented from believing her message. 'Woe unto him that shall offend one of these little ones' (Matt. 18.6). The dogmatically correct delivery of the Christian proclamation is not enough; nor are general ethical principles; what is needed is concrete instruction in the concrete situation. The spiritual forces which sustain the Church are not yet exhausted. The Christians of the world have come closer to one another than ever before. They must join together in performing the tasks of speaking the word of the Church. In brief, the Church must offer solutions for the unsolved problems of the world, and thereby fulfil her mission and restore her authority. We see at once in all this that correct and incorrect ideas are closely interwoven.

2. We ask, is it correct to say that it is the task of the

Church to offer solutions to the world for its problems today? Are there Christian solutions at all for worldly problems? Obviously this depends on what is meant. It is obviously an error if it is meant that Christianity has a solution for *all* the social and political problems of the world, so that one would need only to listen to these Christian answers in order to bring the world into good shape. It is correct if it is meant that on the basis of Christianity there is something definite to be said on the subject of worldly matters. Particularly wide currency has been given in Anglo-Saxon thought to the idea that the Church has at her disposal, in principle, a Christian solution for all worldly problems, but that she has simply not so far taken enough trouble with it. The reply to this is as follows:

(*a*) Jesus concerns himself hardly at all with the solution of worldly problems. When He is asked to do so His answer is remarkably evasive (Matt. 22.15ff.; Luke 12.13). Indeed He scarcely ever replies to men's questions directly, but answers rather from a quite different plane. His word is not an answer to human questions and problems; it is the answer of God to the question of God to man. His word is essentially determined not from below but from above. It is not a solution, but a redemption. His word has its origin not in the disunion of the human problems of good and evil, but in the perfect unity of the Son with the will of the Father. It lies beyond all human problems. That is what must first of all be understood. Instead of the solution of problems, Jesus brings the redemption of men, and yet for that very reason He does really bring the solution of all human problems as well ('All these things shall be added' (Matt. 6.33)), but from quite a different plane.

(*b*) Who actually tells us that all worldly problems are to be and can be solved? Perhaps the unsolved state of these problems is of more importance to God than their solution, for it may serve to call attention to the fall of man and to the divine redemption. Perhaps the problems of men are so complicated and so wrongly formulated that they really are simply insoluble. (The problem of the poor and the rich can certainly never be solved otherwise than by remaining unsolved.)

(c) One of the characteristic features of church life in the Anglo-Saxon countries, and one from which Lutheranism has almost entirely freed itself, is the organized struggle of the Church against some particular worldly evil, the 'campaign', or, taking up again the crusading idea of the Middle Ages, the 'crusade'. Examples of this are slavery, prohibition and the League of Nations. But precisely these examples betray at the same time the critical weakness of these 'crusades'. The abolition of slavery coincided with the coming into being of the British industrial proletariat. (It might be said that the world will have its due.) Prohibition, which was forced through mainly by the Methodists, led to worse experiences than those of the preceding period, so that the Methodists themselves supported its abolition. (This experience was of decisive importance for the American churches.) The League of Nations was intended to overcome national antagonisms, but its result was to intensify them to the highest pitch. Such experiences as these must give food for earnest thought in the face of the question of the extent to which the Church is called upon to solve worldly problems. 'God in their hand' (Job 12.6 [Luther]).

(d) It is necessary to free oneself from the way of thinking which sets out from human problems and which asks for solutions on this basis. Such thinking is unbiblical. The way of Jesus Christ, and therefore the way of all Christian thinking, leads not from the world to God but from God to the world. This means that the essence of the gospel does not lie in the solution of human problems, and that the solution of human problems cannot be the essential task of the Church. Of course, it does not follow from this that the Church has no tasks at all in this connexion. We can perceive what is her legitimate task only when we have found the right point of departure.

3. The Church's word to the world can be no other than God's word to the world. This word is Jesus Christ and salvation in His name. It is in Jesus Christ that God's relation to

the world is defined. We know of no relation of God to the world other than through Jesus Christ. For the Church too, therefore, there is no relation to the world other than through Jesus Christ. In other words, the proper relation of the Church to the world cannot be deduced from natural law or rational law or from universal human rights, but *only* from the gospel of Jesus Christ.

(*a*) The Church's word to the world is the word of the incarnation of God, of the love of God for the world in the sending of His Son, and of God's judgement upon unbelief. The word of the Church is the call to conversion, the call to belief in the love of God in Christ, and the call to preparation for Christ's second coming and for the future kingdom of God. It is, therefore, the word of redemption for all mankind.

(*b*) The word of the love of God for the world sets the congregation in a relation of responsibility with regard to the world. In word and action the congregation is to bear witness before the world to the faith in Christ; it is to prevent offence or scandal, and it is to make room for the gospel in the world. Whenever this responsibility is denied, Christ, too, is denied; for it is the responsibility which answers to the love of God for the world.

(*c*) The congregation acknowledges and bears witness to God's love for the world in Jesus Christ as law and as gospel. The two can never be separated; nor can they ever be identified. There can be no preaching of the law without the gospel, and no preaching of the gospel without the law. It is by no means the case that the law is intended for the world and the gospel for the congregation. Both the law and the gospel are alike addressed both to the world and to the congregation. Whatever the Church's word to the world may be, it must always be *both* law *and* gospel.

1. This implies a denial of the view that the Church can speak to the world on the basis of some particular rational or natural-law knowledge which she shares with the world, that is to say, with an occasional temporary disregard for the gospel. The Church of the Reformation, unlike the Catholic Church, *cannot* do this.

321

II. From this there follows the denial of the idea of a double church morality, *i.e.* one morality for the world and another morality for the congregation, one for the heathen and another for the Christians, one for the Christian in the secular sphere and another for the *homo religiosus*. The whole law and the whole gospel of God belong equally to all men. If it is objected that in the world the Church demands the maintenance of justice, of property and of marriage, but that from Christians she demands the renunciation of all these things, if it is objected that in the world retaliation and violence must be practised, but that Christians must practise forgiveness and unlawfulness, then these objections, which have as their goal a double Christian morality, and which are very widespread, proceed from a false understanding of the word of God. If the decalogue demands observance in the name of God of the right to life, marriage, property and honour of man, that does not mean that these legal institutions in themselves possess an absolute divine value, but simply that it is only in them and through them that God desires to be honoured and adored. That is why the second table is never to be separated from the first. These institutions are, therefore, not a second divine authority, side by side with the God of Jesus Christ; but they are the place at which the God of Jesus Christ secures obedience to Himself. The word of God is not concerned with the institutions themselves, but with obedience in faith within these institutions. Again, when Jesus calls upon men to follow Him in renouncing their own right, and to give up life, marriage, honour and property for the sake of fellowship with Him, He is not establishing a new table of absolute values, as, for example, self-denial in the place of self-assertion; there is no mention of self-assertion anywhere in the decalogue either, but only of the right and honour of God. On the contrary, both Jesus and the decalogue are concerned with concrete obedience to God and it is possible that precisely in the renunciation of one's own right, of property and of marriage, for the sake of God, one may be rendering higher honour to the true origin of all these gifts, to God Himself, than by an

322

insistence upon one's own right, which might easily distract attention from the right of God. When Jesus tells the rich young man to give up one of his rights, this makes it particularly clear that the man's 'keeping of the ten commandments from his youth up' has not been obedience to God, but that he has had no thought for the living God, while still always observing the so-called divine ordinances (Matt. 19.16ff.). The decalogue and the Sermon on the Mount are not, therefore, two different ethical ideals, but one single call to concrete obedience towards the God and Father of Jesus Christ. Responsible acceptance of the institution of property in faith in God is not essentially different from renunciation of property in faith in God. Neither the 'struggle for one's rights' nor the 'renunciation of one's rights' is anything in itself, or can itself be, for example, a topic of the Church's proclamation, but in faith both are submission to the right which belongs only to God. Consequently there are not two scales of values, one for the world and one for the Christians, but there is the one and only word of God, which demands faith and obedience, and which is addressed to all mankind. Moreover, it would also be wrong to lay greater stress on the struggle for rights in the proclamation to the world and to lay greater stress on the renunciation of rights in the proclamation to the congregation. Both apply to both world and congregation. The assertion that it is not possible to govern with the Sermon on the Mount arises from a misunderstanding of the Sermon on the Mount. The government of a state may also be able to honour God both by its struggle and by its renunciation, and this is the sole concern of the Church's proclamation. It is never the task of the Church to preach the natural instinct of self-preservation to the state, but only obedience to the right of God. That is quite different. The proclamation of the Church to the world can never be anything other than Jesus Christ in the law and the gospel. The second table cannot be separated from the first.

III. The Church summons individuals and peoples to faith and obedience towards the revelation of God in Jesus Christ, and in so doing she defines an area within which this faith and this obedience are at least not rendered impossible. This area is delimited by the ten commandments. Wherever there is no sign of transgression of the ten commandments, there, at least, there is no offence or scandal to prevent belief. The Church cannot indeed proclaim a concrete earthly order which follows as a necessary consequence from faith in Jesus Christ, but she can and must oppose every concrete order which constitutes an offence to faith in Jesus Christ, and in doing this she defines, at least negatively, the limits for an order within which faith in Jesus Christ and obedience are possible. In their most general form these limits are given in the decalogue; and *in concreto* they will have to be defined ever anew. In everything which the Church has to say with regard to the institutions of the world she can only prepare the way for the coming of Jesus Christ; the real coming of Jesus Christ itself lies within His own freedom and grace. It is because Jesus Christ has come and is coming again that the way must be prepared for Him everywhere in the world, and it is therefore also solely for that reason that the Church is concerned with the secular institutions. Consequently what the Church has to say about the secular institutions follows solely from the preaching of Christ, and the Church possesses no doctrine of her own which is valid in itself with regard to eternal institutions and natural or human rights such as might command acknowledgement even independently of faith in Christ. The only human and natural rights are those which derive from Christ, that is to say, from faith.

iv. The question arises here whether the world and men really exist only for the sake of faith in Jesus Christ. This question is to be answered affirmatively in the sense that Jesus Christ existed for the world and for men, and that therefore it is only when everything is directed towards Jesus Christ that the world becomes really world and man becomes really man, in accordance with Matt. 6.33. The true significance of the world and of man is recognized precisely when it is perceived that all created things exist for the sake of Jesus Christ and consist in Him (Col. 1.16ff.).

v. On this basis the Church has a definite interest not

only in the *punctum mathematicum* of belief but also in such empirical factors as the formation of a particular attitude with regard to secular problems as well as in particular earthly conditions. There are, for example, certain economic or social attitudes and conditions which are a hindrance to faith in Christ and which consequently destroy the true character of man in the world. It must be asked, for example, whether capitalism or socialism or collectivism are economic forms which impedes faith in this way. In this respect the conduct of the Church is twofold, on the one hand, drawing negative limits, she will, by the authority of the word of God, necessarily declare those economic attitudes or forms to be wrong which obviously obstruct belief in Jesus Christ, and on the other hand, positively, not by the authority of God but merely on the authority of the responsible advice of Christian specialists and experts, she will be able to make her contribution towards the establishment of a new order. A strict distinction is to be drawn between these two tasks. The first task is that of the office, and the second is that of the *diakonia*; the first is divine, and the second earthly; the first is that of the word of God, and the second is that of Christian life. But here Luther's dictum is applicable: *doctrina est coelum, vita est terra.*

VI. This provides a basis for the solution of the much-discussed problem of the autonomy of the secular institutions. There is good reason for laying stress on the autonomy of, for example, the state in opposition to the heteronomy of an ecclesiastical theocracy; yet before God there is no autonomy, but the law of the God who is revealed in Jesus Christ is the law of all earthly institutions. The limits of all autonomy become evident in the Church's proclamation of the word of God, and the concrete form of the law of God in commerce and industry, the state, etc., must be perceived and discerned by those who work responsibly in these fields. Here, so long as it is not misunderstood, one might speak of a relative autonomy.

VII. Reason—law of created things—of existent things[1]

1 *Editor's note.* Unfinished.

V

WHAT IS MEANT BY
'TELLING THE TRUTH'?

FROM the moment in our lives at which we learn to speak we are taught that what we say must be true. What does this mean? What is meant by 'telling the truth'? What does it demand of us?

It is clear that in the first place it is our parents who regulate our relation to themselves by this demand for truthfulness; consequently, in the sense in which our parents intend it, this demand applies strictly only within the family circle. It is also to be noted that the relation which is expressed in this demand cannot simply be reversed. The truthfulness of a child towards his parents is essentially different from that of the parents towards their child. The life of the small child lies open before the parents, and what the child says should reveal to them everything that is hidden and secret, but in the converse relationship this cannot possibly be the case. Consequently, in the matter of truthfulness, the parents' claim on the child is different from the child's claim on the parents.

From this it emerges already that 'telling the truth' means something different according to the particular situation in which one stands. Account must be taken of one's relationships at each particular time. The question must be asked whether and in what way a man is entitled to demand truthful speech of others. Speech between parents and children is, in the nature of the case, different from speech between man and wife, between friends, between teacher and pupil, government and subject, friend and foe, and in each case the truth which this speech conveys is also different.

It will at once be objected that one does not owe truthful speech to this or that individual man, but solely to God. This

326

objection is correct so long as it is not forgotten that God is not a general principle, but the living God who has set me in a living life and who demands service of me within this living life. If one speaks of God one must not simply disregard the actual given world in which one lives; for if one does that one is not speaking of the God who entered into the world in Jesus Christ, but rather of some metaphysical idol. And it is precisely this which is determined by the way in which, in my actual concrete life with all its manifold relationships, I give effect to the truthfulness which I owe to God. The truthfulness which we owe to God must assume a concrete form in the world. Our speech must be truthful, not in principle but concretely. A truthfulness which is not concrete is not truthful before God.

'Telling the truth', therefore, is not solely a matter of moral character; it is also a matter of correct appreciation of real situations and of serious reflection upon them. The more complex the actual situations of a man's life, the more responsible and the more difficult will be his task of 'telling the truth'. The child stands in only one vital relationship, his relationship to his parents, and he, therefore, still has nothing to consider and weigh up. The next environment in which he is placed, his school, already brings with it the first difficulty. From the educational point of view it is, therefore, of the very greatest importance that parents, in some way which we cannot discuss here, should make their children understand the differences between these various circles in which they are to live and the differences in their responsibilities.

Telling the truth is, therefore, something which must be learnt. This will sound very shocking to anyone who thinks that it must all depend on moral character and that if this is blameless the rest is child's play. But the simple fact is that the ethical cannot be detached from reality, and consequently continual progress in learning to appreciate reality is a necessary ingredient in ethical action. In the question with which we are now concerned, action consists of speaking. The real is to be expressed in words. That is what constitutes

truthful speech. And this inevitably raises the question of the
'how?' of these words. It is a question of knowing the right
word on each occasion. Finding this word is a matter of long,
earnest and ever more advanced effort on the basis of
experience and knowledge of the real. If one is to say how a
thing really is, *i.e.* if one is to speak truthfully, one's gaze and
one's thought must be directed towards the way in which the
real exists in God and through God and for God.

To restrict this problem of truthful speech to certain
particular cases of conflict is superficial. Every word I utter
is subject to the requirement that it shall be true. Quite
apart from the veracity of its contents, the relation between
myself and another man which is expressed in it is in itself
either true or untrue. I can speak flatteringly or presumptuously or hypocritically without uttering a material untruth;
yet my words are nevertheless untrue, because I am disrupt-
ing and destroying the reality of the relationship between
man and wife, superior and subordinate, etc. An individual
utterance is always part of a total reality which seeks expression in this utterance. If my utterance is to be truthful it
must in each case be different according to whom I am
addressing, who is questioning me, and what I am speaking
about. The truthful word is not in itself constant; it is as
much alive as life itself. If it is detached from life and from
its reference to the concrete other man, if 'the truth is told'
without taking into account to whom it is addressed, then
this truth has only the appearance of truth, but it lacks its
essential character.

It is only the cynic who claims 'to speak the truth' at all
times and in all places to all men in the same way, but who, in
fact, displays nothing but a lifeless image of the truth. He
dons the halo of the fanatical devotee of truth who can make
no allowance for human weaknesses; but, in fact, he is
destroying the living truth between men. He wounds shame,
desecrates mystery, breaks confidence, betrays the community
in which he lives, and laughs arrogantly at the devastation
he has wrought and at the human weakness which 'cannot
bear the truth'. He says truth is destructive and demands its

victims, and he feels like a god above these feeble creatures and does not know that he is serving Satan.

There is a truth which is of Satan. Its essence is that under the semblance of truth it denies everything that is real. It lives upon hatred of the real and of the world which is created and loved by God. It pretends to be executing the judgement of God upon the fall of the real. God's truth judges created things out of love, and Satan's truth judges them out of envy and hatred. God's truth has become flesh in the world and is alive in the real, but Satan's truth is the death of all reality.

The concept of living truth is dangerous, and it gives rise to the suspicion that the truth can and may be adapted to each particular situation in a way which completely destroys the idea of truth and narrows the gap between truth and falsehood, so that the two become indistinguishable. Moreover, what we are saying about the necessity for discerning the real may be mistakenly understood as meaning that it is by adopting a calculating or schoolmasterly attitude towards the other man that I shall decide what proportion of the truth I am prepared to tell him. It is important that this danger should be kept in view. Yet the only possible way of countering it is by means of attentive discernment of the particular contents and limits which the real itself imposes on one's utterance in order to make it a truthful one. The dangers which are involved in the concept of living truth must never impel one to abandon this concept in favour of the formal and cynical concept of truth. We must try to make this clear. Every utterance or word lives and has its home in a particular environment. The word in the family is different from the word in business or in public. The word which has come to life in the warmth of a personal relationship is frozen to death in the cold air of public existence. The word of command, which has its habitat in public service, would sever the bonds of mutual confidence if it were spoken in the family. Each word must have its own place and keep to it. It is a consequence of the wide diffusion of the public word through the newspapers and the wireless that the essential character and the limits of the various different words are no longer clearly felt and that, for example, the special quality of the personal word is almost entirely destroyed. Genuine words are replaced by idle chatter. Words no longer possess any weight. There is too much talk. And when the limits of the various words are obliterated, when words become rootless and homeless, then the word loses truth, and then indeed there must almost inevitably be lying. When the various orders of life no longer respect one another, words become untrue. For example, a teacher asks a child in front of the class whether it is true that his father often comes home drunk. It is true, but the child denies it. The teacher's question has placed him in a situation for which he is not yet prepared. He feels only that what is taking place is an unjustified interference in the order of the family and that he must oppose it. What goes on in the family is not for the ears of the class in school. The family has its own secret and must preserve it. The teacher has failed to respect the reality of this institution. The child ought now to find a way of answering which would comply with both the rule of the family and the rule of the school. But he is not yet able to do this. He lacks experience, knowledge, and the ability to express himself in the right way. As a simple no to the teacher's question the child's answer is certainly untrue; yet at the same time it nevertheless gives expression to the truth that the family is an institution *sui generis* and that the teacher had no right to interfere in it. The child's answer can indeed be called a lie; yet this lie contains more truth, that is to say, it is more in accordance with reality than would have been the case if the child had betrayed his father's weakness in front of the class. According to the measure of his knowledge, the child acted correctly. The blame for the lie falls back entirely upon the teacher. An experienced man in the same position as the child would have been able to correct his questioner's error while at the same time avoiding a formal untruth in his answer, and he would thus have found the 'right word'. The lies of children, and of inexperienced people in general, are often to be ascribed to the fact that these people are faced with situations which they do not fully understand. Consequently, since the term lie is quite properly understood as meaning something which is quite simply and utterly wrong, it is perhaps unwise to generalize and extend the use of this term so that it can be applied to every statement which is formally untrue. Indeed here already it becomes apparent how very difficult it is to say what actually constitutes a lie.

The usual definition of the lie as a conscious discrepancy between thought and speech is completely inadequate. This would include, for example, even the most harmless April-fool joke. The concept of the 'jocular lie', which is maintained in Catholic moral theology, takes away from the lie its characteristic features of seriousness and malice (and, conversely, takes away from the joke its characteristic features of harmless playfulness and freedom); no more unfortunate concept could have been thought of. Joking has nothing whatever to do with lying, and the two must not be reduced to a common denominator. If it is now asserted that a lie is a deliberate deception of another man to his detriment, then this would also include, for example, the necessary deception of the enemy in war or in similar situations.[1] If this sort of conduct is called lying, the lie thereby acquires a moral sanction and justification which conflicts in every possible way with the accepted meaning of the term. The first conclusion to be drawn from this is that the lie cannot be defined in formal terms as a discrepancy between thought and speech. This discrepancy is not even a necessary ingredient of the lie. There is a way of speaking which is in this respect entirely correct and unexceptionable, but which is, nevertheless, a lie. This is exemplified when a notorious liar for once tells 'the truth' in order to mislead, and when an apparently correct statement contains some deliberate ambiguity or deliberately omits the essential part

[1] Kant, of course, declared that he was too proud ever to utter a falsehood; indeed he unintentionally carried this principle *ad absurdum* by saying that he would feel himself obliged to give truthful information even to a criminal looking for a friend of his who had concealed himself in his house.

of the truth. Even a deliberate silence may constitute a lie, although this is not by any means necessarily the case.

From these considerations it becomes evident that the essential character of the lie is to be found at a far deeper level than in the discrepancy between thought and speech. One might say that the man who stands behind the word makes his word a lie or a truth. But even this is not enough; for the lie is something objective and must be defined accordingly. Jesus calls Satan 'the father of the lie' (John 8.44). The lie is primarily the denial of God as He has evidenced Himself to the world. 'Who is a liar but he that denieth that Jesus is the Christ?' (I John 2.22). The lie is a contradiction of the word of God, which God has spoken in Christ, and upon which creation is founded. Consequently the lie is the denial, the negation and the conscious and deliberate destruction of the reality which is created by God and which consists in God, no matter whether this purpose is achieved by speech or by silence. The assigned purpose of our words, in unity with the word of God, is to express the real, as it exists in God; and the assigned purpose of our silence is to signify the limit which is imposed upon our words by the real as it exists in God.

In our endeavours to express the real we do not encounter this as a consistent whole, but in a condition of disruption and inner contradiction which has need of reconciliation and healing. We find ourselves simultaneously embedded in various different orders of the real, and our words, which strive towards the reconciliation and healing of the real, are nevertheless repeatedly drawn in into the prevalent disunion and conflict. They can indeed fulfil their assigned purpose of expressing the real, as it is in God, only by taking up into themselves both the inner contradiction and the inner consistency of the real. If the words of men are to be true they must deny neither the Fall nor God's word of creation and reconciliation, the word in which all disunion is overcome. For the cynic the truthfulness of his words will consist in his giving expression on each separate occasion to the particular reality as he thinks he perceives it, without reference to the totality of the real; and precisely through this he completely destroys the real. Even if his words have the superficial appearance of correctness, they are untrue. 'That which is far off, and exceeding deep; who can find it out?' (Eccl. 7.24).

How can I speak the truth?

1. By perceiving who causes me to speak and what entitles me to speak.

2. By perceiving the place at which I stand.

3. By relating to this context the object about which I am making some assertion.

It is tacitly assumed in these rules that all speech is subject to certain conditions; speech does not accompany the natural course of life in a continual stream, but it has its place, its time and its task, and consequently also its limits.

1. Who or what entitles or causes me to speak? Anyone who speaks without a right and a cause to do so is an idle chatterer. Every utterance is involved in a relation both with the other man and with a thing, and in every utterance, therefore, this twofold reference must be apparent. An utterance without reference is empty. It contains no truth. In this there is an essential difference between thought and speech. Thought does not in itself necessarily refer to the other man, but only to a thing. The claim that one is entitled to say what one thinks is in itself completely unfounded. Speech must be justified and occasioned by the other man. For example, I may in my thoughts consider another man to be stupid, ugly, incapable or lacking in character, or I may think him wise and reliable. But it is quite a different question whether I have the right to express this opinion, what occasion I have for expressing it, and to whom I express it. There can be no doubt that a right to speak is conferred upon me by an office which is committed to me. Parents can blame or praise their child, but the child is not entitled to do either of these things with regard to his parents. There is a similar relation between teacher and pupil, although the rights of the teacher with regard to the children are more restricted than those of the father. Thus in

criticizing or praising his pupil the teacher will have to confine himself to single particular faults or achievements, while, for example, general judgements of character are the business not of the teacher but of the parents. The right to speak always lies within the confines of the particular office which I discharge. If I overstep these limits my speech becomes importunate, presumptuous, and, whether it be blame or praise, offensive. There are people who feel themselves called upon to 'tell the truth', as they put it, to everyone who crosses their path.[1]

[1] *Editor's note.* Unfinished. A letter of December 1943 contains the following passage on this problem. 'I have been thinking again about the problem of talking about one's own fear (in air raids), a problem I wrote to you about quite recently. I believe that under the guise of "honesty" something is here presented as being "natural" which is really fundamentally a symptom of sin; it is really exactly like talking in public about sexual matters. The point is precisely that "truthfulness" does not mean the disclosure of everything that exists. God Himself made clothes for man (Gen. 3.21); and this means that *in statu corruptionis* many things in man are to remain concealed, and that if it is too late to eradicate evil, it is at least to be kept hidden. Exposure is cynical; and even if the cynic appears to himself to be specially honest, or if he sets himself up to be a fanatical devotee of truth, he nevertheless fails to achieve the truth which is of decisive importance, namely, the truth that since the Fall there has been a need also for concealment and secrecy. For me the greatness of Stifter lies in the fact that he refrains from intruding upon the inner life of man; he respects its secret and looks at men, so to speak, only quite discreetly, always from without and not at all from within. Any sort of curiosity is quite foreign to him. It made a great impression on me once when Frau —— told me with genuine horror of a film in which the life of a plant was shown in quick motion. She and her husband had found this intolerable as an unauthorized intrusion into the mystery of life. That is Stifter's point of view, too. But is there not a connexion between all this and the so-called "hypocrisy" of the British, which is contrasted with the "honesty" or "frankness" of the Germans? I think we Germans have never properly understood the meaning of "concealment", that is to say, ultimately the *status corruptionis* of the world. Kant in his *Anthropology* makes the very sound remark that anyone who fails to grasp the significance of the false appearances in the world, and who opposes them, is a traitor to humanity. Nietzsche says that "every profound mind has need of a mask". In my view "telling the truth" means saying how something is in reality, *i.e.* respect for secrecy, confidence and concealment. "Betrayal", for example, is not truth; nor are frivolity cynicism, etc. What is concealed must be disclosed only at confession, *i.e.*, before God.' (*Cf.* the last footnote to the section on *Shame.*)

INDEXES

INDEX OF NAMES

INDEX OF SUBJECTS

Japan, 68
Jews, 69–70, 223
Justification, 88, 94–97, 98–102, 110–111, 143

Labour, 86, 112, 158, 179–182, 228, 245, 246, 295, 308–310
League of Nations, 320
Life, 8, 131–147, 149, 156, 159–160, 187–190, 191–193, 305
Lotteries, 85
Lying, 41, 46, 112, 214, 229, 330–332

'Macchiavellism', 86
Mandates, 179–184, 252–259, 261–267, 295, 308–310, 322
Meditation, 267
Methodists, 320
Monasticism, monks, monasteries, 169, 187, 223–224, 277

Nationalism, 79–81
Nature, the Natural, 121, 123–125, 126, 127–131, 155, 165

Optimism, 125

Passivity, 37
Pharisaism, 12–17, 19, 21, 27–28, 49, 54
Positivism, 166, 243
Predestination, 4–5
Prohibition, 320
Property, 159, 247, 322–323
Prussia, Prussian, 80, 253

Radicalism, 104, 106–108
Reality, 50, 161–168, 169–170
Reason, 11, 47, 49, 76–77, 154, 276, 325
Reformation, 71, 73–74, 76, 78, 98–99, 168–169, 171, 258, 267, 283, 299–300, 321

Responsibility, 48–49, 51, 180, 194–230, 281, 313–315, 321
Roman Catholicism, 70, 73–76, 82, 120, 123, 148, 150–152, 153, 156, 243, 258, 267, 277, 298, 321, 331
Rome, 70, 71–72, 290

Science, 8, 76, 180, 205, 225, 288, 309
Secularization, 75–76, 84
Sex, 7, 86, 93, 132, 133, 154–156, 159, 172, 246, 334
Shame, 6–9, 111, 157, 334
Simplicity, 50–51, 201
Sin, 45, 91, 100–101, 110, 116, 120, 142, 143–144, 172–173, 177, 178, 213, 259, 263, 291
Slavery, Slaves, 111, 114, 157, 158, 159, 220, 223, 287, 289–290, 320
Socialism, 325
State, 154, 287–294, 298–301, 305, 310, 315, 323, 325
Sterilization, 154–156
Success, 56–59, 190, 198
Suicide, 137, 141–147, 211

Technology, 77–78, 80–81
Torture, 156, 157–158
Tragedy, 49, 200–201
Truthfulness, 326–334

Vedas, 261
Vitalism, 125
Vocation, 222–230

War, 72–73, 81, 135, 138, 139, 155, 208, 215, 220, 229
Western world, 67, 68–85, 87, 95–97, 118–119, 201
Wisdom, 50–51

BIBLICAL REFERENCES

REFERENCES TO THE LUTHERAN
SYMBOLIC WRITINGS

The Lutheran symbolic writings referred to in this work include the following:

Confessio Augustana (C.A.). Article XVI: *De rebus civilibus*
The *Apologia Confessionis Augustanae*, the *Apologia* written by Melanchthon for the *Confessio Augustana:*
II *De Peccato Originali*
VI *De Iustificatione*
VIII Appendix of VII: *De Ecclesia*
XVI *De Ordine Politico*
XVIII *De Libero Arbitrio*
XXI *De Invocatione Sanctorum*
Articuli Christianae Doctrinae (A.S.). The Schmalkaldic Articles written by Luther:
C II *Tertia Pars Articulorum;* II *De Lege*
Great Catechism
Formula Concordiae (F.C.):
VI *De Tertio Usu Legis Divinae*
Epitomae (Ep.)—The first part of the *Formula Concordiae*
Solida Declaratio (S.D.)—The second part of the *Formula Concordiae:*
II *De Libero Arbitrio Sive De Viribus Humanis*
IV *De Bonis Operibus*
V *De Lege et Evangelio*
VI *De Tertio Usu Legis Divinae*

The Roman figures denote the articles of the writings, the Arabic figures denote the sections into which the Latin version of the symbolic writings have been divided, rather in the manner of verses in the chapters of the Bible.

Confessio Augustana (C.A.)
XVI, 4   276
Apologia Confessionis (A.C.)
II, 34   279
IV, 5   280
IV, 7   275
IV, 8   274, 275
IV, 22   276, 277, 281
IV, 22–24   276
IV, 24   276
IV, 35   275, 279
VIII, 50   279
XVI, 55–57   276
XVI, 64   277
XIII, 70   276
XVIII, 71f.   276
XVIII, 72   276
XXI, 44   279
Schmalkaldic Articles (A.S.)
C II   274, 279
Great Catechism
Formula Concordiae (F.C.) 280, 291
VI   271
Epitomae (Ep.)
VI   271
VI, 1   274
VI, 6   280
VI, 7   271
Solida Declaratio (S.D.)
II, 24   279
II, 46   279
II, 53   279
IV, 8   279
V, 10   275, 279
V, 12   275
V, 17   272
V, 23   280
VI, 1   271, 272
VI, 9   280
VI, 24   273.